TEOLOGÍA

Teología

AN INTRODUCTION TO HISPANIC THEOLOGY

LUIS G. PEDRAJA

Abingdon Press
Nashville

TEOLOGÍA
AN INTRODUCTION TO HISPANIC THEOLOGY

Copyright © 2003 by Abingdon Press

This book is printed on recycled, acid-free elemental-chlorine–free paper.

Library of Congress Cataloging-in-Publication Data

Pedraja, Luis G., 1963-
   Teología : an introduction to Hispanic theology / Luis G. Pedraja.
    p. cm.
Includes Index.
  ISBN 0-687-09064-4 (pbk.)
1. Hispanic American theology.   I. Title.

  BT83.575.P43 2004
  230'.089'6807—dc22

2003018981

03 04 05 06 07 08 09 10 11 12—10 9 8 7 6 5 4 3 2 1

MANUFACTURED IN THE UNITED STATES OF AMERICA

To my wife, Amber,
Who stands by me day and night,
and
To all who live at the margins of
society,
With whom I will always stand in
solidarity

CONTENTS

ACKNOWLEDGMENTS

Writing a book is always a difficult task fraught with many pitfalls, struggles, dry spells, and productive periods. Without the encouragement of family and friends, this book would have been impossible to finish. Thus, I am grateful to my wife, Amber, who not only encouraged me to write on those days and nights when I lacked motivation, but who was also willing to sacrifice what little time we had alone in the evenings so that I could go to my office to write while she took care of tasks around the house. Her encouragement, along with the encouragement of other friends and family, was invaluable to my work.

I would also like to thank my faculty colleagues and fellow administrators at Memphis Theological Seminary who at times made do without a dean while I closed my door for a few hours on an afternoon to meet a deadline for the book. I am also grateful for their help in providing information or being willing to read a few chapters to offer me feedback when needed. I am also grateful to my student research assistants who were willing to go to the library to fetch a book or track down an article. In particular, I am grateful to Arko Longkumer who helped me proofread the endnotes and bibliographical entries.

Finally, I would like to thank my colleagues in the Latino/a community and all those who stood in solidarity with me in the midst of our struggles, in churches, communities, and academic circles, whose stories, experiences, and scholarship provided me with fertile ground for reflection. I hope to have done justice to their voices and lives in my recollections and reflections.

Luis G. Pedraja
Memphis

CHAPTER ONE

THE CONTEXT OF THEOLOGY

A ll theology is biography, for it is in the context of one's life that we can truly understand the shaping of theologians and their thoughts. Thus, I begin with a glimpse into my own story. I was born in Cuba, under communist rule, and grew up across the street from the Catholic cathedral, where I first came to know the faith of the people who worshiped there. I lived in Spain and later in a Cuban neighborhood in Miami, surrounded by the violence of inner city life. I attended a Hispanic Baptist church, where I felt a call to the ministry. Eventually, I would enroll in college, seminary, and a doctoral program. Along the way, I served as a pastor to a migrant congregation in Florida, a Hispanic ministry in Kentucky, and a blue-collar Anglo church in Virginia. Eventually, I would marry, teach religion, and become dean of a seminary. All these factors shaped who I am. But they also shaped my theology. Neither my theology nor I exist in a vacuum. Hence, it is essential for theologians to know their history and the contexts they inhabit, for it is part of who they are and of the theology that they create.

While I am a Hispanic theologian, I do not speak for all Hispanics. I can only speak out of my own experiences. Since I am a Latino, I do offer a Hispanic perspective on theology and share the stories of my friends and family. While the aim of this book is to introduce Hispanic, or as it is more popularly known now, Latino/a theology, this book is not a survey or an overview. Rather, my intent is to show you how theology is different from a Hispanic perspective. Latino/a theology is a dynamic theology that is still developing. As a result, I intend to give you an initial sketch of themes, issues, and thoughts emerging in this field. But by no means is this an exhaustive taxonomy.

The Tapestry of Life

Human beings are products of their circumstances. We exist in a particular place and time, and, to a certain extent, we are creatures of our circumstances, circumscribed by history, culture, and our own finite place in reality. To a point, our world creates. But, while it is true that we are conditioned by our social and cultural context, we are also able to affect it.[1] To some extent, we are both creatures and creators of our world engaged in an ongoing process that is continually changing and changing us as we contend with it.[2]

All knowledge, culture, and society are conditioned and bound by location and time period.[3] We make history, but we also have a history. We create society, but we also are part of it. We contribute to culture, but we are also creatures of our culture. Similarly, our theology and our faith are no different from other aspects of human experience. Our religious experiences and cultural biases, our upbringing, language, and socioeconomic status all affect the way we envision and express our faith. Throughout our lives, we form a theological framework through which we interpret and express our faith—a framework affected by the same factors that shape us.[4]

Often, I imagine that our lives are like a complex tapestry in the making. Many different strands come together to form the rich pattern that shapes our lives. As we make decisions and choose how to bring these different strands together, we create ourselves. But we are not mere agents of our destiny. The choices of others, as well as our past choices, also affect and construct us. Together, we all form and are formed by the rich tapestry of human history that we inherit, create, and leave as a legacy to our children.[5] This complex tapestry of life is our context—that rich framework of experiences and historical, cultural, social, and spiritual forces that shape our identity and provide us with meaning.[6]

Human beings are born into a particular time and place in history. According to existentialist philosophers, it is this very fact that makes us human—we exist in a particular time and place that defines us. When we are born, we are thrown into a world not of our choosing, a world that defines us and provides us with a certain set of mores, notions, constructs, and words that we acquire as children. Our birth also sets us in the midst of a given history and surrounds us with events, people, and circumstances not of our choosing. History creates us. The decisions of those that precede and surround us impinge upon us, making us into a particular human being living in a particular circumstance. As we come into our own, we might change those circumstances and make our own mark, limited as it may be, upon history. But we can never totally escape our history. We must always contend with it, for we are the children of history, born into the particularity of a given time and people.

Living at the Intersections of Cultures

We all live at the intersections of cultures, as heirs to a history, and as architects of our future. All the products of human life exist within this ever-expanding matrix of forces and constructs that form our context. Within this matrix we create art, literature, science, and history. In its midst we produce capital, wage war, form societies, and carve out our lives. Theology grows within this same complex context of forces that shape all other aspects of human existence. Thus, to study theology without understanding the context from which it comes is like studying the use of a color or set of brushstrokes in a work of art while ignoring the masterpiece itself. While such a painstaking study of a color or brushstrokes in a painting by a master such as Monet might prove useful in learning a particular technique, it becomes meaningless if taken apart from the whole of the masterpiece and the life of the artist who created it.

Yet, often we study theology as if it were a set of disembodied ideas, not realizing that theological thought is always embodied in the particularity of a human being. Theologians construct their theology in their own language, from the particularities of a given time, place, culture, and social location. These particularities inevitably influence and limit theologians' ideas as they react to the thoughts of their contemporaries and express their particular set of concerns about the Christian faith—concerns usually influenced by their surrounding contexts. These concerns might vary from theologian to theologian, the same as interests and concerns vary from person to person. Even we, who live in a different time period from those who have preceded us, will see the world in a different way than our ancestors did. In time, as our progeny bear their own theologies, they too will see the world in a different light than what we saw.

At our very core many of us want to believe that the truths and doctrines that appear to be foundational to our faith are indeed unchanging truths, given to us by an unchanging God and universally applicable to all creation. Yet, although the subject of our inquiry might be God, we who are doing the inquiry are nevertheless fallible, finite human beings, conditioned by our contexts and our biases.[7] Even if we are indeed presented with unquestionable truths in angelic languages given to us by God, these truths once received are conditioned by human language and interpreted by us.[8] Hence, theology is a living and ever-changing set of interpretations, embodied in the particularities of human history, culture, and society. To say otherwise would be to ignore the painting in favor of the brushstrokes.

However, that theology occurs within a living context is not detrimental to it. On the contrary, it is part of theology's strength. Theology is relevant to our lives because it is contextual. We, who are embodied in a flesh and bone existence, living in the everyday particularities of history and society, need theology to speak to us. To do so, our theologies too must be embodied and particular, interpreting the Christian message to each generation, to each culture, to the ever-changing needs of human life.[9] Hence, theology is alive and relevant to us in its very contextuality and pluriform nature. By embracing our contexts, we are better able to address the particularities of the age and place where each occurs, while remaining aware of the distortions, biases, and limitations our contexts bring to our theology. This awareness frees us to speak to particular circumstances, to be relevant to a given situation and culture, without the pretense of universality or "objective" detachment.[10] Even more, it helps us become more self-aware of our biases and limitations, thus crafting theology with humility.[11]

Hispanic theology is contextual, as are all theologies. This does not mean that it, or any other theology for that matter, is irrelevant to those who are not of that same context. What it means is that it, like all theologies, is a way of knowing that emerges out of a given context, bringing its own particularities and rich perspectives to the whole of Christian theology. Hispanic theology lends its voice to the multitude of theological voices that help us understand, interpret, and live out our Christian faith. By engaging theologies emerging from other contexts, the Hispanic voice, along with those of many other theologies, ensures an ongoing discussion that holds all of us accountable for the positions we take.

The multitudes of theological voices that paint the panoramas of theological thought today do not diminish how we understand our faith. Rather, they are individual brushstrokes in a never-ending masterpiece, each brushstroke enriching and expanding the way in which we view God. Within each theological perspective there exists a potential for uncovering new dimensions of our faith that we would never have envisioned otherwise. Each different theological voice we encounter forces us to examine our own understanding of the Christian faith and confront our limitations—limitations that are inherent parts of the particularity of being human and finite—as we attempt to ponder the depths of an infinite God. And, to understand these perspectives, we need to understand the different contexts that affect them.

The Context of Power

One of the most influential forces we encounter in history and society is the unbridled might of power, politics, and domination. What we understand as history is primarily the accounts of the victors. The voices of those less fortunate are muted forever in the dark recesses of history, occasionally uncovered by the thoughtful gaze of an historian biased in their favor. Those in power usually define and create the systems and structures of society, primarily to serve their needs. This makes them blind to how these structures exclude and oppress those who are different and makes it difficult for them to acknowledge their complicity in preserving the status quo from which they benefit.[12] Because it is painful to face our complicity in oppressive systems, we engage in conscious and unconscious avoidance of these systemic realities, often leading to innocent readings of history and social structures that keep us from confronting our inheritance and involvement in oppressive structures.[13]

The church itself, never immune to these forces, has often defined doctrine through the voices of the victors or political pressure. Often the fine line between orthodoxy and heresy is drawn by sheer power and force. Dominant groups often assume that their theological views and position are normative and absolute, aligned with divine will. Thus, they assume that other theological positions are merely contextual, meaning *only* applicable to those within that particular context, offering a *limited* contribution to the whole of theology. Theologies that come from nondominant groups often receive qualifiers that emphasize their contextuality, such as Hispanic theology, Feminist theology, and Black theology, while theologies from dominant groups are simply referred to as theology, giving the impression of being noncontextual, universal, and relevant to the entire church.[14] Hence, one seldom hears of other contextual qualifiers such as white male theology or Western European theologies. After all, it is usually the perspective of those in power that prevails. The intrusion of power into the theological arena is inevitable. Yet, when dominant and powerful groups define theological standards, silencing less powerful voices in theology, we experience a tragic loss of perspectives. Often, this loss of perspective weakens our ability to pursue and even see dimensions of our faith and God that could enrich Christianity. Power even blinds us to the truth.

Barbara Kingsolver beautifully illustrates the reality of how power obscures reality in *The Poisonwood Bible*, a fictional account of an evangelical missionary family in the Belgian Congo. In the book, Orleanna Price, the missionary's wife, tells of an encounter in the African woods with an okapi, a beautiful and strange beast believed by the white explorers to be fictional, in spite of the many accounts from the native inhabitants of its existence. It is not until a white man sees, shoots, stuffs, and brings an okapi to a museum that people actually believe that this type of gazelle-like animal exists. The character in the book muses about the dead, stuffed okapi in contrast with the wild beauty of the uncaptured one she encounters in the wood, wondering how Africa and the okapi would have been different if the white men had never come.[15]

The same can be said about how power and dominance affect theological reflection. The beliefs, faith, and theologies of those without power are in many circumstances considered irrelevant, marginal, or even mythological unless experienced and articulated by those in power. We tend to value most that which best fits into our paradigms, context, and tradition—that with which we are comfortable. While it is important to acknowledge what we value, we must be careful not to readily dismiss positions that challenge our values and that might enhance our perception of others. Theology is not the domain of one culture or one age, it belongs to all and all need to be engaged in it fully if it is to be of value. We should be careful not to dismiss too quickly those who do not play by our rules or fit neatly into our way of thinking, for only through our engagement with them can we grow beyond ourselves.

When we define theology through the narrow lens of a dominant group and the limited perspective of a given culture, we also narrow our ability to envision the fullness of God. To believe that any one of us, or even any single culture or race, has *the* definitive, or *the best* understanding of God, would be sinful hubris on our part. None of us can escape our particularity and our context to achieve a culturally unbiased or an absolute understanding of our faith. No one can assume a privileged position as the sole arbiter of theological truth, whether it is by claims of divine illumination or detached philosophical rigor. If we are not open to the voices of others, our understanding of God and ourselves risks becoming distorted and obscured by our pride. We all have something to contribute. Allowing a singular, dominant voice to define what is to be our entire understanding of God can only leave us with a truncated understanding of our faith, because, ultimately, all of our theologies are contextual, limited, and particular. Elevating the concrete particularity of our faith to an absolute status is also idolatrous, assuming that we can reduce God to ideas constructed by our human intellect.[16]

The Contexts of Cultures

Some of the most powerful, formative forces in our lives are rooted in our cultures, which play a significant role in helping us interpret our experiences and our world. Yet, the very definition of culture is in itself fluid and transitional, caught up in generalities, definitions, and discourses. Since we create culture, there is a sense in which culture defies a given definition.[17] Some define culture as the artifice of humanity, the constructs that define our humanity. Others limit culture to simply the intellectual and artistic creations of a society—things such as philosophy, art, music, and literature. Yet, these standards themselves are merely the refinements of culture as cherished by some, for culture also includes the folk and grassroots expressions of humanity. As the word itself conveys, culture is that which we cultivate, cherish, and produce, composed of the very things that also help define us and differentiate us from each other.[18] But ultimately, culture, like context, is not a singular reality, but a plurality of realities containing our creations and artifacts—creations that sustain, form, and transform us as we continually transform them. Culture cultivates us as we cultivate it.[19]

Among the many cultural factors that shape us, our language is probably the primary artifact.[20] Through language we can grasp the intricacy of the world that surrounds us, creating complex abstract notions that help us understand, remember, and convey particular aspects of our context. Because language is our primary framework for thinking and interpreting reality, it plays a significant role in shaping us. We use language to describe and grasp the world that surrounds us, as well as to communicate our understanding of that world to others. Through language we both receive and disseminate the bulk of our knowledge, experience, and cultural insights. Our thoughts take shape in language as we develop our inner discourse. Language provides the framework by which we organize the world and the experiences that constitute our lives.

Philosophy, Science, and the Context of Modernity

Since the dawn of Western philosophy, the notion that truth is universal and unchanging has dominated our thoughts. Monotheism also contributed to this notion, underscoring the idea that there was a singular, knowable source of truth. Thus, reason and revelation served as the primary pillars and sources of truth. Medieval scholars understood revelation, primarily defined by the Scriptures, as a divinely inspired and trustworthy source of truth. It was inconceivable to doubt these sources. Reason was solely complementary to divine revelation. However, in time, reason would replace these sources of authority as the universal norm by which truth claims could be measured. Philosophers like Immanuel Kant and René Descartes, while retaining a commitment to faith, turned primarily to reason to prove the existence of God and to ground morality.

Descartes's philosophy, among other things, was pivotal in defining the modern ambiance that gives detachment, objectivity, and logic a privileged position. Instead of revelation, for him the starting point of knowledge was the thinking subject, the self, detached from all its contexts. Descartes proposed that logic dictate the norm for adjudicating among the different notions that claimed to be true. Hence, he proposed that truth claims had to be based on clear and distinct ideas upon which all rational human beings could agree and arrive upon logically.[21] The quest for normative objective truths had begun in earnest. Naturally, Descartes's position privileges primarily theoretical forms of reason and assumes that Western notions about reason are applicable to all human beings—at least those deemed rational by him.[22] In addition, he assumes that clear, distinct, verifiable ideas based on logic are normative.

The rise of scientific thought and the questioning of the authoritative status of revealed truth led scholars to search for another norm upon which all could agree. These norms were determined by the same empirical and rationalistic tendencies that led to the effacement of revealed truth as authoritative—the suspicion of subjective claims to authority that were not empirically or logically verifiable. Yet, even scientific thought with its emphasis on empirical quantifiable data still retains a bias and particular interests. Scientists are not disinterested. On the contrary, they approach questions with a preconceived theory, searching for particular data. Power plays as much of a role in the survival of certain theories and the obtainment of research funds as it does in other aspects of human life. Personal success, fame, and financial gain still underlie some of the motivations of scientists as they engage in research. Because those doing the research and interpreting the data are human beings, they too are subject to the same frailties and weaknesses that plague all of us.

Language, Authority, and the Postmodern Context

Language is not only the principal artifact of culture; it is also, along with culture, one of our primary interpretative frameworks in our quest for meaning. In *The Nature of Doctrine*, George A. Lindbeck argues that our culture and language create a framework that provides meaning and shape for our lives. This framework creates the lenses through which we interpret reality, thus shaping and constituting our experience.[23] In other words, we do not experience things in a vacuum, in a pure and uninterpreted manner. It is always filtered and "experienced" within the framework of culture and language.

To some extent, we often construct reality through our language by giving meaning to words through the way we use them and relate them to other words.[24] For example children do not learn the meaning of the word "red" by associating it with the color in some sort of necessary connection. Rather, children learn the meaning through the way others use the word—or more precisely, phrases and uses of the word within a context—so that eventually they learn to use the word red appropriately to refer to the color red. Hence, to a large degree language is determined by its context because it is dependent on the practices and usage of language within a given situation and group.

In recent years, postmodernism has challenged some of our basic assumptions about meaning, authority, truth, and modernity. According to postmodern thinkers such as Jacques Derrida, the meaning of words is not fixed by an external referent. By that, he means that the meaning of words is not necessarily related to some external or ultimate reality. Their meaning or "significance" does not depend on some transcendent or external object that they signify or point to beyond language. The meaning of the word chair, for example, does not come from some ideal object, a chair, that embodies the ultimate and universal meaning of the word, contrary to Plato. The word might apply to a million different seating implements that have very little in common. Some might have four legs, others three or one. We might insist that one is a chair and another is a stool. Others might disagree. We might also use the word to mean the head of a committee. Someone else might use it as a verb, meaning taking the lead. In academia, if it is endowed, it does not mean a comfy seat; although it might mean a comfy job. The context, the way we use it, its location in language—all change its meaning.

This fluidity of meaning is particularly true when we are speaking of a written language. When we are speaking with someone, we often share an immediate context that makes it possible to refer to things in our surroundings to clarify what we mean, even though a certain level of interpretation and mutual understanding continually take place in any conversation.[25] However, this is not the case when we are dealing with a text. The text can be far removed from the environment, context, and intentionality of the author. Hence, this can lead us to interpret the meaning of the text in a variety of ways, often beyond the writer's original intent.

Postmodern critiques of language and human knowledge have opened the door for other forms of reasoning and other perspectives to gain validity. This openness has made it possible for us to engage in a greater and more expansive dialogue among different theological positions. Unfortunately, postmodernism in some of its forms does not provide a means for adjudicating between conflicting truth claims. Since meaning is solely determined by the text, most forms of interpretation, one might argue, can claim a certain level of validity. The result is that while postmodernism validates different perspectives and contextual positions as being viable truth claims, it does not provide a means for one context to criticize the other. Hence, such a position makes it difficult for marginalized groups to offer a critique of dominant notions that may be contributing to their marginalization.[26] In other words, if my claim is as valid as yours, then how am I able to criticize your position, even if that position is responsible for my oppression? After all, to whom can I appeal to make my argument against you? This is the double edge sword of postmodernism. While it opens a space for the voice of minorities to be heard, it dilutes their ability to speak against something.

Postmodernity also raises another important question. How do we know that a particular interpretation is valid and another one is not? To what authority do we appeal? The question of epistemology, how we know things, and the problem of finding foundations upon which to ground our knowledge in a postmodern reality, often plagues theology. While postmodernity brings freedom to explore different perspectives, it also tends to leave us without a standpoint, since there are no foundations upon which we can stand! For theology this can be problematic, since we tend to seek truth and ultimacy. Yet, it is possible to find an alternative to radical nihilism or reactionary orthodoxy. For instance, if we understand the problem in terms of perspective, we can agree that while there is a common event, experience, or reality that we encounter, we each encounter it from a different perspective—which includes our context, culture, and socioeconomic location. Hence, there is sufficient commonality to engage in dialogue and to arrive at certain conclusions about what is valuable and what is not, while recognizing the impossibility of total agreement and of a single universal standpoint.[27]

In the western hemisphere, our central constructs revolve around particular notions of Christianity and God, which we tend to assume are a normative standard for truth by which other theological interpretations should be measured. Even when we consciously hold a philosophical position to the contrary, we still tend to act as if that position itself were universal and unchanging! Hence, postmodern philosophers, process philosophers, and others who might argue against rigid and unchanging truths still take very dogmatic and ideological positions regarding their views. We tend to view those things we value and trust as being authoritative for us. As a result, we tend to call upon them as primary resources and criteria for deciding among conflicting claims. However, since our contexts, values, and sources of authority may vary among us, we never fully resolve the problem of adjudicating between conflicting truth claims. By dialoguing with others, we can better gauge our position and gain a broader perspective than what our own limited position and context may allow, thus expanding our horizons and perspectives.

Living in the Middle

While it is true that the contexts that shape us are unique to us—no two persons share the same experiences in the same way at the same time—it is also true that no context is insular unto itself. Our experiences are part of a multitude of experiences that come to us in continuity with others' experiences, extending well beyond the limits of our own personal and cultural contexts. Because our contexts overlap, they influence one another. Ultimately, all things in life are interrelated and woven together in an ever-expanding, extensive continuum that goes beyond our immediate present and place in history. We live within this seamless continuum of experiences, carving out our own place in history, while at the same time being shaped by it. Thus, defining our context is not a matter of simple location, for we truly inhabit a variety of contexts throughout our life, and we often exist in between overlapping contexts at the same time.

This overlap of contexts is especially true of Hispanic Americans. Latinos and Latinas live at the juncture of cultures, in the hyphen that joins their multiple heritages into one embodied reality. We are both Americans and Hispanics. We often find distinct aspects of both cultures existing together in our lives. Our own bodies often bear the marks of two or more races, each embodied in a particular trait or feature. We exist in a space between worlds, cultures, races, languages, and beliefs—a living legacy to the forces of history in which different worlds came together, often violently. Yet, because we embody different traits and cultures, we live on the boundary between contexts, existing in both as a living bridge between the cultures, races, and contexts that gave us birth.[28]

Hispanics are not the only ones who live at the juncture of different cultures and contexts. Our experience, especially in our current society, with its instant access to information and ease of travel, is truly multicultural and intercontextual in ways never before imagined. To some extent, everyone lives in a complex context, influenced by many different realities, cultures, and values. Because our experiences are interconnected and as such often

21

overlap with that of others, we are able to construct a shared space where we can communicate and compare our experiences with those of others. We are inextricably intertwined with one another, inhabiting a multiplicity of contexts that are interconnected into a multiform webbing that forms the weaves of the tapestry of life. Hence, no context is ever insular unto itself, irrelevant to others, or incommensurable with that of another. Yet, each is unique unto itself.

Is Theology Contextual?

To deny that theology is a product of its cultural context is tantamount to denying the Incarnation and the historicity of Scripture. This may sound like a very drastic statement, yet it is true. Divine revelation inescapably occurs within a particular human cultural matrix. According to the German-born theologian Paul Tillich, God's revelation comes to us enmeshed within a specific historical context.[29] Revelation comes to us in forms that are understandable to humans within their particular place and time in history. Revelation is relevant to a specific cultural context, at a particular time, for a particular purpose. In the Scriptures, when God acts or speaks, God acts in history and speaks to a particular person or group within their cultural parameters. God's acts and God's revelations never occur as abstract universals, detached from the messy realities of human life, which include our cultures, struggles, suffering, and aspirations. When we encounter God, we always do so within the context of history and culture.[30]

Thus, when we read the Bible, we cannot help noting that the Bible is thoroughly situational. Throughout the Scriptures, God acts within a particular social, economic, and cultural context.[31] In addition, God acts in a fashion that is significant to the people being addressed. Hence, for God to address human beings in a manner that they can understand, God must address them within the context of their language and culture. Even if God were to give us an unadulterated, direct divine revelation, the recipients of such revelation would still have to conceptualize and articulate it within the context of their own language and culture. Their own experiences, limited vocabularies, levels of comprehension, and cultural norms would color their interpretation of the event. If we were to hear a voice speaking from heaven, some would interpret it as divine, while others would say it is merely thunder, as occurred during Jesus' baptism. The words of such a voice, for us to understand it, would have to come in a comprehensible human language, which is subject to limitations and nuances. Even our recollection of the events and the words would be interpreted by us in light of our cultural expectations—such as gender bias, nationalist agendas, or religious expectations.

The Incarnation itself becomes the clearest example of God's contextual activity. Orlando Costas, the late missiologist, speaks of the Incarnation as the peak of contextualization, where God enters human history and culture embodied in human flesh.[32] As Christians, we believe that God becomes manifest for us most clearly in the life, death, and resurrection of Jesus of Nazareth. You cannot get more particular than that! As far as we know Jesus spoke Aramaic, followed many Jewish customs, and lived in a particular time and a particular place. In him, God's presence in the midst of humanity is thoroughly contextualized. But even more, Jesus also identified with a particular group of people, the poor and the marginalized, whom he sought to free from their bondage. God's presence in humanity not only makes God accessible to us, it makes God accessible in a particular fashion and in a particular place. In such particularity—enfleshed and fully contextual in the midst of human history, suffering, and struggle—we fashion our theologies and define criteria by their relevance to their own particular reality in light of the reality in which we find God who puts on our human flesh.

Know Thyself

According to the oracle at Delphi, the beginning of wisdom lies in our self-knowledge. The same can be said of theology. Unless we fully understand who we are and our context, we can never fully appreciate our theology or that of others. Through our interaction with other theologies and contexts, all of us can enrich our understanding of ourselves and of God as we see the different brushstrokes take shape within a masterful work of art or as different strands come together to make the tapestry of life.

Understanding that theology is limited and that we need to be aware of these limitations to overcome our own narrow perspectives and biases is not a new proposition. Even some white male European theologians recognize the limitations that culture places on their theology. Paul Tillich, for instance, exemplifies that awareness when he writes:

> Yet it must be conceded at the outset that this attempt is subject to certain essential limitations. Not every situation, not every society, can be understood from the point of view of another situation or society; but only that one which is vitally related to the one from which it is observed. Hence, the present about which we can speak is the life of our Western society. Even this society is divided and is cut across by creedal and national walls, which it is difficult for individuals to surmount. To concede this does not mean

that we are limiting ourselves intentionally but that there are actual limitations which can never be wholly transcended and of which one must remain conscious, particularly when one's point of view is located in the midst of deeply shaken mid-European society.[33]

Tillich recognized the need for different cultures to be vitally connected with one another to truly engage in dialogue and mutual criticism. But Tillich was also aware that he could never completely transcend his context rooted in the turmoil of mid-twentieth-century Europe. The need for a self-aware, contextualized theology leads us to look at ourselves and at how our context affects our theology. Hence, to understand Hispanic theology, one must first understand one's own context, as well as the context from which Hispanic theologies emerge.

Notes

1. Ian Hacking, in his book, *The Social Construction of What?* (Cambridge: Harvard University Press, 1999), provides an examination and valid critique of ways in which we use the notions of "social construction," illustrating the interplay between our behavior and the ideas and terms we use to understand ourselves, pp. 25-28.

2. The late missiologist and Hispanic theologian, Orlando Costas, speaks of all forms of human knowledge as being "processual" in nature, constantly changing and transforming us as we interact with it and each other. *Christ Outside the Gate: Mission Beyond Christendom* (Maryknoll: Orbis Press, 1982), pp. 4-5.

3. According to Costas, there is no form of human knowledge that is timeless, detached, and not connected with other forms of knowledge. Ibid., p. 4.

4. Howard W. Stone and James O. Duke refer to this cumulative theological framework as the person's embedded theology, which is communicated and enhanced by his or her language of faith. *How to Think Theologically* (Minneapolis: Fortress Press, 1996), pp. 13-16.

5. This imagery connotes an image of actual entities and their interconnection in an extensive continuum as developed by Alfred N. Whitehead, *Process and Reality*, corrected edition (New York: Macmillan, 1978).

6. Orlando Costas provides an excellent analysis of the meaning and etymology of "context" in *Christ Outside the Gate*, p. 4. The word "context" means literally "to weave together," its etymology related to such words as "textile" and "text."

7. The problem of ignoring our fallibility and sinfulness in constructing our theologies and worldviews is part of the argument presented by Jean Bethke Elshtain in her article "Beyond Traditionalism and Progressivism, or Against Hardening of the Categories," in *Theology Today*, Vol. 58 (April 2001), pp. 4-13. Particularly, she quotes Czech President Václav Havel's depiction of how a humble message becomes an arrogant one as one begins to think of oneself as the possessor of reason and history, thus becoming the rightful architect of defining a utopian future for all, even those who do not fit in the paradigm, pp. 8-9. This illustrates the danger of seeing one's self as the center, ignoring one's own fallibility and fallenness, thus succumbing to anthropological arrogance.

8. Justo L. González, in *Santa Biblia: The Bible Through Hispanic Eyes* (Nashville:

Abingdon Press, 1996), pp. 11-13, tells a story regarding a question on biblical inerrancy that speaks precisely to this point and the fallibility of our interpretation as human beings.

9. Justo González argues in *Mañana: Christian Theology from a Hispanic Perspective* (Nashville: Abingdon Press, 1990), p. 22, that there is no general theology. Instead, each particular community within the common bonds of the Christian faith brings its own voice to bear on the message of the gospel in the hopes of enriching the whole through new perspectives, correctives, and insights to the shared understanding of our faith.

10. Ada María Isasí-Diaz makes the argument that all claims to objectivity are merely someone's subjectivity made from a position of power.

11. Martin Luther writes that theology must be done with humility, recognizing one's own limitations and the tentativeness of one's theology in the Preface to the Wittenberg Edition of his German writing, *Martin Luther: Basic Theological Writings*, Timothy F. Lull, ed. (Minneapolis: Fortress Press, 1989), pp. 63-68.

12. J. V. Gallos and J. Ramsey, *Teaching Diversity: Listening to the Soul, Speaking from the Heart* (San Francisco: Jossey-Bass, 1996), p. 215.

13. González speaks of innocent readings of history and Scripture in *Mañana*, pp. 38-41.

14. González argues that theologies of dominant groups are seen as relevant to the entire church, but those of minority groups as relevant only to those groups. Ibid., p. 52.

15. Barbara Kingsolver, *The Poisonwood Bible* (New York: HarperCollins, 1998), pp. 6-8.

16. Paul Tillich writes, "The weakness of all faith is the ease with which it becomes idolatrous.... Faith has the tendency to elevate its concrete symbols to absolute validity." *Dynamics of Faith* (New York: Harper Torch Books, 1957), p. 97.

17. Homi Bhabha addresses the duplicity of culture's articulation of the constructs of power that define colonialism, with its desire to reduce cultures to sameness and yet its constant transformation in the multiplicity of cultures into something indefinable. *The Location of Culture* (New York: Routledge Press, 1994), pp. 135-38.

18. Delwin Brown, in his book *Boundaries of Our Habitations: Tradition and Theological Construction* (New York: State University of New York Press, 1994), builds upon the work of Clifford Geertzn and draws from the historical account of Raymond Williams's *Marxism and Literature* (Oxford: Oxford Press, 1977) addressing the idea of how culture before the Enlightenment referred to cultivation, that is, "the care of crops, animals, and human minds." But post-Enlightenment the term became associated primarily with the human aspects and associated with "civilization." Another concept also outlined by Brown and traced to the eighteenth century is that of culture as social process, pp. 59-62.

19. Clifford Geertz develops the notion of culture as contextual and emerging out of the social political and interactive process of ongoing negotiations. See his book, *The Interpretation of Cultures* (New York: Basic Books, 1973).

20. Paul Tillich, *Theology of Culture*, Robert C. Kimball, ed. (Oxford: Oxford University Press, 1959), p. 42.

21. René Descartes, *Discourse on Method* (New York: Penguin Books), p. 27.

22. Other forms of reason beyond the theoretical have always been accepted. Scholars from Aristotle to Tillich have posited different forms of reason, such as practical (moral) reason, poietic (aesthetic) reason, and even ecstatic reason. Often, these other forms are discounted in making reason a theological and philosophical criterion. See Paul Tillich, *Systematic Theology*, volume 1 (Chicago: University of Chicago Press, 1951), pp. 72-75.

23. George A. Lindbeck, *The Nature of Doctrines* (Philadelphia: Westminster John Knox, 1984), pp. 32-41.

24. The notion of the play between words goes back to people such as Ludwig Wittgenstein who speaks of language games in *On Certainty*, G. E. M. Anscombe and G. H. Von Wright, eds., Denis Paul and G. E. M. Anscombe, trans. (Oxford: Basil Blackwell, 1969), pp. 1e-7e.

25. For more see Hans-Georg Gadamer, *Truth and Method*, 2nd edition, Joel Weinsheimer and Donald G. Marshall, trans. (New York: Continuum Press, 1995), pp. 383-405.

26. The incommensurability of differing positions and the inability to adjudicate between these positions occurs primarily in Paul de Man's use of binary opposites, where the result is an aporia of meaning through its ultimate undecidability.

27. See Gavin Hyman, *The Predicament of Postmodern Theology: Radical Orthodoxy or Nihilist Textualism?* (Louisville: Westminster John Knox, 2001), particularly chapter 1.

28. Hispanics exist in a state of hybridity or in-betweeness in a liminal space. Thus, we are able to construct a sense of identity in the fluidity of negotiating a space between the different cultures that we inhabit physically, but to transcend the boundaries of a given culture, as articulated by Homi K. Bhabha in *The Location of Culture*, pp. 1-9.

29. Paul Tillich, *Biblical Religion and the Search for Ultimate Reality* (Chicago: University of Chicago Press, 1955), p. 3.

30. Karl Barth concedes that God's Word is still encountered through the world, along with its brokenness, sin, and secularity. God's word is "an act of God in the reality that conceals him." Ultimately stating that "revelation means the incarnation of the Word of God. But incarnation means entry into this secularity." *Church Dogmatics*, Volume 1, part 1, 2nd edition, trans. G. W. Bromiley (Edinburgh: T & T Clark), pp. 167-68.

31. Orlando Costas maintained that our familiarity with the Bible in its vernacular translation obscures "the distance that separates us from its actors and writers." Because God can only be known within the context of a history and culture, Costas maintains that the Bible's theology is culturally and historically bound. *Christ Outside the Gate*, p. 5.

32. Ibid.

33. Paul Tillich, *The Religious Situation* (New York: Meridian Books, 1956), p. 40.

CHAPTER TWO

DOING THEOLOGY IN A HISPANIC CONTEXT

S itting in a Mexican-theme restaurant in West Tennessee, Afro-Cuban music plays in the background, while the waitress, who is a white Southerner, is taking my order. "You mean *'she-u-rus*, honey" she says with a heavy Southern drawl, trying to correct my pronunciation of Spanish when I ask for *churros* for dessert. This surreal postmodern experience of cultural eclecticism and *mestizaje*—the mixing of European and indigenous cultures—is not uncommon today. Whether eating at a Chinese restaurant in Dallas as Mexican cooks in the kitchen speak Spanish, or having black-bean sushi in a Cuban-Asian fifties-theme fusion restaurant in downtown Nashville, the mixture of cultures is a reality in today's America. Hispanics, who embody and experience this ever-changing mix of cultures as an historical and physical reality, find it amusing at times and frightful at others to see the complexity of our cultural reality and heritage.

We exist in this confusing, complex cultural milieu. We come from different cultures, nationalities, and ethnicities. Yet, we, who call ourselves Hispanic, Latinos/as, Mexicans, Cubans, Puerto Ricans, Salvadorans, Nicaraguans, Costaricans, Dominicans, Guatemantecos, Chicanos, Tejanos, Americans, and other names live in a land that often sees us all only as Hispanics. Although we embrace the culture of our country, the U.S., we are not always embraced by it. Thus we live in a quandary of a confusing and tenuous existence, in a country that loves our Latin music, glorifies hot-blooded Latin sensuality, and devours with gusto our Latin food, yet at times can't seem to tolerate us. It is at this place—in the borderland of cultures, in the in-between space of being insiders and outsiders, accepted and rejected—that we exist as a people, sometimes hidden from the gaze of history and overlooked by the dominant society.[1]

The Context of History

Alfred North Whitehead, in *Adventure of Ideas*, compares the gaze of the historian to a searchlight, illuminating the object of its focus while rendering everything else into obscurity.[2] History is never disinterested and acritical.[3] Because all theology occurs in and emerges out of a particular history, we must look to history as a place of theological reflection, to discover the voices that have been suppressed by the gaze of the historian. For Latinos/as, recovering our history is important, for there are many strands to our history that have been rendered into obscurity by our life in the United States and its accounting of history. But, we are also heirs to the violence of conquests that obscures the histories of those we conquered. Still, both the blood of the conquered and the blood of the conquerors flow together in our veins. Thus, we must reclaim our history as a people, both the good and the bad.

The historical roots of the Latino/a people run deep and far, running not just through this continent, but also through the Iberian Peninsula, now known as Spain and Portugal.[4] During almost 1,000 years of Islamic rule, Christians, Muslims, and Jews coexisted, sometimes in peace and at other times at war. Throughout these centuries there were periods of great cultural exchanges, as well as ethnic and racial blending. Even today, the Spanish language itself contains a large proportion of words that actually come from Arabic, evidence of this rich mixture of cultures.[5] Other influences of the different cultures, ethnicities, and races present then can still be seen in the architecture, traditions, people, and foods of the different regions of Spain.

During this period, many kingdoms and serfdoms, often at war with one another, dominated the region. Christians controlled some regions such as Aragon and Castile. To the south, the Moors dominated regions such as Granada, while Jews dominated some cities throughout the Peninsula. All of this was to change with the marriage between Isabella of Castile and Ferdinand II of Aragon, which forged an alliance between the two kingdoms that set the stage for the "Reconquest" of Spain. On January 2, 1492, the same year that Columbus set sail on his fateful journey, Granada surrendered to the forces of Ferdinand and Isabella after a decade of war, setting the stage for the unification of Spain. While the unification of Spain under the power of the monarchy and Christendom brought stability, it also brought, by royal edict, the expulsion of Jews and Muslims from Spain and the establishment of the Inquisition. The age of religious tolerance, often fostered by political necessity, had come to an end.[6]

However, the cultural milieu of Spain before the Reconquest had a significant impact on the Americas. First, it led to an interesting mix of openness and intolerance by the Spaniards in the Americas. On the one hand, unlike the British settlers of North America, there was more openness to appropriating certain aspects of the native cultures and a greater degree of interaction with the natives. On the other hand, the spirit of the Inquisition and the quest for purity allowed for little, if any, tolerance toward indigenous religions seen as pagan by Spaniards. In addition, years of strife had made the Spanish adept at the art of war. This legacy of violence, coupled with avarice and religious intolerance, were the necessary ingredients that would lead to the bloody conquest, subjugation, and rape of the native people.[7] The *conquistadors*, most young men who had left their families in Spain, seldom had qualms about raping or entering into sexual unions with native women. The result was the creation of a people of mixed heritage in all of the lands occupied by Spain, which would eventually extend to other aspects of religion and culture, preserving some aspects of indigenous cultures.

Although greed and power were the driving forces of the conquest by Spain, theology and religion helped justify it. Some saw conquest as a means of evangelization. Many *conquistadors*, like Cortés, saw themselves as instruments of God and bearers of the gospel, foreshadowing what the U.S. would later use to justify their occupation of Spanish and Mexican territories.[8] Theologian José de Acosta justified enslaving the natives and taking their lands by using Aristotelian categories that defined the natives as barbarians devoid of reason or as "natural men," fierce beasts who only looked human.[9] Many theologians and missionaries did genuinely seek to bring the Christian faith to the natives. Some argued in favor of *encomiendas, decrees that gave native inhabitants over to the control of Spanish settlers,* believing them to be a tool for Christianization through education and evangelism.[10] The actual results of course, were no different from that of indentured servitude. Even though the Spanish crown did not abrogate the right to freedom of the native (with the exception of natives who were cannibals, rebellious, or already enslaved by others), the system was fraught with abuse.[11] Some clerics, such as Bartolomé de Las Casas, a Dominican friar, horrified by the atrocities committed against the indigenous population, their enslavement and decimation, argued fervently on their behalf before authorities and theologians alike.

Laws enacted by Spain to protect the Indians came too late and were difficult to enforce. While remnants of the once proud Aztec, Mayan, and Inca cultures survived, the same was not true for the Caribbean islands where forced labor, disease, and violence led to the death of most of the indigenous population. The need for additional laborers led to the import of slaves from Africa, using similar theological rationalizations to justify it under the guise of evangelism and the claim that they were better off under the "benevolent" tutelage of Christian masters.[12] At first, even Las Casas, believing Africans would fare better, endorsed this idea to help ease the burden on the natives. However, as African slaves endured ocean crossings and forced labor, they fared no differently than the natives. Decades later, after witnessing the barbaric treatment of African slaves, Las Casas recognized his mistake and recanted his endorsement.[13]

Even worse was the role of religion in this tragedy. The final words of the chieftain, Hatuey, exemplify the deep stain the conquest left on Christianity. Captured and about to be burned at the stake by the Spanish, he was given a chance to convert to Christianity. Las Casas writes that upon hearing that Christians would be in heaven, without further thought, Hatuey said that "he did not want to be there, but rather in hell, so that he would not be where they were and to not see such cruel people." Las Casas added this final note to his account: "such is the faith and honor our God and our faith have earned."[14]

The Legacy of Conquest

In the midst of tragedy, remarkable things still happen. And such was the case only a few decades after the fall of the Aztec empire. On Mount Tepeyac in the outskirts of Mexico City the Virgin of Guadalupe appeared to Juan Diego, a poor *mestizo* man. Although the truth of the story is still debated— some think it was actually a tool of the Spanish church to evangelize the natives—the Virgin of Guadalupe has nevertheless remained a powerful symbol for many of the people of Mexico.[15] Her symbolic power can be traced to several factors, some rooted in the violence of the conquest. First, the Virgin did not appear to the Spaniards or to the church officials, but to a lowly *mestizo* laborer of mixed heritage. Second, the Virgin appeared as a *mestiza*. Third, she appeared in a place that was sacred to the natives, dedicated to an Aztec goddess. Ultimately, the Virgin of Guadalupe represents a cultural and religious union, a *mestizaje*, that has not only evoked religious fervor in the people, but also has come to symbolize the *mestizo/a* identity of the people.

This religious and cultural syncretism, exemplified by the Virgin of

Guadalupe, is only one page in our history. Syncretism is not limited to Guadalupe. Many countries in the Caribbean and throughout Central America experienced other forms of syncretism as African slaves brought with them different aspects of their cultures and religions. In time, these would come to influence Latin music, food, and even religion. African religions, such as Yoruba, came to influence Latino/a religion, hiding at times under a veil of Catholicism to become Santeria. Other religious mixtures continued, many gaining popularity, particularly those forms that empowered otherwise powerless individuals. Veiled expressions of indigenous religions also remained, coexisting with Christianity, through *curanderos/as* (medicine men and women), popular practitioners of what some might call witchcraft, and religious art.[16] To this continuous churning of cultures and religions, new elements were added as events brought cultures and peoples further together, often through violent means.

During the nineteenth century and the early part of the twentieth century, the United States became a player in the unfolding drama of the Latino/a people. But we seldom get the full story in our textbooks, since history textbooks are often no more than propaganda tools or "innocent" readings of history that gloss over embarrassing, shameful, or hidden dimensions of our history.[17] History is always a complex reality. During periods of war with Spain, England created propaganda tools that painted Spaniards as backward, lazy, cruel, unsophisticated, and corrupt. While some stories of atrocities were based on half-truths committed during the conquest of the Americas, most were merely propaganda tools.[18] These "dark legends" remained in the consciousness of the English-speaking people and eventually affected American perception of Latinos/as. In addition, a sense of "Manifest Destiny" also dominated American culture and politics for most of the nineteenth and twentieth centuries. Manifest Destiny was a belief in the superiority of Anglo civilization, coupled with expansionist ideals and the notion that the U.S. was the new Israel, God's ordained instrument destined to establish God's reign on earth and to propagate American values throughout the continent. Anglos were hailed as being spiritually, intellectually, and morally superior to Hispanic and native peoples.[19]

The "dark legends" and Manifest Destiny worked together to inspire U.S. expansion into western territories that were at the time part of Mexico. First, Texas—with its many settlers from the U.S., settlers who originally came as immigrants and accepted Mexican rule—successfully rebelled against Mexico in 1836, partially as a result of a dispute with Santa Ana, the Mexican leader at the time.[20] Later, the rest of the Southwest territories, including New Mexico, Arizona, Nevada, and California, came under U.S. control as the result of the Mexican-American War, a war provoked and driven by expansionist views in the U.S. The treaty of Guadalupe-Hidalgo ended the war in 1848, but left stranded many citizens of Mexico, who went to sleep in Mexico and woke up in the United States, engulfed by a new country and culture.

Mexican citizens living in these territories had to contend with their new country, a country that did not always welcome them. The treaty originally guaranteed some rights to Mexican citizens, including the right to keep their language and lands, but the provisions of the treaty were quickly reneged. They were continually pressured by incoming Anglos who wanted to impose their language upon them.[21] Many were cheated out of their land while others were cheated out of their culture. Along with the influx of ordinary people came evangelists who brought Protestantism to this primarily Catholic region. Protestantism brought new opportunities, greater access to the Bible, education, and, for some, even the promise of easier upward social mobility.[22] At the same time, most of the Hispanics who joined these Protestant denominations found segregation, discrimination, and cultural oppression waiting for them in those churches.[23]

Other immigrants soon joined the Mexicans already in the Southwest as immigrants made their trek across the artificially drawn borders. Some came to join family, separated from them by the sudden shift of the borders, and others came to find work. Some came and went as the borders remained porous, and later, they still came in spite of the border tightening. Some worked in the fields for subsistence wages; others found better work in service industries. While it might be easy to assume that most immigrants were unskilled laborers, it would be a mistaken assumption. Many were and continue to be skilled professionals who migrated for different reasons, including political persecution or economic advancement. But all of these new immigrants from other countries soon joined the growing number of Mexicans in the United States.

In 1898, U.S. expansionist desires contributed to the Spanish-American War, resulting in the addition of Puerto Rico and Cuba as U.S. territories. Although Cuba was granted independence by the U.S. in 1902, its influence on Cuban economics and politics continued until Fidel Castro took control of Cuba in 1959. Even before communism took hold in Cuba, many Cubans had already settled in the U.S., primarily in New York and Florida. After the communist revolution, different waves of Cubans migrated to the United States. At first, it was the wealthy, the middle class, and government officials seeking refuge from the new government. Along with them came strong anti-communist sentiments and conservative ideals that often are at odds with that of other Latino/a communities in the U.S. The Mariel boatlift in 1980 brought more blue-collar workers, while, later, others came in small boats and rafts ill-equipped to make the hazardous journey across the Florida straits. Countless people have lost their lives in these crossings, including the mother of Elian González, the little boy who captured widespread media attention not too long ago.

Puerto Rico, on the other hand, remained a territory of the U.S until it became a commonwealth. Yet, at the onset, the island was governed under military rule—the people living as colonists, with truncated rights and limited control of their own destiny.[24] U.S. government policies, often designed to benefit U.S. economic interests, created large-scale unemployment and poverty on the island. Anti-U.S. sentiments led to violent clashes with the government, including the Palm Sunday Massacre in Ponce on March 21, 1937, where soldiers killed twenty-one people in a conflict with Puerto Rican Nationalists. Continued unrest, unemployment, and poverty on the island led many to leave in search of work in the mainland, settling in cities in the Northeast and Midwest. After World War II, there was a steady immigration of Puerto Ricans to the U.S. mainland, numbering more than 1 million by 1960 and nearly 3 million in 2000, not counting the almost 4 million living on the island.[25] Although citizens of the U.S., the status of Puerto Rico and Puerto Ricans remains nebulous and unclear; they are seen as foreigners and not as true citizens.

To this influx of Hispanic immigrants, large groups of Dominicans came in the 1960s, many fleeing unrest in the Dominican Republic—unrest caused by U.S. intervention in a revolt to restore the democratic election of Juan Bosch. Fearing that the revolt would lead to a communist regime, the U.S. sent troops to quench the revolt. This led to the establishment of a right-wing government and the persecution of Bosch supporters.[26] Later, other groups of Hispanic immigrants came from Nicaragua, El Salvador, Guatemala, and other countries of Latin America, many fleeing violence in their own country, violence often fueled by U.S. covert operations. As Juan González writes in *Harvest of Empire*, "this sudden exodus did not originate with some newfound collective desire for the material benefits of U.S. society; rather, vicious civil wars and the social chaos those wars engendered forced the region's people to flee, and in each case, the origins and spiraling intensity of those wars were a direct result of military and economic intervention by our own government."[27]

Whether as refugees or as immigrants in search of betterment, Latinos/as came to the U.S. and continue to come, making this land their new home, accepting its culture, but also bringing their own cultures. Latinos/as in the U.S. were not simply passive pawns of history. They were active contributors, fighting in wars alongside many other immigrants. They built congregations, ordained ministers and priests, and contributed to the growth of the nation, as did other groups of immigrants. But they found it hard to escape discrimination. In their struggle to overcome discrimination, Latinos/as began to develop coalitions from which different movements formed. One of the most influential movements in the Southwest was the Farm Workers Movement led by Caesar Chavez. Through his effort to unify and unionize farm workers, Chavez and his followers were able to bring social change, often with religious overtones.[28] In the 1960s and 1970s, fueled by the Civil Rights Movement, other groups emerged such as the Brown Berets, La Raza Unida, Young Lords, and MECHA. Some became militant and splintered into different factions, while others, like the National Council of La Raza, continued to thrive, along with LULAC and other earlier groups.[29]

A Legacy of Liberation

The different Civil Rights Movements that developed in the United States in the decades of the 1950s and 1960s did not go unnoticed by the church. On the contrary, the church was influential in many of these movements. The inevitable result was the development of theologies influenced by these movements, such as African American theologies—influenced by leaders such as Dr. Martin Luther King Jr., a Baptist minister, and Malcolm X, a Black Muslim. African American theologies were able to recover a rich heritage of spirituality and religion that had already influenced American culture through its music. While Black theology has roots in early spirituals, sermons, and civil rights leaders, the publication of James Cone's *A Black Theology of Liberation* in 1970 signaled its inauguration into the academic world. According to Cone, Black theology tries to mediate between the liberation of blacks and the revelation of Jesus Christ using black experience, black history, black culture, Scripture, and tradition as its sources.[30] In the years that followed, others followed Cone's footsteps, bringing the neglected voices of African Americans to bear on the theological arena.

A second movement of liberation, also rooted in the desire to obtain equality and rights, is the feminist movement, which influenced theology by bringing the voices of many disenfranchised women to bear. Many feminist theologians consider the origins of contemporary feminist theology to be an article written by Valerie Saiving, "The Human Situation: A Feminine View," which appeared in *The Journal of Religion* in 1960.[31] According to Rosemary Radford Ruether, in her well-known book, *Sexism and God-Talk: Toward a Feminist Theology*, feminist theology draws from women's experience and tradition to promote the full humanity of women, rejecting anything that "denies, diminishes, or distorts" their full humanity.[32] Later, these theologies influenced the development of minority feminist theologies, such as Womanist theology in African American circles and Mujerista theology in Latina circles.

However, to a large extent, Latin American liberation theologians are one of the greatest influences on Latino/a theology.[33] Liberation theology is in part a legacy of Vatican II and Pope John XXIII's sweeping changes in the Catholic church, including the papal encyclical *Pacem in Terris* (Peace on Earth) that called for a move toward ecumenism, social work, human dignity, and justice. As a result, Catholic bishops in Latin America called for the church to address the sweeping poverty of the people in Latin America. Protestant churches in Latin America also played a role, issuing similar calls for action.[34] But the key date in the development of Latin American liberation theologies came in 1971, when Gustavo Gutiérrez, a Catholic theologian and priest, published his book *Teología de la liberación, Perspectivas*, later translated into English as *A Theology of Liberation*. In the book Gutiérrez traces his argument for developing an historical theology based on liberative praxis, or reflective action, and focused on God's relationship with the poor. Salvation, according to Gutiérrez, cannot be limited to the spiritual realm. Rather, it must encompass historical and material dimensions, bringing about change in all aspects of humanity by freeing everyone from all forms of sin and all sinful structures inherent in society. Ultimately, for Gutiérrez, sin is not merely an impediment for human salvation in the afterlife; it is an historical reality that breaches our communion with God and with each other.[35]

Examining the Bible, Gutiérrez finds what he calls God's preferential option for the poor, a sense of God being in solidarity with the poor, oppressed, and marginalized throughout biblical history, and he argues that the church as the Body of Christ must also move to be in solidarity with them.[36] Although Gutiérrez brings to light the theme with his unique insights, the notion that God sides with the poor and the oppressed of society is not new to the church, and it is a common theme for the biblical prophets and in the Gospels. Even Jesus is cited as issuing a call for us to stand in solidarity with the least in society (Matt. 25:31-46) and recognize God's presence in their suffering.

As Gutiérrez points out in his lectures and in conversation, even though the church often forgets, God's preferential option for the poor is a result of God's love for humanity. God's preferential option for the poor might not appeal to the sensibilities of some who would prefer a God who loves us all equally. But, if understood in terms of God's love, it makes sense that God identifies and stands in solidarity with the poor, the oppressed, and all other victims of society. God must stand in solidarity with the weak and the oppressed, feeling their anguish and striving for their liberation. After all, what loving parent would not come to the aid of a beloved child, even if the one hurting the child is also another equally loved child? However, God's preferential option for the poor does not mean that there is some inherent innocence in poverty that negates their sin or that God loves others less. It means that God, because of a love for all creation, identifies with those who suffer the brunt of the sins of others, and thus, acts especially on their behalf. God's love demands action on their behalf, because the failure to act would imply God's tacit complicity with the oppressors by allowing those who have power to abuse those without power.[37]

In the years that followed, other theologians, such as Leonardo Boff, Jon Sobrino, Ignacio Ellacuría, José Miguez Bonino, and Juan Luis Segundo added their voices to that of Gutiérrez. But it did not come without a price. Their emphasis on creating just, egalitarian political and economic systems, eradicating the oppression and inequalities created by sinful structures, brought swift and deadly government reprisals. Oscar Romero, the archbishop of El Salvador was killed by an assassin's bullet while observing mass. Later Ellacuría met a similar fate, along with other clerics. Nevertheless, Liberation Theology would come to influence theology everywhere.

Although liberation theologies have influenced Latino/a theology, there are significant differences between them, and the two should not be confused. They do share similarities, including an emphasis on the lived experience of the people, a liberative praxis, and a biblical hermeneutics with an eye to power structures and the role of the oppressed. But, because there are some basic differences in the contexts of Latin America and Latinos/as in the U.S., some basic differences between the two can be expected. For instance, for Latinos/as in the U.S., social and cultural marginalization is as significant theologically as poverty and oppression. Furthermore, Latino/a existence in the borderland of various cultures also affects Latino/a theology, forcing it to examine issues of identity, hybridity, and race. Additionally, the emphasis on culture and the experience of Latinos/as in the U.S. also brings a new theological focus beyond that of poverty and oppression. By using culture as an instrument of social change and theological reflection, Latino/a theology opens new theological perspectives and brings about changes beyond the scope of Latin American Liberation theology with its emphasis on politics and economics.[38] Ultimately, Latino/a theology redefines many key theological concepts using multicultural, organic, historical, and diverse perspectives that surge from the lives of historical subjects.[39]

To some extent, Latino/a theology even influenced Latin American theology, forcing it to confront some of its own theological lacunas. For instance, María Pilar Aquino, a Latina theologian, traces four areas Latino/a theology forced Latin American Liberation theology to re-examine. First,

Latino/a theology challenged Liberation theology's limited focus on the political and economic, to the exclusion of cultural, aesthetic, and racial dimensions of society. Second, Latino/a theologians critiqued Liberation theology's failure to explore popular religion—the popular religious expressions of the people—as an important source for theological reflection. Third, *Femenista* and *Mujerista* theologians criticized Liberation theology's failure to address issues of sexism. Finally, Latino/a theologians challenged the dismissive attitudes and the assumptions that Latino/a theologians are compromised and sold out to the oppressive systems of the U.S. As a result of these dialogues, Latino/a theology has not only been influenced by Latin theologies of liberation, but has also influenced them.[40]

The Emergence of Latino/a Theology

Latino/a theology emerged as its own distinct theology in the 1970s, heralded by the establishment in 1972 of the Mexican American Cultural Center (MACC) in San Antonio, founded by Virgilio Elizondo, who served as the center's first president.[41] Soon, several centers and programs developed in some seminaries, such as the Mexican American Program at Perkins School of Theology. These centers served as catalysts for discussion and writing that laid a foundation for Latino/a theology. *Apuntes*, published in 1981 by the Mexican American Program in cooperation with the United Methodist Publishing House and edited by Justo L. González, became the first journal exclusively dedicated to Latino/a theological reflections. The following year, 1982, saw the publication of Virgilio Elizondo's book *Galilean Journey*, another landmark in Latino/a theology.

In the latter part of the 1980s and in the early part of the 1990s Latino/a theology saw a "boom" in publication, marked by a proliferation of publications in the field.[42] During this time, there was a surge of new organizations and resources with an emphasis on Latino/a academic reflection, scholarship, and theological education. In the American Academy of Religion, the Hispanic American Religion, Culture, and Society Group and *La Comunidad*, an organization of Latino/a scholars in religion, were created. During this time the Academy of Catholic Hispanic Theologians of the United States (ACTHUS) came into being and launched *The Journal of Hispanic/Latino Theology*. *La Asociación para la Educación Teológica Hispana* (AETH), focusing on the theological education of Hispanics; and AMEN, an association of Latino/a evangelical ministers, also developed during these decades. Later, the Hispanic Summer Program, gathering Latino/a professors of religion and students for intensive summer studies at member seminaries and schools, was formed. In 1996 Pew Charitable Trusts created the Hispanic Theological Initiative (HTI) to promulgate advanced theological studies by Latino/a students and junior faculty. As a result, Latino/a theology continues to proliferate in the United States, with new books and scholarly projects emerging annually.

Latino/a theology did not emerge in a vacuum. It took shape in a particular context and is part of an historical legacy—a legacy marred by violence, domination, and oppression, both against us and by us. We cannot do Latino/a theology without acknowledging our history. We are heirs of atrocities committed by us, including our complicity in the genocide of Native Americans and the enslavement of Africans. We are guilty of racism and classism, as are other cultures and groups.[43] We are also the victims of violence, discrimination, and oppression. We are the fusion of the conquerors and the conquered, the slaves and the enslavers, the oppressed and the oppressors. Thus we live the embodied reality of the fusion of cultures and peoples. But we are also heirs of the sacrifices, dreams, and struggle for liberation of people like Bartolomé de Las Casas, Bernardino de Sahagún, José Marti, Oscar Romero, and Caesar Chavez.

Understanding the context of history shows us how theology can become a tool for justifying domination and atrocities, helping us uncover the "skeletons in our closets." Learning from the dark periods of our history that are still a part of our legacy today, we might avoid making the same mistakes. Learning from our history also serves as part of our catharsis and repentance. As we confess the sins of our fathers and mothers, as well as our own, we can begin to accept that who we are today is inextricably connected to that past we would rather not see. By appropriating our honest and full history, we learn from whence we come and are better able to see where we are going.

On Naming Our Present[44]

Theologians often attempt to identify the ethos of their age, yet these are often veiled attempts to identify abstractions detached from the complex reality of their present context. Simply put, their naming of the present ignores the reality and voices of the marginalized and the oppressed persons, as well as the particularities of concrete historical subjects. Ultimately, as David Tracy wisely observes, these attempts are merely too "self-centered and narrow." Yet, those communities who are in power in the Western world, who as the center of history and theological reflection define the "norm," cannot truly come to terms with their own identity without entering into dialogue with those who are different from them.[45]

One of these communities, vital to the self-understanding of the church and of Western culture, is the Hispanic world and the voices coming from the margins of society, a margin in which many Latinos and Latinas live. Yet, naming the present reality for Hispanics is a difficult process and fraught with the inherent problems. In understanding the present context of the Hispanic community, we must not ignore the complexity of our context or over-simplify it. Rather, we must look at the present situation of Latinos/as in the United States. Nor should we forget that the process of naming can enlighten and obscure simultaneously, for as we name, we also unname. When we identify something, we also constrict and control it, reducing it to the parameters of what the name implies. When the naming is imposed from without, it becomes an expression of power over the one being named, reducing the one named to the limits that the name imposes upon it, limits determined by the power of the one doing the naming.

Biblically, most of us are aware of the power of the word and of a name. In Genesis, God creates by the very power of the word. Later on, humans gain dominion over creation, and in part, that dominion comes through the power of naming given to humanity by God (Gen. 2:19-20). The power inherent in the act of naming continues as a motif in the Bible as we find prohibitions against taking God's name in vain and see the special treatment given to God's name in both the Scriptures and the religious practices of the Jewish communities, where the name of the most Holy is not spoken. One of the clearest examples of the role of names in the Bible occurs in the discourse of Moses and God at the burning bush. Moses asks God's name, yet the name given to Moses by God is an assertion of God's identity more than a defining name.[46] It is a name that retains the openness of self-definition, rather than of being limited to a specific identification.[47] *Yahweh*, I am who I am. God is who God is.

The practice of naming as an assertion of power over others in contrast to self-determination of one's own identity is significant for Hispanics and an essential part of our history too. Our names are an expression of our own self-identity, and the power to name who we are is part of our power of self-determination. When we read through the different texts and historical accounts of our people, we discover a diversity of names used by Hispanics to identify themselves—names coming from their countries and ethnicities.[48] Even today, the name we chose to call ourselves helps determine our sense of identity and our connections with different groups. We might refer to ourselves in terms of our country of origin, by a hyphenated term such as Mexican-American or Cuban-American, or by a politically charged term such as Chicano or Chicana. We may even accept terms imposed on us by the government, such as Hispanic, in order to foster a common identity with other groups.

There is a darker side to the process of naming and identifying. Our own history is filled with accounts of how the *conquistadors* named the lands and inhabitants, imposing their own notions and terms upon them. When Columbus came to this continent, his first acts were to give new names to the lands and to name the inhabitants "Indians," mistakenly believing he had arrived in the Indies. His act of naming the places and the people revealed his own sense of superiority and his belief that the Western European worldview and Christendom were the determinants for the rest of the world. In the act of naming, he exerted control and dominance over the inhabitants and their land.[49] Naming was an assertion of dominance and power, the first act of and a foreboding of the conquest that was to come. Thus, to name our present, we must do so with the awareness of the inherent dangers in any act of naming.

In naming the present reality of the Hispanic population we must also take into account the fluidity and changing nature of the Hispanic reality. Descriptions are always dated in and of themselves—a glimpse at our recent past, a snapshot that freezes the action into a static instant. Census figures are always inaccurate to a certain degree and already dated when they come out. By the time this book is published, the facts and the figures in it will reflect a reality that no longer exists, since things have changed since the time I originally wrote these words. Even I may have changed my opinions and perceptions as the contexts that affect me continue to change.

The Present Hispanic Context

Just a few years ago, population projections from the census indicated that, discounting any new immigrants and undocumented immigrants who are seldom counted, Hispanics would be the largest minority population by the year 2005. According to the 2000 census, Hispanics comprised 12.5 percent of the population in the U.S.—over 35 million people. In comparison, African Americans comprised only 12.3 percent of the population.[50] By July 2001, the Hispanic population had grown to 37 million, a 4.7 percent increase, constituting 13 percent of the population, while the African American population only grew by 2 percent to 12.7 percent. That the Hispanic population of the U.S. grew so quickly in such a short period of time to become the largest minority is indicative of how easily it outpaced growth projections.[51] Of course, it is important also to note that Latino/a and Hispanic are ethnic categories, not racial categories. Hispanics embody a wide variety of races. Some are of African origins, while others are of Indigenous origins. Some come from Western European ancestry, while others share Asian heritage, including some of my cousins. Others are a mix of several of these races, as is the case with *mestizos* (Spanish and Indigenous) and mulattos (Spanish and African).[52]

Hispanic populations in the Midwest and Midsouth have also grown dramatically in the past years. In the city of Memphis, where I currently reside, Hispanic populations have doubled in the last ten years, soaring in some official figures from about 5,000 to 57,000. Some Hispanic leaders in the area put the figure even higher at close to 125,000.[53] Regardless of figures and projections, one only needs to look around to see the growth of the Hispanic populations around the country. Just blocks from my house in East Memphis, there is a Hispanic bakery, three *taquerias* (restaurants), six markets, and a Spanish-language Christian bookstore. Even the local Kroger grocery store has a well-stocked Hispanic section. These are not indications of a small enclave of Hispanics, but of a vibrant, thriving community with even more *taquerias*, groceries, and rapidly growing Hispanic churches scattered throughout the city.[54] This same story is being repeated in cities across the U.S. like Omaha, Nebraska, and Kansas City, Missouri.

Hispanic Americans are not merely the fastest-growing minority segment of the U.S. population, they are also the youngest and, in many cases, one of the poorest. Latinos/as are considerably more likely to be unemployed than non-Hispanic whites, and although they compose only 13 percent of the total population, 22.8 percent live in poverty. In comparison, only 7.7 percent of non-Hispanic whites live in poverty. Yet, while figures vary among different groups, Latinos/as are also less likely to have finished high school or gone to college.[55] In comparison to other minority groups, the number of Latinos/as attaining a high school education has not grown proportionately to the population.[56]

Concerns about Generation X in the media and academic circles pale in comparison to those about Generation Ñ, a term coined by Bill Teck, whose parents are Cuban-American, to designate the thriving young Latino/a population who did not fit into the rubric of Generation X.[57] Studies indicate that 35.7 percent of Hispanics are under 18 years of age, compared to 23.5 percent of non-Hispanic whites, and over 40 percent are under the age of 44.[58] Some of these young Hispanics are second generation, speak little or no Spanish, enjoy rock and rap music as much as they might enjoy Latin and *Tejano* music. In contrast to recent immigrant groups who speak little English and work primarily in manual labor, Generation Ñers are upwardly mobile.

Our music also reflects our diversity from the Afro-Cuban music that has been popularized in the United States through the movie *The Buena Vista Social Club*, to the Polka influence in Tejano music, to the rock-Latino music mix popularized by Gloria Estefan. In addition, with the rise of stars such as

Jennifer Lopez and Ricky Martin, new mixes and influences are beginning to take shape in the American and Latin musical scene.[59] The influence of Latino/a culture upon the general American culture also demonstrates the porous nature of multiple contexts and cultures. The way in which Hispanic culture has permeated into American pop culture is astounding. Salsa has replaced ketchup as the condiment of choice in the U.S. Latin music is one of the top favorites of American teens—Hispanic and Anglo alike. Hispanic entertainers such as Jennifer Lopez, Marc Anthony, Christina Aguilera, and Ricky Martin have easily achieved superstar status.

As with any group, there are always exceptions to the rule. Economically, Hispanics range from the lower socioeconomic range of field workers and day laborers to the upper range of professionals and CEOs of large corporations. Many Hispanics no longer speak Spanish, especially the younger generations. Hispanic activism and political affiliations vary from the union organizers in the farm labor movement, to Puerto Rican nationalists who desire independence, to right wing conservative Cubans in South Florida. Still, we have some common traits, such as a shared linguistic heritage, family values, and sense of spirituality that run like threads through many of the different groups, though not all. Only one single element traverses all our cultures and nationalities—the legacy of the Spanish conquest of the Americas. Due to this diversity, attempts at self-definition of the group as a whole are nearly impossible. Yet, at times we are galvanized by our fight against discrimination and anti-Hispanic sentiments.

We live and participate in the changing dynamics of the American culture. We are shaped by it, just as we also shape it. American values, food, and pop culture influence us as we influence them. We intermarry with one another. We fight for shared causes side by side with other Americans. We are as much a part of America as America is a part of us. As the Latino/a population of the U.S. continues to grow and gain influence, our own self-definitions will also change. We might become one people, or we might fragment into different groups guided by individual interests. Who we are is continually in flux.

The Hidden People

I remember the first time I ate Mexican food. I was twelve years old, attending an international cultural fair in Miami. As a Cuban-American, I was more used to my roast pork, black beans and rice, and fried plantains. Although I was aware of other Hispanic cultures, I had very little exposure to them. Yet, this is difficult for non-Hispanics to understand. Hispanic is an artificial construct created by the government in the United States to define people that come from Mexico, the Caribbean, Central America, and South America—including recent immigrants as well as those who have lived in the U.S. for generations. Yet, because the term has a leveling effect on all Latinos/as, our differences are often hidden or subsumed under some amalgam of what a person may think a Hispanic is like.[60]

In the United States, most of the race dialogue occurs within a white-black paradigm, often excluding Latinos/as, Asians, and even Native Americans. This exclusion was most evident during segregation, as Virgilio Elizondo writes in his book, *The Future Is Mestizo*: "I remember well the problems we experienced just trying to go to the toilet. If we went into the ones marked "colored" we were chased out by the blacks because we were not technically black. Yet, we were often chased out from the ones marked "white" because we had dark skin. So we didn't even have toilets to which we could go."[61] The exclusion of Latinos/as from the categories that defined race in America left them without a clear place in society and often excluded them from politics, the media, and public life. Outside of a few exceptions, like Desi Arnaz's Ricky Ricardo television character in *I Love Lucy* and a few sports figures, Latinos/as had little presence in pop culture and in the public life of the United States.

History texts often fail to mention that the first permanent European settlement in what is now the United States was St. Augustine, Florida, a Spanish colony. Nor do they mention the thousands of Mexican Americans who fought in the Civil War, the lands that were taken in the Mexican American and Spanish American wars, nor the resistance movements organized by Hispanics.[62] These omissions keep the accomplishments and contributions of Hispanics hidden, giving the impression that most of us are recent interlopers and freeloaders, living off the wealth of America without contributing much in exchange.

Latinos/as still remain a hidden people in other ways. Today, many persons still assume that all Latinos/as are alike based on whatever preconceived notion of a Latino/a the person has. At times, this preconception comes from the general traits we perceive as common to the predominant Latino/a population in our area. For instance, people who live in the Southwest, where Latinos/as are primarily of Mexican ancestry, may tend to assume all Latinos/as have traits similar to the ones they know. So they may assume all Hispanics eat Mexican food. These people are not bigots; they are just human. They make assumptions based on their experience as all of us do. Unfortunately, even people in academia and from other minority groups make these assumptions and erroneously gloss over the complexity of the Latino/a reality in the United States.[63]

As the presence of Latinos/as in the United States continues to grow, along with their economic, social, and political impact, they are beginning to be discovered by communities, businesses, and churches. Latinos/as are still marginalized and disenfranchised—and in many communities they still remain hidden or ignored. Even worse, many still live in poverty, while others are victimized by systemic racism, bias, and stereotyping. As a church, we cannot ignore the needs of this rapidly growing community, nor forgo receiving the many gifts Latinos/as bring to the church and to our culture. In time, Latinos/as will no longer be a hidden people. Yet, there will always be people in our communities who are hidden, marginalized, and disenfranchised. As a church we must always strive to uncover these people and be their advocates.

Notes

1. See Virgilio Elizondo's account regarding this experience of being insiders-outsiders in *The Future Is Mestizo: Life Where Cultures Meet* (New York: Crossroads, 1988), p. 21.

2. Alfred North Whitehead, *Adventure of Ideas* (New York: Free Press, 1967), p. 43.

3. Ibid., p. 4. The historians' judgment and interests affect their description of the past.

4. Parts of this section are from my introduction to *Más Voces: Reflexiones Teológicas de la Iglesia Hispana,* ed. by Luis G. Pedraja (Nashville: Abingdon Press, 2001).

5. Spanish words like Naranja, Almendra, and Camisa come from Arabic instead of Latin.

6. Dates and historical data found in "Isabelle I," by Ramón Ruiz Amado, *The Catholic Encyclopedia, Volume VIII*, Online Edition (New York: Robert Appleton Company, 1910; Online Edition Copyright © 1999 by Kevin Knight).

7. See Luis N. Rivera Pagán's analysis and account of the violence of the conquest and how theology was used to justify it. *Evangelización y violencia: La Conquista de América* (San Juan: Editorial Cemi, 1990), especially chapter IX on the holocaust of the natives and chapter XI on the theological debate and the criticism of Spanish greed by clerics like Fray Tomás Ortiz, Motolinía, and others, pp. 423-24. The English translation of this book can be found under the title *A Violent Evangelism: The Political and Religious Conquest of the Americas* (Louisville: Westminster, 1992).

8. Ibid., pp. 79, 82, 86-94.

9. Ibid., p. 165. Also, see José de Acosta, *Predicación del evangelio en las Indias,* "Promio," pp. 43-48.

10. Pagán, *Evangelización y violencia,* pp. 191-99.

11. Ibid., pp. 161-75.

12. Ibid., 305-7. As Pagán notes, the enslavement of the Africans occurred, supposedly, at the hands of other Africans when found by the Portuguese. Hence, the Spanish did not believe themselves to bear the moral burden for their enslavement.

13. Ibid., 305. Rivera Pagán cites a letter by Las Casas admitting his previous stance and recanting it after becoming aware of the injustices brought upon the slaves.

14. Bartolomé de Las Casas, *Brevísima relación de la destrucción de África: Preludio de la destrucción de Indias. Primera Defensa de los guanches y negros contra su esclavvizacion,* ed. by Isacio Pérez Fernández (Lima: Instituto Bartolomé de Las Casas, 1989), p. 45. Also cited by Rivera Pagán in *Evangelización y violencia,* p. 423.

15. Virgilio Elizondo provides a good account of the story of the Virgin of Guadalupe and its significance in his book *Guadalupe: Mother of the New Creation* (Maryknoll: Orbis, 1997), pp. 65-67, 81-87. He also addresses the controversy regarding the story and offers arguments in favor of the account, p. 84.

16. See Luciano C. Hendren, "Daily Life on the Frontier," in *Fronteras: A History of the Latin American Church in the USA Since 1513*, ed. by Moisés Sandoval (San Antonio: Mexican American Cultural Center, 1983), pp. 123-30.

17. See James W. Loewen, *Lies My Teacher Taught Me: Everything Your American History Textbook Got Wrong* (New York: Touchstone Books, 1996) for a wonderful account of the distortions and lacunas found in history texts. Also Justo L. González, *Mañana: Christian Theology from a Hispanic Perspective* (Nashville: Abingdon Press, 1990), pp. 38-41.

18. See Giacomo Cassese's examination of the "Black Legends" and their origin in "Hispanos bajo la sombra de la Leyenda Negra: Historia de una contraversia religionsa," in *Apuntes*, 18/1 (Spring 1998), pp. 14-27.

19. Paul Barton's article "Inter-ethnic Relations Between Mexican American and Anglo American Methodists in the U.S. Southwest, 1836–1938," addresses the effect of Manifest Destiny in the Southwest in *Protestantes/Protestants: Hispanic Christianity Within Mainline Traditions*, ed. by David Maldonado (Nashville: Abingdon Press, 1999), pp. 60-62, 68-69.

20. Carlos Fernandez Shaw, *The Hispanic Presence in North America: From 1492 to Today*, trans. by Alfonso Bertodano Stourton, et al. (New York: Facts on File, 1991), p. 188, provides a good overview of different aspects of Hispanic presence in the United States by state and offers brief historical details.

21. Ibid., p. 201, which addresses particularly the situation in New Mexico, but is equally applicable to other territories that came under U.S. rule as a result of the treaty.

22. Tomás Atencio provides an example of the educational and economic impact of Protestantism in New Mexico in his article "The Empty Cross: The First Hispanos Presbyterians in Northern New Mexico," in *Protestantes/Protestants*, pp. 47-57.

23. Paul Barton addresses these problematic relationships between Hispanics and the denominations they joined. *Protestantes*, pp. 70-74.

24. For a good look at Puerto Rican culture and development in relationship to the United States, see Juan Flores, *From Bomba to Hip-Hop: Puerto Rican Culture and Latino Identity* (New York: Columbia University Press, 2000), particularly in relation to the colonial status of Puerto Rico, pp. 9-10.

25. See Juan González, *Harvest of Empire: A History of Latinos in America* (New York: Penguin Books, 2000), pp. 81-85.

26. Ibid., p. 118.

27. Ibid., p. 129.

28. Susan Ferris and Ricardo Sandoval, *The Fight in the Fields: César Chavez and the Farm Workers Movement* (Orlando: Paradigm Production, 1997) provides a good account of the movement, including how the Virgin of Guadalupe served as one of the movement's symbols see pp. 119-20.

29. Juan González, *Harvest of Empire*, pp. 170-77.

30. James H. Cone, *A Black Theology of Liberation: Twentieth Anniversary Edition* (Maryknoll: Orbis Press, 1970, 1990), pp. 23-38.

31. According to Susan Brooks Thistlewaite, in *Sex, Race, and God: Christian Feminism in Black and White* (New York: Crossroad, 1989), p. 77, Saiving's article is believed by many women to be the beginning of modern feminist theology.

32. Rosemary Radford Ruether, *Sexism and God-Talk: Toward a Feminist Theology*, tenth anniversary edition (Boston: Beacon Press, 1983, 1993), pp. 12-19.

33. This translates and builds on material found in my introduction to *Mas Voces*.

34. See José Miguez Bonino, *Faces of Latin American Protestantism* (Grand Rapids: Eerdmans, 1995), pp. 19-22.

35. Gustavo Gutiérrez, *A Theology of Liberation: 15th Anniversary Edition* (Maryknoll: Orbis Press, 1988), pp. 83-85.

36. Gustavo Gutiérrez, "Option for the Poor," in *Mysterium Liberationis: Fundamental Concepts in Liberation Theology*, ed. by Ignacio Ellacuría and Jon Sobrino (Maryknoll: Orbis Press, 1993), pp. 239-50.

37. Roberto S. Goizueta offers one of the best illustrations for understanding God's preferential option for the poor using the example of a fight between his older daughter and his younger son. Although he loves both equally, if he did not intervene on behalf of his son, by default he takes his daughter's side, who, by being stronger and bigger, would inevitably win. *Caminemos con Jesús: Toward a Hispanic/Latino Theology of Accompaniment* (Maryknoll: Orbis Press, 1995), pp. 175-76.

38. Daniel M. Bell analyzes these two theologies, particularly culture as being the key difference, in "Crossing the Postmodern Divide: Hispanic and Latin American Liberation Theologians in the Struggle for Justice," *Apuntes*, 21/1 (Spring 2001), pp. 4-14.

39. Maria Pilar Aquino argues that the assumptions made by systematic theologians, their negation of their historicity, and their role in defining normative theology serves to colonize other theologies. "Theological Method in U.S. Latino/a Theology, " in *From the Heart of Our People: Latino/a Explorations in Catholic Systematic Theology*, ed. by Orlando O. Espín and Miguel H. Diaz (Maryknoll: Orbis Press, 1999), pp. 8-9.

40. Ibid., pp. 16-17.

41. For a good overview of the historical development of Latino/a theology, see Eduardo C. Fernández, *La Cosecha: Harvesting Contemporary United States Hispanic Theology (1972–1998)* (Collegeville: Michael Glazier Books/Liturgical Press, 2000), pp. 35-92.

42. Allan Figueroa Deck presents an overview of these events and refers to this time period as the year of the "boom" in his article "Latino Theology: The Year of the 'Boom,'" in *The Journal of Hispanic/Latino Theology*, 1/2 (February 1994), pp. 51-63.

43. See my article "Building Bridges Between Communities of Struggle: Similarities, Differences, Objectives, and Goals," in *The Ties That Bind*, pp. 205-19.

44. With apologies to David Tracy, who used the title *On Naming the Present* (Maryknoll: Orbis Press, 1994) originally in the *Concilium* article which serves as the lead chapter to his book, pp. 3-24, addressing the theological questions raised by Modernism, Anti-Modernism, and Postmodernity. There he asks the question "Where, in all the discussions of otherness and difference of the postmoderns as well as the moderns and the antimoderns, are the poor and the oppressed? These are the concrete others whose differences should make a difference," adding that the lack of these voices in the conversation also tells the Western center about itself, p. 21.

45. Ibid., p. 20.

46. Walter Brueggemann, in *Theology of the Old Testament: Testimony, Dispute, and Advocacy* (Minneapolis: Fortress Press, 1997), addresses some of the complexities of Genesis 3:14, citing arguments that indicate that the phrase is indicative of God's presence or of God as the one who acts, pp. 123-24, note 17. Yet, in either

case, God's name is not defined by Moses or by human standards, but by God's action and presence. The name never delimits or defines God outside of God's activity and initiative.

47. Ibid., pp. 184-85. Brueggemann speaks of the first three commandments as indicative of Yahweh as a God who "cannot be captured, contained, assigned, or managed by anyone or anything, for any purpose." The prohibition against making images and taking God's name in vain indicate the power and inherent dangers of naming and imaging God.

48. Timothy Matovina and Gerald E. Poyo, in the introduction of their edited work, ¡Presente! U.S. Latino Catholics from Colonial Origins to the Present (Maryknoll: Orbis Press, 2000), acknowledge the power of names in self-determination and attest to the variety of names used by different people in their writings and historical documents to name themselves, while noting how the more inclusive terms such as Hispanic, Latinos, Latinas, and Spanish-speaking began to be used later to assert a sense of unity, p. xx.

49. Luis N. Rivera Pagán gives a wonderful account of how Columbus's naming of the lands was a precursor and an indication of his intent on domination. In addition, Rivera Pagán also addresses the inherent power of the act of naming. Evangelización y violencia: La Conquista de América (San Juan: Editorial Cemi, 1990), pp. 16-17.

50. Profile of General Demographic Characteristics for the United States: 2000, United States Department of Commerce, Table DP-1.

51. U.S. Census Bureau, news release, January, 21, 2003, CB 03-16.

52. Newsweek provides a summary of the 22 nationalities and the races that made up the Latino/a community in 1999, as well as their political leanings, use of Spanish, educational attainment, and other traits in the article by Brook Larmer, "Latino America" (July 12, 1999), pp. 50-51.

53. Estimates based on figures provided by Latino Memphis Connection.

54. Good Morning America had a segment on the changing face of race in America, focusing on the growing Latino/a population of Memphis (Good Morning America, ABC News, June 4, 2001).

55. Melissa Therrien and Roberto R. Ramirez, The Hispanic Population in the United States: March 2000 (Washington: Current Population Reports, P20-535, U.S. Census Bureau, March, 2001), pp. 4-6.

56. Jennifer Cheeseman Day and Kurt J. Bauman, "Have We Reached the Top? Educational Attainment Projections of the U.S. Population," Population Division (Washington: U.S. Bureau of the Census, May 2000).

57. John Leland and Veronica Chambers, "Generation Ñ," Newsweek, Vol. 134, No. 4 (July 12, 1999), p. 53.

58. Therrien and Ramirez, The Hispanic Population in the United States, pp. 2-3.

59. Both the article by Leland and Chambers, "Generation Ñ" and the article by Christy Haubegger, "The Legacy of Generation Ñ," provide a good glimpse of the changing dynamics of culture as influenced by Latinos/as in the U.S. in 1999, including the mix of cultures found in the younger generations who were exposed to American pop culture as much as to Latino/a culture. Newsweek (July 12, 1999), pp. 52-61.

60. See my essay "Guidepost Along the Journey: Mapping North American Hispanic Theology" in Protestantes/Protestants, pp. 124-27, where I address how differences are obscured, sublimated, and leveled by the dominant culture.

61. Virgilio Elizondo, The Future Is Mestizo, p. 18.

62. Ilan Stavans mentions these and other omissions in *The Hispanic Conditions: Reflections on Culture and Identity in America* (New York: HarperCollins, 1995), 23.

63. Lee H. Butler, Jr., in "African American Christian Churches: The Faith Tradition of a Resistance Culture," in *The Ties That Bind: African American and Hispanic American/Latino/a Theologies in Dialogue*, ed. by Anthony B. Pinn and Benjamin Valentin (New York: Continuum Press, 2000), says language is one of the most significant barriers in African American and Hispanic dialogues, not realizing that this is not true for many Hispanics who are bilingual or who speak only English, p. 233.

CHAPTER THREE

MAPPING OUR JOURNEY: THE TASKS OF THEOLOGY

E very journey must begin somewhere, go somewhere, and follow a given path. This is true for our lives. It is also true for our theological journeys. In the previous chapters we looked at context and the beginnings of Latino/a theology. Now we turn our attention to the task, the sources, and the methods of theology. To continue with the analogy of a journey, our context and historical legacy set the stage for our theological journey, guiding our choices and direction. In a sense, our context and history serve as a map that shows us where we are and how we got there. It is like the maps we find at malls and airports with a big arrow signaling, "You are here." As theologians it is important to know our location before embarking on our theological journey. To throw ourselves into our theological endeavor without getting our bearings can be disastrous, leading us to make erroneous assumptions, taking us down the wrong path, and causing us to wander aimlessly. We must know who we are and where we are before going forth.

Theology as Map Making

I like using the analogy of a map to describe the work of theologians for several reasons. First, maps are not pictures that depict a snapshot of reality to be hung on a wall or bound in an album. Maps are <u>functional</u>. They serve a <u>purpose</u>. They are not meant to be admired. They are meant to be used. In addition, their function determines their nature. That is, what the map is for determines the kind of map it is. Thus, a map can be simple, rough, drawn on a napkin guiding you from the restaurant to a friend's house. Such a map might not be to scale. It probably will not include all of the landmarks and features along the way. It may not even give you exact directions. But if it gets you to your friend's house it has served its purpose well. Other maps, such as topographical maps might contain more accurate depiction of elevations and features in the landscape, but if it does not get you to your friend's house, then it is not a good map for such purposes! The <u>value</u> of maps depends on the purpose of the map. The same can be said for theology. Our theological work should be measured by its <u>purpose</u>, that is, its <u>tasks</u>.

Maps are also like theology in another way. Maps are <u>never exact replicas</u> of the realities they depict. Regardless of their accuracy, maps always distort some aspect of reality. Depending on the type of map, you will notice that in some the top edges are elongated, while in others the sides are shortened. In trying to represent a three dimensional reality in the bounds of two dimensions, we cannot prevent certain distortions. Even the most detailed globes lack certain minute features found in the real globe we live on. Maps are even <u>influenced</u> by political agendas, such as the drafting of borders. They can be <u>affected by the power status</u> of the culture or the perspective of the cartographer. For instance, most maps give preference to their country by placing it at the center of the map, while others draw the northern hemisphere as larger and on top.[1] If we mistake the map for reality, we <u>misconstrue its purpose</u> and allow the distortions to enter into our perceptions and we miss the features that are absent from the map. Just because a map does not depict a street or a city does not mean that they do not exist. Maps need to be compared with reality for accuracy and updated from time to time.

The same can be said for theology. Theology tries to <u>depict our under-standing of God from a human perspective</u>. It is the same as trying to fit a three-dimensional world into a two-dimensional map. There are always some things missing, and some distortions will inevitably take place. Thus we must <u>not adhere so closely to a theological perspective</u> that it will blind us to other dimensions of God and God's interaction with humanity that might be absent or distorted by our particular theology. In addition, from time to time we need to re-examine our theology and our beliefs to see if they conform with reality as we currently understand it—if there are distortions that need correcting and details that need updating.

Maps are also artificial. They are not unadulterated depictions and expressions of reality. People with particular intentions, limitations, and preconceptions make them. Maps have an uncanny ability to <u>reflect the perceptions</u>, biases, and assumptions of the map maker. As a child, I wanted to visit the border between states and countries to see the line. I imagined that there was an actual line drawn in the land and a change in color of the dirt, just as we saw it on the map. Of course, I was sorely disappointed. Boundaries and borders are ultimately artificial creations emerging out of human struggles, politics, and compromises. Thus, to some extent, maps are political creations that reflect structures of power and domination. For instance, North America and Europe are generally depicted as bigger than they actually are and as being on top on maps. There is no reason this needs to be the case. Rather, it is merely a reflection of the power structures of our present reality.

Theology, by the same token, also bears the marks of politics, domination, and human struggles. We cannot deceive ourselves into thinking that theology is somehow pristine and pure, devoid of all the biases and prejudices that are part of the human condition. To do so would not only be naïve, but it would also be dangerous. Theology is an artificial enterprise. It serves a purpose in our quest to understand God. But it also bears the marks of our sinfulness, of our politics, and of our prejudices as well as our hopes and our dreams. We must always look to theology with the realization that at times the boundaries it draws and the colors it depicts are mere creations of human beings, reflecting their own frailty and not the truth of God.

Finally, theology is also similar to cartography, the art of map making and reading, in that we can easily misread a map. We might even be unable to correctly read a map at all! Reading a map incorrectly can lead us astray of our destination. Being unable to read the map can render the most detailed map useless. Not knowing the purpose or type of map we are using can also cause us problems. Similarly, we must also learn to "read" theology correctly. We must learn to identify the purpose and type of theology we are using and make sure that we are using the proper form of theology for our purposes in a correct manner. In a sense, we are all cartographers, finding our way through uncharted lands. But as we move into the future, into what Shakespeare would call the undiscovered country, we must begin to chart our own course and to draw our own maps. To do so, we can follow the paths others before us have trod or make our own way as we seek to understand how our particular context shapes our understanding of theology, as well as informs our choices and the tasks before us.

The Tasks of Theology

Doing theology merely for its own sake is like making maps that lead nowhere. Theology has a given purpose and direction. Like a map, the tasks or purposes set forth for our theology guide the shape that it will take. Generally, theologians, guided by their purpose, context, and definitions, identify different tasks for theology. At its most basic, we can say that theology is discourse about God. The word *theology* itself is a combination of two Greek words, *theos* meaning "God" and *logos,* a word of various meanings, including "word," "reason," "discourse," "order," and even "creative word." Whatever meaning the theologian eventually chooses is telling because it hints at the theologian's understanding of theology and its tasks. Thus, I would like to take a more integral approach to our theological tasks by examining some of theology's many different interpretations and possible tasks.

Friedrich Schleiermacher, considered by many as the father of modern theology, defines theology primarily by its tasks, which include the development of church leadership and a focus on examining the capacity of faith in humanity.[2] This approach, focused on human spirituality as the object of reflection, emphasizes the subjective dimensions of faith as the location of theological study. This is an attempt by Schleiermacher to give theology a degree of scientific legitimacy while safeguarding it from the critiques leveled by the, at the time, emerging hard sciences such as chemistry and physics. As a result, faith, defined by Schleiermacher in terms of the feeling of absolute dependence, becomes the central focus for theological scrutiny.[3] Theology begins with human capacity and experience. It then proceeds to examine the ramifications of this experience in the context of the church.

In the twentieth century, Karl Barth defined theological dogmatics as "the scientific self-examination of the Christian Church with respect to the content of its distinctive talk about God."[4] This concise statement points to what for Barth are three key constitutive ingredients of theology. First, by scientific, Barth does not mean what we would call today the "scientific method." What he means is that theology is, like any other discipline of inquiry, a human attempt at understanding an object of knowledge that must follow a given and consistent method, and be accountable for it to itself, to the church, and to the other disciplines. Second, theology is a practice of self-examination, that is, critical inquiry into the discourse of the church about its beliefs and practices. Third, theology has a distinct object of reflection. For Christianity, the object that provides distinctiveness and content of the church's discourse is the uniqueness of God's revelation to humanity through Christ.

Thus, Barth could say that theology is the church's discourse about God in its broadest sense, but in a narrower sense, theology is also an ongoing examination, critique, and revision of this discourse in recognition of the frailty and fallibility of humanity.[6] Unlike Schleiermacher, Barth does not believe faith to be the result of human capacity or action. Rather, it is constituted by

God's free and gracious address to humanity through the presence and activity of Jesus Christ, God's ultimate revelation. The task of theology comes from our understanding of God's revelation—primarily, God's revelation in Christ. As a result, Jesus Christ becomes the criterion for examining our theological discourse about God. In other words, God's revelation in Jesus Christ serves as the yardstick of theology as we examine whether the church's talk about God is faithful to that revelation and relevant to our present situation. Thus, the task of theology according to Barth involves not only examining the accuracy of the church's discourse about God in light of the criterion of Jesus Christ, but also in speaking to our lives today.[7]

Schleiermacher emphasizes human faith in God as the subject of our theological exploration. Barth places the emphasis upon God's revelation in Christ as the object of our theological exploration. Rudolf Bultmann, a contemporary of Barth, provides a third alternative, arguing that the task of theology actually involves both. In his book, *What Is Theology*, Bultmann argues that we cannot look simply at the nature of our faith without understanding the object of our faith and vice versa. Both how we believe and in what we believe are relevant to the task of theology according to Bultmann.[8] Paul Tillich, a contemporary of Barth and Bultmann, identifies the task of philosophy as making a correlation between religious and philosophical language by matching up the questions of philosophy with the symbols of religion that might provide the answer.[9] Tillich's argument resolves the tension between the subjective experience of faith and its object in the act of faith that unites the two.[10]

Theology cannot simply look at the object of its faith, its understanding of God and doctrine. It needs to look at how the people of faith believe and relate to the object of their faith. Both are necessary dimensions of our theological task that should not be separated from each other. In Latino/a theology, this is an essential balance that we must preserve, for the faith of the people—that is, how the people believe—is an important aspect of our theology. At the same time, we must not lose sight of the object of faith in the development of our theological insights. We must always try to relate our understanding of the faith of the people to the history, doctrines, and revelatory experience of the church.

One often cited classical argument used by Anselm, defines the task of theology as *fides quaerens intellectum*, faith seeking understanding. This approach focuses on "reason" as the primary definition of *logos* while keeping faith as an integral component of theology. At times, we professional theologians forget this connection, focusing solely on reason almost to the exclusion and minimization of faith and belief as a component of theological inquiry. By understanding theology as faith seeking understanding we acknowledge the primacy of faith in theological inquiry, that is, our experience of faith precedes the application of reason.

More recently, this is the approach Daniel Migliore uses in his aptly titled book *Faith Seeking Understanding*, where he initially defines theology in its most basic form as "faith venturing to inquire, daring to raise questions."[11] People of faith inevitably raise questions about the nature of their faith, its object, its relation to their present situations, and a quest for truth.[12] Given this definition, Migliore ultimately interprets the tasks of theology as a "faithful, coherent, timely, and responsible articulation of the Christian faith."[13] This task of theology requires that theologians examine whether the practices and proclamations of the church are true to the legacy of the gospel message, whether they are relevant to our present context, whether they have a transforming influence on our world, and whether they are full and consistent expressions of the gospel.[14]

But faith is also an intricate part of who we are, shaping our self-understanding and guiding our actions. Our faith is not just intellectual; it is emotional and personal. We want our faith to be true and worthy of our trust, but because it is so significant to us, it is difficult for us to question and examine it. Our faith also transcends the bounds of our lives, since we are part of a faith community and heirs to a tradition.[15] We must risk trying to understand, examine, and articulate our faith. Yet we must not forget that faith is more than a body of doctrines and a set of beliefs, it is part of our lives and a way of life. It determines what we value and how we evaluate our context as well. Our faith shapes and affects us. It guides what we do. Faith is more than an intellectual exercise; it is also part of our praxis, our doing.[16] It has consequences in our lives and affects the lives of others. Thus, it is necessary to look at more than our belief system. We must also look at faith practices, actions, and the consequences—both intended and unintended—of our faith. At times, we realize that our actions reveal our true faith and belief, maybe in ways we had not realized—in ways that are better than words, dogmas, or cognitive ideologies.

Latino/a theologians, like most theologians, take all of these tasks we have discussed seriously. But they also build upon them, for even these basic tasks can be building blocks of further inquiry. For instance, the task of faithfulness to the gospel must take into consideration how we read and interpret the gospel. We can easily interpret the gospel in a manner that is oppressive, as did conquerors who interpreted the call to evangelize the world as a mandate to conquer and subjugate people of other faiths. The gospel in hurtful hands, as our history has shown, can be a very dangerous weapon. Theology can also become so enamored with being relevant to its present situation that it can lose its sense of continuity with the Christian faith. The same can be said about any aspect of our theological tasks.

The Forms of Reason

If we think of the task of theology primarily as faith in search of understanding, both of how we believe and in what we believe, reason immediately comes to our minds as the means for scrutinizing our faith and beliefs. But what does it mean for us to use reason to reflect upon our faith, both in its content and expression? Generally when we think of the term "reason," we think primarily of the cognitive functions of the mind. However, the Greek term, *logos*, is far richer than our basic view of reason as a cognitive function. It encompasses how we order reality, think about things, make judgments, and relate to our world. Through reason, we grasp the world around us and interact with it.[17]

Truth, we are told in John's Gospel, will set us free (John 8:32). In many ways, reason, in its quest for truth, can set us free. However, reason can just as easily become an instrument of oppression. As Herbert Marcuse warns in his epilogue to *Reason and Revolution*:

> Freedom is on the retreat—in the realm of thought as well as in that of society...with the increasing concentration and effectiveness of economic, political, and cultural controls, the opposition in all these fields has been pacified, co-ordinated, or liquidated....It [reason] helps to organize, administer, and anticipate the powers that be.[18]

In many ways, reason can become an instrument of domination that establishes a totalitarian and monolithic understanding of truth through which we measure all things. In equating truth with reason and reason with reality, we make the quest of reason simply a question of determining what is "truly" real—that is, what actually exists or is the case. The result is the reduction of reason to a simple form that merely orders, clarifies, and qualifies "reality" without ever recognizing that there is also a dimension of potentiality and possibility inherent in reality—a dimension that must also qualify reality by exploring not merely what is the case, but also what ought to be the case.[19]

In aligning itself with the process of describing the status quo and then asserting it as the truth, reason becomes an instrument of oppression that excludes the voices of those who present alternate interpretations or demand change. Ideas that do not conform to this simplistic view of reason are labeled irrational or false, further perpetuating the status quo. Such is the case when men preserve sexist structures by charging that women, who may use a different way of reasoning, are irrational and unfit for performing the same task as a man. It was also the case in the conquest of the Americas, where the subjugation of indigenous people and the enslavement of Africans was justified by claiming they were inferior because they did not fit into our ways of knowing or reasoned in a different fashion. Even the ways we define reason can lead us to exclude most people from ever engaging in it, since most people, burdened with the necessity of working to subsist do not have the luxury of spending time in pure contemplation. Such a limited view of reason limits "rational thought" to the privileged few who can afford the luxury of contemplating reality and denies it to the majority of people who must work to subsist from day to day.[20] If this definition of reason is indeed the case, then it excludes the majority of humanity from being rational!

Given the richness and diversity of what reason means and the dangers it embodies, when we speak of theology in terms of reasoning about God, we must be careful not to limit ourselves to a simplistic view of reason that reduces it to a descriptive, cognitive, or analytical function. From early on, philosophers spoke of at least three types of reasons used by human beings to relate to their world: theoretical, practical, and aesthetic. Let us take a closer look at each of them.

Theoretical Reason

The first type of reason, theoretical reason, is the one we most often think of in relationship to the term reason, and it is an essential component of the practice of theology. Its very name, "theoretical," comes from the same Greek word meaning "god" that lies at the root of the word "theology." We might even say theoretical reason is the form of reason that tries to divine the mind of God! Of course, in reality, it is the form of reason that searches for the order of things and for the truth—ideally what and how God has ordained things to be. In theoretical reason, we relate to the world around us primarily through a cognitive and analytical framework, where we thinking subjects examine the world of objects around us to determine their nature, that is, what they are. This is the realm of scientific study, empirical data, critical reflection, and logic. Accordingly anything can be an object of our scrutiny, including people. What we try to determine is the nature of the things we are examining, not as subjects themselves, who have their own thoughts and self-definitions, but as objects of our reason and determinations. We gaze upon the objects of our reflection, trying to penetrate into their innermost place, dissecting them, manipulating them, and analyzing them—in part to understand them and in part to determine them.[21] This is why being objective is the primary attribute of theoretical reason. One objectifies in order to subtract all that is subjective out of any given situation. According to this view, the better one can make subjects into objects, the purer the theoretical reasoning becomes.

Theoretical reason relates us to the world through perception, examination, logic, and analysis. We order and structure reality, develop categories, and make determinations about the world that surrounds us. With theoretical reason we analyze statements about our world and determine the truth and accuracy of these statements.[22] Through theoretical reason we try to determine whether things are the way we think they are and examine the coherence of our thoughts—how our thoughts hang together and how well they reflect the state of things around us. Theoretical reason examines whether we are thinking correctly about the world. Within the scope of religion, it plays a major role in our quest for truth and orthodoxy to see if we believe the right thing.

Naturally, this type of reason is crucial for understanding God and important for theology as we examine our beliefs, doctrines, and language about God. After all, our faith in God is a serious matter that cannot be taken lightly. We are never merely satisfied with believing in something. We also want what we believe to be true, coherent, and cogent—that is, to be reasonable. We need to examine and articulate our faith, as well as relate it to other aspects of our world including scientific innovation and world politics. At times, we might even need to engage in some level of speculation based on our faith experience and belief, drawing out the logical implications of our faith and its possibilities. But theology must not stop there in its use of reason.

Practical Reason (aka Moral Reason)

Practical reason, also known as moral reason, relates to the world of action and how we should interact with other subjects in the world. Aristotle's works distinguish theoretical reason from practical reason by indicating that we do not simply want to know what courage and justice are (theoretical reason) but we want to be courageous and just (practical reason).[23] Hence, merely having theoretical knowledge is not sufficient. One must also be able to act accordingly, and this requires a certain measure of rational deliberation to ensure that our actions correspond to our beliefs and vice versa.

In religion, beliefs alone are not sufficient. Action is also an essential part of our world. As a result, we must apply our judgment to how we should act in the world, since our thoughts themselves often influence what we do. Generally, in religion and philosophy, we associate practical reason with the field of ethics. This association of practical reason with ethics is important and essential to our thought as we determine the right course of action in specific circumstances, develop both a sense and a rationale for moral judgment, and ascertain the values inherent in our decision-making process.

However, we must also look beyond the field of ethics. In theology, for instance, liberation theologies address the need to include practical reason as a part of our theological reflection, primarily through their emphasis on praxis and orthopraxis. Praxis pertains primarily to human action, and in the strict Aristotelian sense, it is an end in itself and a process of self-determination.[24] However, Karl Marx understands praxis as an action that produces an external result, including social transformation.[25] Thus, as we can see, the term *praxis* is filled with ambiguity. It is not merely our behavior or mere action, but a deliberate action, an intentional way of life with an end in sight. As Liberation theologians use the term it typically refers to a liberating activity as part of the struggle for liberation from poverty, oppression, injustice, and death—a struggle for life. But in particular, it applies to a specific Christian commitment to justice.[26]

Our beliefs and thoughts many times do drive our actions, and it is important for theologians to think about the practical implications of our faith in our decision-making processes and in judgments of value regarding the rightness or wrongness of our actions. But our actions do not always reflect our beliefs. We do things that often are opposed to our belief and value systems that may be driven by circumstances, by moral failings, or by arriving at our decision through other means.[27] In some ways, our actions might reflect hidden beliefs or agendas, even some we might not even be aware of consciously.[28] Thus, it is necessary for us as theologians to examine not only our beliefs, but also our actions in light of what we believe to see if they conform to our faith.

While theoretical reason focuses on determining the case and its search for "truth," practical reason focuses on determining the right course of action with questions about what is right and wrong, or what ought to be the case.[29] In a sense, it also raises the questions of justice and righteousness. Naturally, such questions are important in the development of any theology and are essential questions raised by Liberation theologies, including Latino/a theologies. The role of theology in transforming the lives of individuals and society is a central tenet of Liberation theologies, and as a whole cannot be ignored in our theological reflection. Theology influences our actions, and our actions reflect our theology. The two must be looked at side by side.

Aesthetic Reason (aka Poietic Reason)

A third form of reason is what we call aesthetic or poietic reason. In Aristotle's work, this third form of reason serves a creative function, producing something in the world, whether as an art form or as a material product, such as a tool or building.[30] This form of reason traditionally seeks to determine the beauty, symmetry, and sublime nature of something. Whether it is in art or in production, we invoke our rational capacities as we examine the beauty and appearance of what lies before us. We know whether a work of art is beautiful or whether something serves the purpose for which it was created. There are certain aesthetic qualities that we seek and a certain level of judgment that we invoke to determine whether something is truly a work of art or kitsch.

While theoretical and practical reasons are primarily directed toward an object or a subject, aesthetic reason has a dual nature. We use our aesthetic reason to create a tool, a work of art, to bring something to life. But at the same time, we can be grasped by something—a piece of art or even an idea that enthralls us or beckons us to give it life. Let me give you two examples. First, most of us can recall being at a play or gazing at a work of art that fully enthralls us, engages our imagination, and draws us into that world. In a sense, we lose ourselves in the world of the play and its characters or become immersed in the piece of art to such an extent that we lose our sense of present reality and are transported briefly in our minds into another world. In that sense, we are grasped by the object as much as we grasp it.

Second, we can also think of an idea, a tune, or an image that beckons us to make it into an actual reality. We may call it inspiration or the muses, but whatever it might be, the notion grasps us and takes hold of us until we bring it into being. The inspiration of the artist or the "eureka" moment of the inventor is such a moment in which we not only grasp an idea, but we are also drawn to it in such a way that the idea takes hold of us. Such is the nature of the aesthetic dimension of reason; we grasp the object, as we examine it and judge its beauty, symmetry, and purpose, but the object can also take hold of our imagination in such a way that it draws us into itself, much like a good novel engrosses us in its plot or an artistic creation draws us into itself.[31]

Generally, we do not tend to see the connection between aesthetic reasoning and theological reflection. As a result, we tend to remain focused primarily on the theoretical and practical aspects of reason for most of our theological reflection. But as we saw above, the term praxis, as creative and productive, carries some of the nuance of Aristotle's original intent for aesthetics, that is, of producing something. In addition, the creation of symbols, a powerful tool for religion, also involves elements of the aesthetic! The theologian Paul Tillich, for instance, argued that the ultimate concern of our faith, the object of our faith, could only be expressed in symbolic language. Symbols point beyond themselves to a reality that is greater than they are and in which they participate. They derive their meaning and their power from this greater reality to which they refer and in which they participate. A flag, the illustration used by Tillich, has a power and meaning that is greater than the cloth and colors that compose it; they have power and meaning because of the nations they represent.[32] Symbols come to life, not by artificial design, but in their power to capture the imagination and open dimensions of reality otherwise inaccessible. If symbols play a central role in theology, then it should be clear that theology has an aesthetic dimension. Symbols can be rich and complex in nature, incorporating dimensions of art, culture, and religion.[33] Their aesthetic value cannot be ignored, nor can we ignore the role of aesthetic reason in theology.

This is an area where Latino/a theology takes the forefront. Rituals, symbols, art, and other expressions of faith and culture are central foci of Latino/a theological reflection. As we explore popular expressions of faith and cultural symbols, we examine the role that they play in resisting oppressive impositions, expressing our struggle, and opening new dimensions for understanding our Christian faith. As Roberto Goizueta argues, "the very emphasis on beauty, aesthetics, and celebration then—and only then—becomes, *de facto*, a subversive act in a society geared toward the accumulation of economic and political power."[34] Goizueta's work makes a strong argument for the power of aesthetics in theology in relation to praxis. In the same manner, as Alejandro García-Rivera argues in his book, *The Community of the Beautiful: A Theological Aesthetics*, the symbolic-cultural dimensions of Hispanic theological reflection allow Latino/a theology to develop a cultural aesthetic that can face up to suffering and reveal new dimensions of our Christian faith.[35]

Aztec theologians realized the value of the aesthetic for theological language, arguing that the divine could not be grasped by words; the divine could only be expressed by song and flower. Latino/a theology recognizes that at times our faith too can only be expressed by song and flower. Symbols, art, and cultural expressions of faith often reveal dimensions of our theological framework that remain hidden from our intellectual prodding. A theology that lacks an aesthetic dimension is incomplete.

Theology and the Forms of Reason

If we look simply at these three forms of reason and the role they play in theological reflection, it is easy for us to see that theology, defined in the traditional sense of "faith seeking understanding," requires that we have a fuller understanding of reason and its role in theology. If we consider the role of theoretical reason in theology, then we must strive to attain clarity, truth, and an accurate depiction of God in light of the fullness of human understanding and of our knowledge of the world in which we live. This means that we must not only attempt to conform to the rigors of logic and philosophical insight, but also to articulate our faith in light of scientific knowledge, historical research, and psychological, political, cultural, and philosophical insights encompassing the fullness of human thinking. Theology must resonate with our world.

At the same time, theology must also consider the role of practical reason in its reflection. Our faith and beliefs must be examined in light of their implications for action and transformation in our world, and our actions should be scrutinized to see whether they conform to what we claim to believe. Theoretical thinking cannot be separated from praxis. Theology should empower us to act; it should free us to believe and to live in accordance with our faith. It should empower and inspire us to life and to freedom. But we must not stop there. We must also consider the aesthetic dimensions of our faith—the role of symbols, art, and cultural expressions of faith in our theological insights. Theology must be creative. It must be able to open new dimensions as it reveals new aspects of our faith in God. Theology should have dimensions of creativity, beauty, and celebration. But theology should also evoke faith and empower us to believe, which brings me to a fourth dimension of reason.

The Reason for Following *(aka ecstatic acoulothetic reason)*

So far, we have explored the three traditional forms of reason. But I think that we must also consider a fourth. We can call this fourth form of reason the reason for following or believing—ecstatic reason or acoulothetic reason.[36] Any summons to believe something or to follow something, such as a person or a cause, requires us to deliberate and think through it to a certain degree. When Jesus summoned his disciples to follow him, they responded by following him. He clearly evoked that response from them.[37] But why did they follow? For that matter, what evokes a faith response from us leading us to believe? Why do we choose to believe some things and reject others? It may be that the object of faith evokes something in us that helps define who we are or that we experience something that calls us to be part of something greater than ourselves. While faith might indeed involve more than our reason, reasoning does play a role in our believing and in our faith.[38] We obviously do not put our faith in everything. While we wholeheartedly commit to some things, we reject others. Hence, we have criteria and ways of deliberating about what we believe and in whom we put our faith. Ultimately, theology should reflect on the reason of faith—that is, why we believe in something—while at the same time it should empower our faith.

Theology should not hinder our faith, but engender our faith and assist us in the ongoing process of discerning its validity, ensuring that our faith is not wasted on something false or idolatrous.[39] In this task of theology, reason is a necessary component. But we must look at reason in all its forms to avoid presenting a truncated and unbalanced theology that emphasizes only one dimension of human reason. While some might argue that many contextual theologies or theologies that come from a minority perspective are anti-rational, parochial, or confessional in nature because of their inclusions of culture, praxis, or grassroots faith expressions, I believe the opposite is true. I will even venture to argue that many of these theologies, and particularly Latino/a theologies, tend to be more complete because they incorporate the many dimensions of reason often ignored by academic disciplines fixated upon solely theoretical, philosophical models for doing theology, such as aesthetic cultural expressions of faith. As we will see, the methodology and sources of theological reflection incorporated in Latino/a theologies, as well as many other minority theologies, draw from multiple disciplines and incorporate dimensions of aesthetic and faith that often are absent from many more "traditional" models of theology, such as some forms of systematic and philosophical theologies.

Notes

1. A good illustration of this aspect of how power plays a role in the design of maps can be found in Miguel A. De La Torre and Edwin David Aponte's book, *Introducing Latino/a Theologies* (Maryknoll: Orbis Press, 2001), pp. 9-11.

2. Friedrich Schleiermacher, *Brief Outline of Theology as a Field of Study*, trans. by Terrence N. Tice (New York: Edwin Mellen Press, 1988), § 1-6; pp. 21-22.

3. Friedrich Schleiermacher, *The Christian Faith*, volume I, ed. by H. R. Mackintosh and J. S. Stewart (New York: Harper & Row, 1963), § 4, pp. 12-18.

4. Karl Barth, *Church Dogmatics*, vol. I, part 1, trans. by G. W. Bromiley (Edinburgh: T & T Clark, 1975), p. 3.

5. Ibid., p. 7.

6. Ibid, p. 3.

7. Ibid., pp. 12-18.

8. Bultmann, Rudolf, *What Is Theology?* Ed. by Eberhard Jüngel and Klaus W. Müller; trans. by Roy A. Harrisville (Minneapolis: Fortress Press, 1997), p. 49.

9. Paul Tillich, *Systematic Theology*, Vol. 1 (Chicago: University of Chicago Press, 1951), p. 62.

10. Paul Tillich, *The Dynamics of Faith* (New York: Harper & Row, 1957), pp. 10-11.

11. Daniel L. Migliore, *Faith Seeking Understanding: An Introduction to Christian Theology* (Grand Rapids: Eerdmans, 1991), p. 2.

12. Ibid., pp. 2-4.

13. Ibid., p. 10.

14. Ibid., pp. 10-12.

15. As Dorothee Sölle states in *Thinking About God: An Introduction to Theology* (Philadelphia: Trinity Press International, 1990), p. 4, "Faith is certainly my personal affair, but it is always also more than just my private affair. The faith of Christianity was there before I was born, and it will be there after my lifetime. It lives in and through society. It is the faith of the church."

16. Ibid., pp. 5-6.

17. According to Paul Tillich, in his *Systematic Theology*, Volume 1, reason "is the structure of the mind which enables the mind to grasp and to transform reality. It is effective in the cognitive, aesthetic, practical, and technical functions of the human mind" (Chicago: University of Chicago Press, 1951), p. 72.

18. Herbert Marcuse, *Reason and Revolution*, 2nd ed. (New York: Humanities Press, 1954), pp. 433-34.

19. Herbert Marcuse, *One-Dimensional Man: Studies in the Ideology of Advanced Industrial Society*, 2nd ed. (Boston: Beacon Press, 1964, 1991), pp. 130-33.

20. Ibid., pp. 128-29.

21. Here in particular, I am thinking of Michel Foucault's work in *The Birth of the Clinic: An Archaeology of Medical Perception*, trans. by A. M. Sheridan Smith (New York: Vintage Books, 1973), particularly the role of "the gaze," dissection, and perception in the constitution of knowledge.

22. Aristotle in *Nicomachean Ethics* speaks of a distinction in the rational principle of the soul where one part is calculative and the other is scientific, the calculative grasping a principle and the scientific as contemplative. *The Basic Works of Aristotle*, ed. by Richard McKeon (New York: Random House, 1941), 6.1.1139; p. 1023.

23. Aristotle, *Eudemian Ethics*, in *A New Aristotle Reader*, ed. by J. L. Ackrill (Princeton: Princeton University Press, 1987) 1.5.1216; p. 484.

24. Aristotle, *Politics*, in *The Basic Works of Aristotle*, 1.4.1254; pp. 1131-33.

25. Roberto S. Goizueta argues this in *Caminemos con Jesús: Toward a Hispanic/Latino Theology of Accompaniment* (Maryknoll: Orbis Books, 1995), pp. 80-86.

26. Ibid., p. 87. Roberto Goizueta's definitions of praxis and liberating praxis are an excellent exploration of the theme.

27. See how circumstances might affect how people act in Langdon Gilkey, *Shantung Compound: The Story of Men and Women Under Pressure* (New York: Harper & Row, 1966) and *Night* (New York: Bantam Books, 1982), Elie Wiesel's haunting book about the Holocaust.

28. Joerg Rieger refers to ideologies not just as the justification of positions taken, as Schubert Ogden refers to them, but as the justification of positions of which we are not even aware. Hence, oppression may come not just from those who are intent on oppressing us, but also from those who may be unwittingly participating in oppressive structures and practices. *Remember the Poor: The Challenge to Theology in the Twenty-first Century* (Harrisburg, Penn.: Trinity Press International, 1998), p. 58.

29. Aristotle, *Nicomachean Ethics*, in *The Basic Works of Aristotle*, 6.5.1139; p. 1026.

30. Aristotle, *Physics*, in *The Basic Works of Aristotle*, 2.8.199; pp. 249-50.

31. Goizueta, in *Caminemos con Jesús*, offers a similar explanation in terms of how musical pieces can grasp us as he describes Vasconcelos's concept of the special pathos of beauty, pp. 91-92.

32. Paul Tillich, *The Dynamics of Faith*, pp. 41-54.

33. I connect Tillich's theology of culture to Latino/a theology in a paper that was published in the *North American Paul Tillich Society Newsletter* (1999) entitled "Tillich's Theology of Culture and Hispanic American Theology." Although I do not address the notion of symbols in the paper directly, it does make the connection on the role culture plays in religious symbols.

34. Goizueta, *Caminemos con Jesús*, p. 129.

35. Alejandro García-Rivera, *The Community of the Beautiful: A Theological Aesthetics* (Collegeville, Minn.: Liturgical Press, 1999), pp. 54-55. In his work, García-Rivera examines the aesthetic dimensions of Latino/a Theology using several lenses, including the theology of Hans Urs von Balthasar, one of the leading Catholic theologians of the twentieth century, to explore the role of aesthetics in theological reflection.

36. Robert P. Scharlemann proposes this fourth form of reason, which he also refers to as a christological reason or ecstatic reasoning as the rationality that takes place as we determine if something is worth believing or whether a summons is worth following. See his book, *The Reason of Following: Christology and the Ecstatic I* (Chicago: University of Chicago Press, 1991), particularly pp. 86-96.

37. Ibid. Scharlemann uses this illustration of Jesus' summons to follow him to demonstrate the need for arguing for a fourth form of reason that addresses the question of how following can be compared to knowledge, moral action, or aesthetics, and argues in favor of placing Christology within the realm of philosophical theology through its role in developing this fourth form of reasoning, pp. 88-99.

38. See Paul Tillich's definition of faith "as being ultimately concerned" and as a "centered act of the whole personality," which includes the intellect, but cannot be reduced to it alone. *Dynamics of Faith*, pp. 30-35.

39. Ibid., pp. 95-98. Tillich offers us some of the criteria for faith and the truth of faith in this section of his book. The essential element of his argument is the recognition that faith needs to be examined, subjected to criteria, and that doubt is always an essential element in our faith.

FINDING OUR WAY: METHODS AND SOURCES OF THEOLOGY

I f theology is a map that helps us navigate our faith, theological methods are the compasses, sextants, and tools that help us find our way. They are the measures and instruments we use to explore our landscape and read our maps, as well as to draw them. We might find ourselves using more than one tool or instrument to find our way to our destination. To navigate the seas, for instance, we might use a compass and a sextant. We might also use more sophisticated instruments like global positioning satellites, radar, and telecommunication equipment. To draw a map, we might use rulers, pencils, or computers. We might also use other tools if we want to read a map, including a flashlight and a magnifying glass! The same is true for theology.

Methods, like the tools we use for our journey, help us achieve our theological objectives. Some are better suited for certain tasks than others.[1] We might even use several methods to develop our theology, and at times, the methods that we use might be in part determined by the theological task at hand. For instance, most of us are familiar with the scientific method that employs a hypothesis, observation, experimentation, and the forming of theories. A biologist uses different methods of experimentation than a physicist since they are looking at different objects with different criteria. Even though they might both adhere to the broader scientific method, they each have specific methodologies that are more suitable to their particular type of research. Some methods are generic and overarching, while others are more specialized.

The same can be said of theology. Our methods and criteria might change depending on the type of research we are doing. Biblical theology might rely more on methods of interpretation of the text, while philosophical theology might lean more toward logical analysis. But this does not mean that one would totally exclude the other or that both could not come into play at the same time. For instance, interpreting a philosophical text can be an important element of its analysis. Because some methods are more general and overarching while others are more specialized, someone might use several specific methods as part of an overarching method. Of course, this does not mean that we can switch from one method to another midstream. But it does mean that at times there might be more than one method at play. But the many specific methodologies must still fit the goals and larger purposes of the overarching method.

Methods, Criteria, and Theological Sources

Distinguishing between methods, criteria, and sources of theological reflection is also important. When teaching students, they frequently mistake one with another. In part, this confusion can be aggravated because a method, criterion, and source of theological reflection can look very much alike. Thus, a few definitions are in order. First, a criterion is a measure or standard by which you judge the value of something. For instance, you might use the Bible or tradition as a criterion to determine the value of a theological assertion by examining if it flows from it or is contrary to it.

Second, the method is the way you do your theology and arrive at your conclusions. It may involve the way you determine what your criteria are and how you will use them. It can be how you do your reflection on a theological issue and the tools that you use to do it. For example, you might break down a particular doctrine into its components to see how well they hold together or you might examine the similarities and differences that exist between two theological approaches. If we compare theology to a journey, the method is how you get from one place to the other. It includes different aspects of your theological journey, from where you chose to start, to what you consider authoritative, as well as the parameters you set. A good way of distinguishing criteria from a method is that a criterion is what you use to judge a theology to determine its value, while a method is the way you do the theology and choose the criteria.

Finally, the sources of theology are your references for theological study, the objects or subjects of your reflection. These may include Scripture, tradition, cultures, or people. They may even include a particular theology or a relevant doctrine. For instance, while I use Scripture, tradition, and other theologies in my work, culture and the Hispanic people are key sources for many aspects of my theology. Again, it is easy to see how someone can confuse a criterion and a theological source, since at times the two might be the same. The key to the distinction is how you are using it. For instance, the Bible is a criterion when you use it as a standard to determine the value of a theological assertion; but it is a theological source when you are examining it to develop your theology!

Overarching Methods

The methods we use as theologians vary. While some are quite specific to the task, some are fairly common throughout most theological works. These methods that are more general and broadly used by theologians are "overarching methods" in contrast to methods that are more particular to a specific theology, such as Latino/a theology. Also, some methods, as we shall see later, are more specialized versions of these broader methodologies. The list of methods I give in this book is not exhaustive. Even within Latino/a theology, the methods vary, often as much as the people that use them; and new approaches can easily emerge. My intent is solely to highlight some of the most common theological methods in general and those of Latino/a theologians in particular. I also intend to draw attention to the methodology of Latino/a theologians to show how the diverse methods they use are more comprehensive and draw from a broader field of disciplines than the methods more traditionally used. Hence, I will venture to say, Latino/a theologies are not more limited than their Western European counterparts, but are actually more expansive in the areas from which they draw.

Deductive and Inductive Methods

Two widely used methods are deduction and induction. These methods of logic are familiar to us through their use by television detectives and science. The first, deduction, is a process, often involving elimination, by which we arrive at a conclusion based on principles. In a criminal investigation, for instance, a detective can eliminate suspects and arrive at a conclusion by making inferences from the evidence. Through this process we arrive at a conclusion regarding an unknown by seeing what logically follows from the known factors and principles. Typically, the process moves from the general, a vast array of data and factors, to the particular. Induction, on the other hand, is the opposite of deduction and is common in scientific work. A scientist can use induction to move from a series of particular results, such as the data from a series of experiments, to a general conclusion or theory that might apply to all instances of that same nature.

Analytic and Synthetic Methods

More specific than deduction and induction, but still fairly general, are two methods often used by theology and philosophy: the analytic and synthetic methods. In an analysis, we break down a complex matter into its components and examine them and the role they play in the whole. Naturally, in theology this examination might look at many factors, such as the historical and cultural context of a theology, its methods, sources, criteria, and the supporting documentation that went into the development of the particular theology or doctrine. Analysis is a general methodology that can take more specific characteristics depending on how and for what one uses it. Synthesis, on the other hand, involves building something new from existing components. For instance, we might take two somewhat different theological assertions to create a new theological approach or assertion. Another way to think about the two is that an analytic method takes the whole apart, assuming that one can learn about the whole by looking at the parts. The synthetic method begins by looking at the parts, to see how one can put them together.

Dialectic Method

A third method often used in philosophy and theology—including in the works of Hegel, Marx, and to some extent Barth and Tillich—is the dialectic method. Some might argue that this method is the same as the synthetic, since it involves a dynamic tension between the thesis (positive assertion) and the antithesis (an assertion contrary to the thesis) that finds a resolution in a synthesis, which brings them together to form a new thesis. However, I think that while one might argue that the dialectic method is a form of synthesis, I think the opposite does not hold true. While the dialectic method brings together two concepts in a synthesis, the two concepts are opposite and the process generally follows a dynamic movement. However, a synthesis might not always involve opposites or contradictions. It might simply involve different concepts that are brought together. Hence, the two methods are not necessarily the same.

Correlation Method

A fourth method, also common in theology and often confused with the synthetic method, is that of correlation. This method, common to the work of Paul Tillich who developed it, basically correlates, or matches, concepts from one area with those that correspond to it in another area. As used by Tillich, the method of correlation involves the matching of theological symbols that seek to answer the questions raised by us through philosophy.[2] For instance, we might correlate the question: "What is the source of our being?" with the theological symbol of God in the statement, "God is being itself."[3] Naturally, in bringing two concepts together, the method is in some ways synthetic, but in a very specific way. In this method philosophy raises questions that are answered by theology. However, one is not limited to correlating philosophical questions to theological symbols. It is entirely possible to find other forms of correlations, including David Tracy's use of critical correlation, where theology also interrogates the symbols of culture and society, making the question and answer process of correlation flow both ways.[4]

Analogy

Another method, not as common today, but still important, is analogy. Analogy draws comparisons between different qualities assuming that the relationship between things we understand can help us understand the relationship between other things, possibly those that are beyond our comprehension. Thomas Aquinas, the medieval theologian who greatly influenced the development of Catholic theology, relied on this particular method. Primarily, Aquinas relied on the argument that if all created beings came from God, then they would manifest some of God's essence, even if imperfectly, making it possible to draw a comparison between the relationships between beings in creation and God's being by an analogy of being (*analogia entis*).[5] This method allows us to speak about God in terms of comparisons, proportionality, and relationships. We actually use analogy all the time in speaking about God. When we say that God is like a father or mother, we are using an analogy that compares God's relationship to us to our relationship with our parents. Even Jesus used analogies in his teaching, as when he compares the kingdom of heaven to a mustard seed and to leaven (Matt. 13:31-33). Many of the divine attributes are also the result of analogies made between us and God.

Hermeneutics

Finally, hermeneutics, the art of interpretation, can be another method by which we interpret and seek the meaning of theological assertions. Hermeneutics is a difficult term to define.[6] The use of hermeneutics in theology is not new, although the technical term, hermeneutics, is a more recent development attributed in part to Paul Ricoeur. When we interpret the Scriptures, study their meaning or significance for our lives, we are engaging in hermeneutics. Generally, when we speak of hermeneutics, the implication is that there is a text or written document that we are interpreting. It may mean we are trying to understand the meaning of the text, performing some sort of exegesis, trying to understand how the context of the text affects its meaning, or trying to understand how it may be applicable to different situations. In applying hermeneutics to theology, one might mean simply the act of interpretation that takes place in theology. After all, most theology occurs as language and text. But lately, it means a bit more. In some cases, the texts being interpreted go beyond the bounds of simple discourse and writing, and extend to areas of human action and thought, which too can undergo scrutiny and interpretation.[7] For instance, when we ask what a particular action by someone might mean, we are engaging in hermeneutics. By interpreting and seeking the meaning of actions, social conventions, laws, and cultural expressions, we extend hermeneutics to areas of society, politics, and culture, which in turn can bring these areas into contact with theology.

While all of these methods are common to many theological works, the list is by no means exhaustive. Methods can vary from theologian to theologian, from age to age, and from culture to culture. A theologian might use a combination of analysis and correlation to explain a theology to readers, breaking down the concepts to match them to the concepts of another theology. Theology might use exposition to explain the theology, or it can use rhetoric to convince the reader of its merits by exposing the weaknesses of different potential objections, addressing foreseen implications, and providing arguments in its favor—a common practice in early Christian theology.

Some types of theological inquiries might favor certain methods.

Theologies can take the form of apologetics, defending and explaining the position taken. They can also be systematic in their approach, looking at theologies through a particular conceptual lens or system to see how they hold together. They can even be constructive, creating new theological insights, often through synthesis with other theological or disciplinary perspectives. Naturally, it is impossible to cover all the contingencies, but I hope to have provided you with a taste of what is possible as far as methods go. I would like to turn our attention now to the particular methods prevalent in Latino/a theologies and how they compare with these broader theological methods.

Methodology in Latino/a Theologies

Latino/a theologies use many of the same methodologies as other theologies. They do analysis, synthesis, and correlation, and they engage in hermeneutical exercises. But it is the way they use these methodologies that sets them apart. In addition, there are methodologies that are common to Latino/a theologies that seldom occur in other mainline theologies. For instance, Latino/a theologians often work in collaborative ventures, forging their theology in a cooperative dialogue with one another, something we call *teología en conjunto*.[8] Contrary to the standard Western academic norms where theology is typically done individually and in isolation, Latino/a theologies grow out of collaborative ventures.

Doing theology as a collaborative venture often takes the shape of an ongoing dialogue, a dialogue that engages different interlocutors.[9] These partners in dialogue might be other Latino/a theologians, people from the church, communities, or the broader public. But doing theology in dialogue implies that Latino/a theologians do not see theology as merely a contemplative and objective enterprise done in isolation. Rather, they see it as a collaborative venture, a theology that takes shape in the tensions and relationships of discourse as a community of faith. Theology is not the possession of a few elite intellectuals, but the reflection and work of the community as a whole.

In the same manner, Latino/a theologians engage in analysis, but often go beyond the bounds of traditional theological and philosophical analysis, and draw from broader disciplines. For example, *Mujerista* theologians—such as Ada María Isasi-Díaz and other Latinas doing theology from the perspective of Hispanic women—often draw from the field of anthropology using ethnographic analysis both as a method and a source of theological reflection. Ethnographers describe cultures. Just like a map maker, they map cultures through their descriptions. Rather than looking at general assertions, ethnographers work with the particular—with the intentions, reasons, and practices of a people—to understand them better.[10] Ethnography rejects the vacuous and artificial creations of studies that provide some abstract person or ideal in favor of actual individuals who exist in an actual context, engage in self-description, use practical rationality in their everyday life, and interact in social settings.[11] Basically, ethnography attempts to describe the rich complexity of social interaction in a culture or group of people with integrity, taking care to examine many of the components that create the social world these people inhabit to truly understand what they do and believe.[12] The ethnographer engages the people and enlists their participation in developing the method and assuring the accuracy of the description.

The process of ethnographic analysis uses a variety of other methods in developing theology. There is an element of dialogue in which the ethnographer engages the community, a characteristic of Latino/a theologies. It also correlates characteristics from different communities to develop a broader picture, a meta-ethnography. It even uses analogy in an attempt to avoid reductionism. But most of all, the ethnographic analysis done by *Mujerista* theologians allows the religious views of the participants to emerge, providing the people with a voice, empowering them to construct their own theology, validating their lived-experiences and their capacity to reflect theologically on their faith as a community of faith.[13] In this sense, *Mujerista* theologians draw from a broad range of methods and provide a rich theological perspective that grows from the community, instead of reducing the believers to some preconceived typology or forcing them into predetermined theological categories. This allows the theology to emerge from the people and makes for a richer theology than many traditional philosophical and analytical approaches. Thus, Latino/a theology is not less rational or academic in its contextual nature and its methodology, but richer and far more diverse in its scope.

Hermeneutics also plays a key role in Latino/a theology. Particularly, the use of what we often refer to as hermeneutics of suspicion. This term, first used by Paul Ricoeur, has roots in the thinking of Karl Marx, Sigmund Freud, and Friedrich Nietzsche. Hermeneutics of suspicion casts doubts on the interpretative works of any form of theological reflection, science, and philosophy by pointing to the underlying role of personal desires, unconscious motivations, social classes, cultures, power, and politics.[14] Ultimately, hermeneutics of suspicion shows us how our political views, cultural mores, social position, power structures, biases, and prejudices always color our perceptions of the Bible, traditions, history, science, philosophy, and theology. Thus, when we read any of these texts or examine any of these practices, we must look with discernment at the political, cultural, and power constructs that lie at their heart, as well as at the heart of our interpretation of these texts. Thus, Justo González warns us to be aware of "innocent" readings of both history and Scripture that ignore the political agendas and dynamics of power that play a role in their formation and interpretation.[15]

For example, when I asked a group of students to do a reading of the Bible from a minority perspective, one student gave me his reading of the parable of the Good Shepherd. His interpretation, he said, took the perspective of the hireling, which he thought would be with whom a minority person might identify. His reading went on to argue that the hireling ran away when the wolf came because the sheep were not his own, while the shepherd defended the sheep because they belonged to him. Obviously, this student's cultural biases had seeped into his interpretation without him realizing it, thus arguing on behalf of property owners and against those who are hired! When I pointed out to him that a different reading might identify the minorities, the weak, and the marginalized with the sheep that are in danger of being devoured by exploitation; the owner with God; and the hireling with pastors like himself, the student was aghast, but dejectedly realized the implications of the parable for him and his previous assumptions.

The same kinds of issues can be extended to theology, since theology never occurs in a vacuum nor is it ever completely devoid of political agendas, cultural values, and issues of power. For instance, during the early controversies of the church, the winners were often determined by who held power or had the ear of the emperor or pope. In some cases, such as during the Council of Ephesus in 431 C.E., the two sides met separately and excommunicated each other! Today, cultural and political agendas still impinge on the theological arena and our interpretations of the Bible as we contemplate the events of September 11, 2001, preemptive war, capital punishment, and abortion. Reading the Bible and doing theology from the perspective of the oppressed, from the margins of society, and through the eyes of the poor changes the way we read the Bible and do theology. Liberation theologians, for instance, use a hermeneutics of suspicion in their analysis of history to conclude that poverty is not the result of individual insolence or societal backwardness, but rather the result of oppression and sinfulness.[16] Also, Gustavo Gutiérrez's reading of Scripture lead him to conclude that in the Bible God displays a preferential option for the poor, standing in solidarity with the oppressed.[17]

Taking seriously the role of the poor and of those people who live at the margins of society tends to lead us to read and interpret the Scriptures differently. For example, as Justo González illustrates in *Santa Biblia*, an unemployed worker might read the commandment regarding the Sabbath (Deut. 5:13) not as demanding that we take time for rest and relaxation, but as implying that everyone should be able to find sufficient work for six days.[18] This allows us to see the passage from a unique and different perspective that we would have missed otherwise. In fact, taking the biblical and theological interpretations of the poor seriously allow us to gain a deeper insight into Scriptures and into our own theology.

Standing in solidarity with those living at the margins of society also provides us with a different approach to the method of correlation. Instead of correlating the questions of human existence raised by philosophy to religious symbols, we are able to correlate our struggles, suffering, and life experiences to those of others who have shared similar fates in our Scriptures and traditions. Hence, African Americans can correlate their enslavement and oppression with the experience of the Hebrew people in Egypt. In the same way, Latinos/as view their existence at the margins of society and in the borderland of cultures as similar to that of Galilee.[19] The result is a correlation with God's actions during those times and an expectation of what God requires of us in our present situation, allowing us to shape our theology and consequent actions.

Latino/a theologies do not stop at a hermeneutics of suspicion. Latino/a hermeneutics use other tools as well. Cultural symbols, for instance, play an important role in theological construction and interpretation. Since theology always occurs within the matrix of a cultural context, Latino/a theologians give attention to how culture influences theology and how religious symbols manifest themselves through cultural expressions and practices. In a similar manner, Latino/a theology takes the bilingual and bicultural reality in which Latinos/as exist as another hermeneutical tool. Existing in between cultures and languages, we can discern and express the subtle differences and tensions that exist between cultures, as well as the peculiarities of each. Since Latinos/as exist at the border and boundaries of cultures we are able to negotiate both to interpret, contrast, and compare how theology occurs in both cultures, making explicit the unique insights into God each culture offers. From this perspective in between languages and cultures, we can discern the interplay of differences in the meanings and nuances attributed to various words and cultural symbols. For example, in English the exclamation "Jesus!" is considered cursing, in Spanish it is not. In Hispanic cultures we also name children Jesus, something unheard of in English, as well as in many other languages and cultures. These different ways of using the word point to underlying differences in how we understand Christology in each culture.[20]

Praxis and aesthetics also play important roles in the construction of our theology. Theological interpretations do not end with theoretical assumptions, but move toward examining the implications of our actions. As we examine aesthetic practices and symbols for theological content, we find how they influence expressions of faith. Even the faith of the people, the faithful intuition that leads people to a particular faith, plays a role in our theology as a tool for interpreting how people internalize and understand their faith. It even serves as a criterion and a source of reflection as we intuitively judge, with the guidance of the Spirit, that a particular doctrine or activity does not concur with the gospel message.

Latino/a theologians draw on many hermeneutical tools that create new insights into our understanding of God and religion. In this sense, Latino/a theology transgresses the narrow bounds of theological interpretation that often limit some theological works. The result is an enhanced theological landscape that offers multiple views and perspectives that are rich in imagery, color, and depth instead of a flat, monochromatic, and narrow viewpoint. Some scholarly disciplines provide a narrow focus, which might be useful for doing detailed analysis. However, we must not forget that it is through multiple yet distinct views that we gain a sense of depth. As we might recall from science experiments in school, our sense of depth perception relies on seeing through both eyes at slightly different perspectives. The same is true for theology. A single, narrow perspective loses the richness of depth. In drawing from diverse disciplines and offering diverse perspectives, Latino/a theology and other similar theologies offer us a richer understanding of our faith and larger array of interpretative tools.

The Sources of Theology

The sources of theology for Latino/a theology often are the same as those of other traditions. The Bible is the primary source of God's revelation to us and as such is an important source of Latino/a theology. We, like other theologians, also value the role of tradition and the many historical doctrines of the Christian church. We use reason, logic, and philosophy for our theological investigations just as many other theologians. The classical sources of theology are as much a part of our theological work as in any other. Where Latino/a theology varies from many other theologies is in the way we use those sources, as was the case with our methodologies. For example, how we interpret the Scriptures often allows us to find different insights into the Bible and its application. The same is true for tradition. When we use tradition in theology, we give serious consideration to the way power, politics, and context play a role in the shaping of our faith.

Even our culture and cultural memories affect our theological reflection and our understanding of tradition. As Latina theologian Jeanette Rodriguez points out, tradition involves content, that which is handed down, as well as the process of handing it down. This process involves people who live in a society and culture that carry memories, all occurring within political, historical, and social contexts. All of these processes involved in remembering and handing down tradition also carry and evoke the affections, images, ideals, hopes, and feelings of the people who inherit and pass on their traditions. Thus, all these factors along with other aspects of their sociocultural location inevitably affect the interpretation and product of this process of traditioning.[21]

As I am fond of reminding my students, historically, a great deal of our theology came about as a response to heresies and perceived dangers to the faith, as well as cultural and political pressures. At times, who was designated a heretic was determined by who wielded greater power in the church. Heretics were the losers of battles fought often to the death. Furthermore, we also recognize that tradition is not a simple monolithic body of truth, but a multifaceted strand of intertwined threads that often bind together and that other times unravel. What we call tradition is merely the strands we choose or are told to follow. As theologians we are not obligated just to examine and use the traditions of Western Europe that so often dominate theology in the West, but also to consider theologies and traditions of the Third World and the cultural traditions that form part of our legacy as Latinos/as.

The same can be said about the way we use reason in its fullest sense, by not stopping with a theoretical approach to reason, but also including dimensions of praxis and aesthetic in our theological reflection. Like liberation theology, Latino/a theology goes beyond theory and looks at the praxis of theology as it is lived out by us. In addition, Latino/a theology also looks at aesthetics in terms of cultural symbols and religious practices. Hence, it goes beyond a one-dimensional view of reason to develop a multidimensional approach.

While Latino/a theology might come from a particular perspective, it is comprehensive in its approach. For instance, while experience has always been a source of theological reflection, it plays a central role in our theology for various reasons. First, human experience is at the core of all our encounters with God, since revelation occurs as part of our experience. We receive tradition and wisdom through our experiences. All aspects of our life and knowledge come mediated through experience.[22] We might reflect upon these experiences, compare them to that of others, develop criteria to judge them, canonize them into scriptures, and shape them into doctrines transmitted through tradition; but they come from experience and are transmitted through experience.

Second, our experiences are central to who we are. They shape our being and our knowledge, as is the case with all theologies. Take the example of

Black theology. The experiences of slavery and discrimination are central to African American self-understanding and faith. Their unique theological insights and contributions to the church's understanding of theology come out of their experiences. The experiences of women also play a role in their self-understanding and in their theological insights. Their understanding of God, power structures, and bodily existence ultimately enriches theology as a whole. To these experiences, women of color have added their experience as marginalized minorities, drawing deep insights from their sense of double marginalization and struggle, giving birth to Womanist and *Mujerista* theologies that offer us new and useful theological insights.

Latino/a theology is no different; it draws heavily from the experience of the Latino/a people. Our sense of struggle, marginalization, oppression, and cultural mixing gives us deeper insights into our faith and theological reflection. Latinas, for instance, intentionally engage in a praxis of liberation infused with religious insights that offer a far richer understanding of our faith than detached abstract reflection. Out of their lived-experience and struggle, they engage in a type of rationality that resists the intellectual impositions of the dominant groups that would deny rational value to these insights.[23] The lived experiences of the Latino/a people, their faith, and their practices are fertile sources of theology, for in those experiences we encounter and try to understand God.[24] Of course, we do not only expand our reflection on the traditional sources of theology, we also go beyond them.

There are five areas, in some ways related to particular aspects of our experience as Latinos/as, that serve as fertile sources for our theological reflection. These sources of reflection are central to Latino/a theology and often go beyond the more basic theological sources of Scripture, tradition, reason, and experience. The five areas are culture, identity, popular religion, the *sensus fidelium* (faithful intuitions), and *lo cotidiano* (daily experience).

Culture

First, as one might easily assume, culture is a central source of theological reflection. Our practices, *ethos,* and language serve as a rich resource for our reflection. Cultural symbols and practices, whether religious or not, convey many valuable insights into our self-understanding and faith. Because our experience of God and our interpretation of that experience occur within this cultural matrix, theological reflection must look carefully at culture.

A significant part of any culture is language. Because language is so central to our self-understanding, if we fail to examine its role in the development of theology, we lose sight of how different nuances and shades of meaning affect how we understand our faith. For instance, studies have shown that the way we speak about God, using masculine or feminine imagery, actually affects the attributes we associate with God. Those images that are masculine tend to favor attributes of power and justice in contrast with feminine images that attribute compassion and nurture to God.[25] Similarly, cultural and linguistic imagery can affect our theological perspective. In the same manner that the dynamic tension of the different languages we speak as a bilingual and bicultural people can serve as a hermeneutical method for our theology, language itself can serve as a source of reflection.[26]

Beyond language, other elements of our culture also become fruitful sources of theological reflection. The importance of *fiesta* for instance as an essential part of Hispanic culture attains theological significance for some that articulate its importance as an affirmation of life in the midst of suffering.[27] Similarly, cultural heroes, particular symbols, and values such as family and dignity also become important areas for theological reflection. Even religious festivals such as *las posadas*, where children recreate Joseph and Mary's search for a place to stay, can become significant places for theological reflection.

Identity

Second, our identity as Hispanics is a focus of theological reflection, particularly our understanding of being a people in-between cultural, racial, and national identities. The terms *Mestizaje* and *Mulatez* are two key concepts in this reflection. Both terms mean the same thing, a mixture. *Mestizaje* comes from the Latin and refers to the mixture of the Iberian and the indigenous people of this continent. *Mulatez* comes from the Arabic, and usually refers to the mixture of Iberians and Africans, particularly common in the Caribbean. Naturally, the mixture of cultures and races that make up our hybridity and bicultural nature is not easily reduced to fit into a simple *mestizo* or *mulato* paradigm. While other terms might be found to address and better describe the mixture of heritages, cultures, and races embodied by the Latino/a people, *Mestizaje* and *Mulatez* are by far the two most prominent in Latino/a theologies.

Mestizaje as a place of Latino/a theological reflection came into use in the theological writings of Virgilio Elizondo, but it has roots in the work of the Mexican political activist, minister of education, and philosopher José Vasconcelos. At the onset, people tended to view *mestizaje* as a sign of inferiority and lack of pureness. However, Vasconcelos's work redefined the understanding of *mestizaje*. Asserting the value of aesthetic reason and of particularity over abstraction as a way of knowing and relating to others, Vasconcelos interprets *mestizaje in terms of an aesthetic fusion* that stands against tendencies toward homogeneity and opposition that foster interaction among cultures.[28]

The concept of *mestizaje* was later used by Andrés Guerrero in his book *Chicano Theology* in a more expansive way to understand the possibility of liberation and unity inherent in the term by virtue of its inclusion of others and its uplifting of what had been rejected as inferior.[29] Given this expanded definition, Latino/a theologians such as Fernando Segovia, Orlando Espín, Ada María Isasi-Díaz, and Roberto Goizueta began using the notion of *mulatez* to reflect the Caribbean reality in which Africans and Iberians were mixed.[30] Today, the concepts, *Mestizaje*, and by extension, *Mulatez*, express the concrete and particular fusions of races and cultures that many Latinos/as embody. Through this fusion and juncture of cultures, Latino/a theologians hope that a true understanding of each other can occur, while preserving the integrity and uniqueness of each person and culture.[31]

Mestizaje, as used by Vasconcelos and *Mestizaje-mulatez* as used by Latino/a theologians today do not mean a mixture that dissolves the uniqueness of each race and culture. The *mestizo-mulato* is keenly aware that he or she is both Spanish and Aztec, or Spanish and Nigerian, and so forth.[32] Both cultures and races exist in tension with one another in the *mestizo-mulato*, brought together in a particular instantiation of a living human being that can understand and identify with both. Vasconcelos hoped that eventually this ongoing mixture of races and cultures would lead to a new humanity, *la raza cósmica*, the cosmic race, of which the *mestizo/a* was a precursor. This new humanity would allow and affirm diversity while serving as a source of enrichment for all of humanity.[33] The hope of using *mestizaje-mulatez* as a vision of the future would later become expanded to include other aspects of our hybrid reality, such as language and culture. This serves as a paradigm for creating a community where differences are not eradicated, but rethought in relational terms, seeing differences not as barriers to be overcome or as intrinsic natures that make one inferior and another superior, but as something that is relative, constituted by the nature of the relationship and formative of it.[34] This allows *mestizaje-mulatez* to be a source of theology, a hermeneutical lens for understanding our situation, and an eschatological hope.

The "mixing" of the particulars that come together in *mestizaje-mulatez* take on a religious dimension in that, for Vasconcelos, human desire for an aesthetic union is part of our yearning for union with God.[35] *Mestizaje-mulatez*, along with other aspects of our location in the borderland of cultures and races has led to many insights for theological anthropology, Christology, and even eschatology as we shall see in the following chapters. Thus, the state of being in-between cultures and races, which we embody as Latinos/as, serves not only as a methodological hermeneutic, but as a rich source of theological reflection.[36]

However, while *mestizaje* may serve as a source of inclusion and interchange between cultures and races, we who live on the borderline of cultures also face the reality of exclusion as well. Our identity as Latinos/as, on the borderline of cultures and races, puts us in a tenuous state in which we do not belong in the countries where we or our family originated, but are also not accepted by the dominant society of our present home in the U.S. and Canada. Not being accepted in either culture, while embodying the tension between the cultures in our very being, places us in a difficult and emotionally painful situation as individuals. But it also serves as a fertile ground for theological reflection and cross-cultural/racial dialogue, and allows us to see the perspectives of each culture and to reflect theologically on our being as a people in the middle.[37]

Of course, identity is a more complex reality than our simple state of being in the interstices of cultures and races. Our identity also involves the cultural context that shapes us in relation to our community, family, and faith. While some Westerners try to form their identity through separation and differentiation, seeking their identity by autonomy and by distancing oneself from family and community to establish their independence, Latinos/as find their identity in their ties to family, community, and faith.[38] Ultimately, as we shall see later, our very identity and being is an essential source of theological reflection for Latino/a theologians because our theology finds its roots in who we are and in the people to whom we belong.

Popular Religion

A third area of theological reflection is what we call popular religion. The first thing that must be said about Latino/a popular religion is that it does not mean popular in the sense of what is in style or in vogue or widespread.[39] It is popular in the sense that it refers to the grassroots practices, symbols, and rituals that emerge from the people. Popular religion is a term rooted in the Spanish term *religiosidad popular*—as these practices came to be called in Latin America—a term that was often translated as "popular religiosity" in earlier works of Latino/a theology. The term refers to those concrete expressions of the faith of the people that emerge from within their cultures as innovative practices, rituals, and symbols, often in resistance to the established practices of the institutional church.[40] These practices often become vehicles for empowerment to people trying to make sense of and to control their reality—a reality that is usually defined by oppression and marginalization.[41] At times, popular religion becomes a means of expressing aesthetically, through symbols and rituals, the liberative praxis of the community trying to affirm their identity, voice, culture, and call for justice.[42] These creative and innovative practices are at times a form of resistance to heterogeneous impositions, ways of gaining power, and hermeneutical tools by which they can interpret their world.

Many times, the practices of popular religion are syncretistic in nature, not simply using symbols and practices from Christianity, but also incorporating aspects of Native American or African religions. In part, this syncretism is the result of a particular vacuum that Christianity has failed to fill, in areas such as sexuality, bodily existence, or faith and healing—areas that are often considered taboo or abandoned by Christianity and easily filled by these other religious traditions that incorporate them in their faith.[43] But because these practices express intentional attempts at articulating, affirming, and asserting the faith of the people, they are significant and fertile loci of theological reflection for Latino/a scholars.

The aesthetic rituals and symbolism in Catholicism often make it more suitable for these expressions of popular religion than in Protestant congregations, but they are by no means exclusive to Catholicism. While it is true that the anti-Catholic self-definition of many Hispanic Protestants and the syncretistic elements of some popular religious expressions might be looked at with disdain and as idolatrous by some Protestants, the reality is that there are forms of popular religion that can be found in Latino/a Protestant churches. The key difference is that while Catholic forms primarily revolve around certain forms of imagery and rituals, Protestant expressions tend to be linguistic and word centered.

Protestants, for example, might not display images of the Virgin on their walls. But they proudly display Bible verses such as John 3:16. They may also give *testimonios* (testimonies) in worship services. These testimonies serve as forms of empowerment for those offering them. Often women and laypeople who otherwise lack a voice and role in worship can thus have a space for expressing their lived experiences with God and their understanding of Christian faith.[44] Similarly, the *coritos* (choruses) found in loose-leaf folders and sung in both Protestant and Catholic churches provide cultural expressions, interpretations, and teachings of the faith often tailored to the particular situation and accompanied by lively music more appropriate to our Hispanic culture.[45]

Ultimately, both Protestant and Catholic expressions of popular religion are creative expressions of the people's faith as a form of resistance and empowerment. But popular religion is also an extension of the sacramental nature of Hispanic Christianity. For Latinos and Latinas, God is immanently present in our world and in our lives, infusing all of creation with a sacramental presence. This sacramental understanding of reality becomes a source of empowerment and self-expression, often resonating with other indigenous and African religious traditions that also understand reality as sacred. In contrast, many Western traditions, even those with strong sacramental theologies, tend to see the world as materialistic and devoid of spirituality while being more cognitive in their understanding of their faith. Such a view does not resonate with the Hispanic sense of deep spirituality, mystery, and sacramentality that is part of our *ethos*.

Even Protestant Latinos/as maintain this deep sacramental understanding of their faith when they take the Eucharist, enter a church, and hold their Bibles. At times, mainline Protestant Hispanics have more in common with Pentecostal traditions than with their own denominations because Pentecostal traditions still view the world as Spirit-filled and God as actively present in our midst. Thus, while mainline Hispanic Protestants might not incorporate aspects of Native and African religions in their popular religion, they incorporate elements of Pentecostal traditions into it, even when they might go to great lengths to suppress other charismatic tendencies in their worship. In the same way, elements of Catholicism representing deep cultural meaning, such as the Virgin of Guadalupe, can be found in individual Protestant churches and families.

Popular religion is by no means limited to Latino/a culture. Many other cultures, if scrutinized carefully, might find elements of their culture and faith manifesting themselves in popular religious expressions. Furthermore, it is not always liberating, because popular religion often serves to perpetuate certain stereotypes.[46] But it is an expression of faith and an articulation of the people's lived experience. Thus, popular religion is not only significant to Latino/a theology, but it is an essential place for theological reflection to occur.

Sensus Fidelium

Orlando Espín describes popular religion as an expression of the *sensus fidelium*, the faithful intuition of the people as guided by the Holy Spirit.[47] I include it as a source of theological reflection because I believe it transcends popular religion even if it often works in concert with it. This faithful intuition is a part of the Christian tradition expressed through symbols, culture, and language. It sits at the center of our sacramental understanding of reality and serves as a basis for exploring culture, symbols, experiences, and practices for theological meaning. At its core is the belief that God is continually active in our midst, is working in our lives through continual encounters, self-disclosure, and guidance, and is informing our Christian understanding of faith as a continual witness of God's presence in our lives.[48] This does not mean that any religious sensibility, expression, or intuition is fair game. There are criteria that must be considered, including, as Espín suggests, those of its coherence with Scripture, its continuity with traditions, and its results.[49] But to deny the sacramental and active presence of God in the Christian church as transcending the rigid bounds of dogma, institutions, and established traditions is to deny the continual work of the Holy Spirit in our midst.

Lo cotidiano

Finally, a fifth and related source of theological reflection that I believe merits its own place is that of *lo cotidiano*, the daily lived experience of women and men in their struggle, praxis, work, and care for the preservation and nurture of life. Many spiritual traditions value the spirituality of the ordinary, of the daily activities and experiences of life. Buddhism, for instance, values mindfulness, an awareness of what we do. Our work sustains us as we struggle to produce anything from food to ideas, earning wages that, when we are justly compensated, allow us to live. In all of these activities, there is a nourishment of life and a deep-seated spirituality that must be explored. *Lo cotidiano*, of course, is more than the ordinary and has a specific technical meaning for *Mujerista* theology. In *Mujerista* theology, it is an epistemological and hermeneutical framework that finds theological significance in the everyday lived experience and praxis of Latinas through their life and struggle.[50]

Our Ongoing Dialogue

While the methods and sources of Latino/a theologians bear a bit of overlap with traditional theological methods, they also go beyond them in their focus and in the breadth of disciplines from which they draw. The incorporation of different disciplines, their exploration of diverse contexts, and their inclusion of various approaches strengthen the resulting theology, not only in its Latinó/a dimension but also in the insights and perspectives they offer to the theological enterprise of the Christian church as a whole. We may be tempted to assume that the only theologies that offer rigorous scholarship are those that incorporate philosophical and traditional approaches in their theological reflection, but we would be mistaken. Those theologies, I contend, are actually truncated abstractions, often removed from the fullness of reality and life. While such theologies are as important as any other theological approach, they are limited in their application.

In contrast, Latino/a theologies take seriously the particularities of life and provide us with rich insights into God, grounded in the life and experiences of a particular people. In this sense, they take seriously the insights of Garfinkel, who developed ethnography, and those of Vasconcelos, both of whom argued against abstractions and in favor of understanding reality, people, and God from the particular. In this sense, Latino/a theology is a theology grounded in the particularities of a people and a culture. It is through these insights derived from their particularity that we can draw comparisons and better understand other peoples and cultures. As we shall see in the following chapters, these insights help us gain new and exciting perspectives on how we understand ourselves (as human beings), God, and our faith. In this sense, Latino/a theology is not just for Latinos and Latinas. Nor is it just for those who want to better understand Hispanic people and culture. It is for anyone who wants to gain a deeper insight into humanity and into our common faith.

In looking at these methodologies, I noted several key methods and sources for Latino/a theology that distinguish our theology from others. However, this does not mean that Latino/a theology should be the norm—on the contrary, it should help us realize that no single theology should be taken as normative. Rather, what this helps us recognize is that theology as a whole benefits from different perspectives and should continually engage other theologies in dialogue to gain new insights. Hence, Latino/a theology is not just a theology for Latinos/as. It is a theology for the whole church, a gift from the Latino/a community to the broader community of faith. In the following chapters, I attempt to help the readers gain a sense of Latino/a theology not by providing an overview of what different Latino/a theologians say about a given topic. Instead, recognizing that at the heart of Latino/a theology we find a practice of doing theology jointly and in dialogue, I have sought to weave the different voices of Latino/a theology, including my own, into a broader dialogue with other theological perspectives. Thus, we can get a sense of what Latino/a theologians can offer to some of the different theological themes that have emerged throughout the ages. In this process some voices are heard more than others, for it is impossible to fully bring to it the broad richness of thoughts, experiences, and theological works that has blossomed in the last twenty years.

Notes

1. Paul Tillich writes that a method "is a tool, literally a way around, which must be adequate to its subject matter." Hence, a method well suited for one task might be inappropriate or even destructive to another. *Systematic Theology*, Vol. 1, p. 60.

2. Ibid., pp. 60-66.

3. Ibid., pp. 235-36.

4. See David Tracy's argument in *The Analogical Imagination: Christian Theology and the Culture of Pluralism* (New York: Crossroad, 1981), pp. 25-27; 373-76.

5. See Thomas Aquinas, *On Being and Essence*, trans. by Armand Maurer, 2nd edition (Toronto: The Pontifical Institute of Mediaeval Studies, 1968), pp. 61-71. Also, for a description of Aquinas's methodology, see Frederick Copleston, *A History of Philosophy*, Vol. II, Medieval Philosophy (New York: Image Books, 1993), pp. 347-62.

6. For instance, Mark K. Taylor struggles with the many meanings and difficulties in defining hermeneutics in his book, *Remembering Esperanza: A Cultural-Political Theology for North American Praxis* (Maryknoll: Orbis Press, 1990), pp. 48-56.

7. Ibid., p. 50.

8. Justo L. González proposes this model for theological inquiry when he speaks of doing *Fuenteovejuna Theology* in his book *Mañana: Christian Theology from a Hispanic Perspective* (Nashville: Abingdon Press, 1990), pp. 28-30.

9. For more on theology as dialogue see my article "Doing Theology as Dialogue in the Hispanic Community," *Journal of Hispanic/Latino Theology* (February 1998).

10. See the description of ethnography given by James V. Spickard and J. Shawn Landres in the introduction to *Personal Knowledge and Beyond: Reshaping the Ethnography of Religion*, ed. by James V. Spickard, J. Shawn Landres, and Meredith B. McGuire (New York: New York University Press, 2002), where they compare the more generalizing inquiries that seek to form overarching patterns with the particularizing practices of ethnography, pp. 1-4.

11. Ada María Isasi-Díaz provides a good overview of ethnography, which I summarize here to some extent. *En La Lucha / In the Struggle: A Hispanic Women's Liberation Theology* (Minneapolis: Fortress Press, 1993), pp. 65-66. See also the work of Harold Garfinkel who developed this methodology as a critique of the social sciences, *Studies in Ethnomethodology* (Cambridge, England: Polity Press, 1984).

12. Isasi-Díaz, *En La Lucha*, p. 65.

13. Again, see Isasi-Díaz's overview. Ibid., pp. 68-75.

14. See Charles Winquist, *Desiring Theology* (Chicago: University of Chicago Press, 1995), pp. 28-29.

15. Gonzalez, *Mañana*, pp. 78-87.

16. Clodovis Boff, "Epistemology and Method of the Theology of Liberation," in *Mysterium Liberationis: Fundamental Concepts of Liberation Theology*, ed. by Ignacio Ellacuría and Jon Sobrino (Maryknoll: Orbis Press, 1993), pp. 74-84.

17. Ibid., Gustavo Gutiérrez, "Option for the Poor," pp. 235-50.

18. Justo L. González, *Santa Biblia: The Bible Through Hispanic Eyes* (Nashville: Abingdon Press, 1996), p. 59.

19. Virgilio Elizondo, *Galilean Journey: The Mexican American Promise* (Maryknoll: Orbis Press, 1983), pp. 49-53.

20. In *Jesus Is My Uncle: Christology from a Hispanic Perspective* (Nashville: Abingdon Press, 1999), I examine how the words "Jesus" and "incarnation" carry different nuances and uses in Spanish and in English.

21. Jeanette Rodríguez, "*Sangre llama a sangre:* Cultural Memory as a Source of Theological Insight," *Hispanic/Latino Theology: Challenge and Promise* (Minneapolis: Fortress Press, 1996), pp. 118-19.

22. This idea is not unique to Latino/a theology and is found in the works of Paul Tillich. For instance, see his *Systematic Theology*, vol. 1 (Chicago: University of Chicago Press, 1957), pp. 40-42.

23. Ada María Isasi-Díaz, *En la Lucha*, pp. 167-79. The term "lived-experience" applies particularly to those aspects of our experience that are intentional, differentiating it from ordinary experiences, p. 173.

24. Orlando Espín in *The Faith of the People: Theological Reflections on Popular Catholicism* (Maryknoll: Orbis Press, 1997) argues that the incarnation reveals to us that it is possible to encounter God's presence through humanity and that our basic experiences of God occur within the realm of human experience, pp. 12-13.

25. Mark R. McMinn, et al., "The Effects of God Language on Perceived Attributes of God," *Journal of Psychology and Theology* 21 (Winter 1993), pp. 309-14.

26. I address the issue more thoroughly in my book, *Jesus Is My Uncle*, pp. 16-31.

27. See Virgilio Elizondo's use of *fiesta* as an affirmation of life and resurrection in *Galilean Journey*, pp. 30-31.

28. Goizueta presents an excellent and accessible overview of Vasconcelos's concept of *mestizaje* in *Caminemos con Jesús*, pp. 89-100. I am particularly indebted to his descriptions on pp. 96-98. For more detailed information, see José Vasconcelos, *Obras Completas*, 4 vols. (Mexico: Libreros Mexicanos Unidos, 1958–61).

29. Andrés G. Guerrero, *A Chicano Theology* (Maryknoll: Orbis Press, 1987), pp. 17-26; 148-51.

30. Ada María Isasi-Díaz provides an account of how this history develops in an excellent article entitled "A New *Mestizaje/Mulatez:* Reconceptualizing Difference," in *A Dream Unfinished: Theological Reflections on America from the Margins*, Fernando Segovia and Eleazar S. Fernandez (Maryknoll: Orbis Press, 2001), pp. 206-09.

31. Goizueta, *Caminemos con Jesús*, p. 98. Goizueta elaborates on Vasconcelos's notion that while homogeneous communities impose unity by means of exclusion or assimilation, the *mestizo* community achieves unity by inclusion and empathic love, while preserving their uniqueness.

32. Ibid.

33. Goizueta also elaborates on this concept in "*La Raza Cósmica?* The Vision of José Vasconcelos" in *The Journal of Hispanic/Latino Theology* 1/2 (February 1994), pp. 5-27.

34. See Ada María Isasi-Díaz's development of this argument in "A New *Mestizaje/Mulatez,*" pp. 209-19.

35. *Caminemos con Jesús*, p. 94. See Vasconcelos, *Obras Completas*, volume 3, p. 1137.

36. See for example Virgilio Elizondo's essay by the title "*Mestizaje* as a Locus of Theological Reflection" in *Frontiers of Hispanic Theology in the United States*, ed. by Allan Figueroa Deck (Maryknoll: Orbis Press, 1992), pp. 104-23.

37. See Virgilio Elizondo's use of *mestizaje* in *The Future Is Mestizo: Life Where Cultures Meet* (New York: Crossroad, 1992), pp. 82-86.

38. Goizueta makes this point in "Rediscovering Praxis: The Significance of U.S.

Hispanic Experience for Theological Method," in *We Are a People: Initiatives in Hispanic American Theology*, ed. by Roberto Goizueta (Minneapolis: Fortress Press, 1992), p. 65.

39. Orlando Espín makes this point in his essay, "Popular Religion as an Epistemology (of Suffering)," *Journal of Hispanic/Latino Theology*, 2:2 (November 1994), p. 66. Goizueta, agrees with him but feels that one cannot easily dismiss the definition of "popular" in terms of popularity, offering a good argument for not quickly rejecting such an interpretation in *Caminemos con Jesús*, p. 22, note 10.

40. Definitions of popular religion vary depending on whether you look at them from a socio-scientific or theological perspective. Anthony M. Stevens-Arroyo has a good overview of definitions and issues involved in *Discovering Latino Religion: A Comprehensive Social Science Bibliography*, ed. by Stevens-Arroyo and Segundo Pantoja (New York: Bildner Center for West Hemisphere Studies, 1995), pp. 28-33.

41. See Espín's definition of Latino/a popular Catholicism in his essay "Popular Catholicism: Alienation or Hope?" in *Hispanic/Latino Theology: Challenge and Promise*, ed. by Ada María Isasi-Díaz and Fernando Segovia (Minneapolis: Fortress Press, 1996), p. 308.

42. Goizueta, "Rediscovering Praxis," *We Are a People*, pp. 62-64.

43. Anthony M. Steven-Arroyo, *Discovering Latino Religion*, pp. 27-28.

44. For more on *testimonios*, see my essay "Guideposts Along the Journey: Mapping North American Hispanic Theology," in *Protestantes/Protestants: Hispanic Christianity Within Mainline Traditions* (Nashville: Abingdon Press, 1999), pp. 132-36.

45. See Edwin Apontes's article, "Coritos as Active Symbols in Latino Popular Religion," *Journal of Hispanic/Latino Theology* 2/3 (February 1995), pp. 62-65.

46. Stevens-Arroyo raises these questions in *Discovering Latino Religion*, pp. 29-30.

47. Orlando Espín, "Tradition and Popular Religion," in *Frontiers of Hispanic Theology in the United States*, pp. 64-65.

48. Ibid.

49. Ibid., pp. 65-67.

50. Ada María Isasi-Díaz, *Mujerista Theology*, pp. 66-73.

CHAPTER FIVE

¡DIOS MIO! MY GOD!

I t is a common exclamation, both in English and Spanish. ¡Dios Mio! My God! We say it in the face of tragedy or surprise, almost as a prayer. But the words themselves express more than a mere exclamation. There is something profound in their meaning and use. The words imply a relationship where we speak of God as our God. In this utterance we speak about God, not by conjuring up thoughts about the gods of others or by categorical abstractions. We are speaking of our God, of the one with whom we live in relationship—the God we have experienced through our lives, culture, and tradition. It is a cry to God, but not to any God. It is an appeal to *our* God.

This expression has led me to wonder and to ponder its significance for how we speak about God in general. When we say God, do we all mean the same thing? Or is God, when we use the word, always *my* God? Ultimately, I must admit that the very term *God* is somewhat ambiguous. True, we know how to use the term. We also may know or assume that it refers to the ultimate, the divine, the creator, the object of our faith. But even those terms are themselves still loaded with nuances and different shades of meaning. Could it be that the very meaning of God might be colored and affected by who we are, by our culture, our biases, and our assumptions? I will venture to say yes. Our language, concepts, and terms about God are inevitably colored by our culture, personal and social biases, assumptions, and traditions. Even the fragmented and limited nature of our language affects how we speak about God. So in a sense, when we say God, we really mean "my God," that is, "God as I understand God to be."

Speaking About God

Whenever we speak about God, we speak about God using human languages and terms. Our language about God is subject to the same limitations of any language. Since every language is a product of a specific culture, all languages—including theological language—carry the particularities, nuances, biases, and distortions of their culture. Even divine revelation occurs within the contextual matrix of a specific human language and culture.[1] This in itself is not bad. After all, we have no other language in which to talk about God. For God to communicate with humanity, God must speak in human terms and be subject to all the frailties and distortions inherent in human language. God must risk being subjected to the distortions of human language and culture. Otherwise, revelation would be beyond our grasp and ability, akin to an adult explaining quantum physics to a small child. After all, the Bible was not written in angelic tongues; it was originally written in Hebrew, Greek, and Aramaic. When we read the Bible today our study has been further conditioned by the language into which it has been translated. Even the Incarnation serves as a living testament to revelation occurring within the particular context of a specific culture, people, and time.[2]

To assume that divine revelation is unconditioned and unadulterated truth untouched and unaffected by human vicissitudes is ludicrous. Revelation is not *data* or *information* about God furnished to us, information that otherwise would remain hidden.[3] Rather, revelation is an unveiling, a self-disclosure of God that can occur through many means, including events, nature, people, culture, and language. We do not simply hear a voice from heaven that tells us something about God. We encounter God and experience God's activity in nature and in history. Furthermore, we must also acknowledge that even if such pure and unadulterated truth was given to us in some form of mystical vision or religious experience that the revelation would still need to be grasped, understood, interpreted, and articulated by human beings and in human language with all its frailties and limitations.[4] Revelation is given by God to us, and it is us limited and fallen human beings who receive it.

The danger we face with any form of revelation is that we tend to assume that the revelation we receive and our interpretation of this revelation is indeed the unadulterated truth given to us by God![5] This dangerous assumption leads to several disastrous results. First, in assuming we have the sole truth, we fall prey to hubris, believing ourselves to be chosen and superior to others who in our eyes lack this special insight into God. Second, as presumed keepers of the truth, we also tend to silence the voices of others and even the voice of God. We impose our culturally affected interpretations upon others as normative, often through violence and coercion. We burn heretics for believing otherwise, and we silence dissenting voices. We disengage from dialogue and lose sight of the cultural biases, aberrations, and distortions that inevitably seep into our understanding of God. Finally, we codify belief, idolatrize it, and fossilize it, leaving no room for the prophetic spirit of God's ongoing revelation to us.

Our knowledge about God is unavoidably limited and fragmented. Even the apostle Paul recognized that our knowledge of God is limited and partial, as he wrote in 1 Corinthians 13:9-12:

> For we know in part and we prophesy in part, but when perfection comes, the imperfect disappears. When I was a child, I talked like a child, I thought like a child, I reasoned like a child. When I became a man, I put childish ways behind me. Now we see but a poor reflection as in a mirror; then we shall see face to face. Now I know in part; then I shall know fully, even as I am fully known. (NIV)

However, our theology always runs the risk of forgetting the fragmented nature of our knowledge about God. Hence, we begin to speak of terms and concepts as if they were absolutes and unequivocally valid expressions of divine truth, forgetting their broken and tentative nature. Instead, we need to recognize that all theology is temporary and fragmented. As Karl Barth reminds us in his *Dogmatics*, all theology is *teologia viatorum*, theology done along the way.[6] Theology can never capture God in a system or explicitly exhibit its object; it can only point to it with fragmented thoughts and concepts that try to understand God from different perspectives.[7]

This fragmentation and tentativeness of our knowledge leads us to the epistemological problem, the question of how we can have any kind of knowledge about God and verify it. If our knowledge of God is indeed tentative and fragmentary, colored by our culture and biases, and subject to human limitations and liabilities, then how can we know anything about God or be able to speak with any certainty about the divine? Even if we did receive a pure and unadulterated word from God, it would occur within the realm of our language in order for us to understand it. Then it would have to be articulated through human language. Given this problem, how can we even presume to be able to say *anything* meaningful about God?

It is possible to speak about God, but it is not easy. First, we need to realize that while revelation can occur through language, it is not exclusively linguistic data. Revelation is not merely hearing a word from the heavens or information about God. It is also an encounter with God—a God who acts in history and interacts with us. Revelation is an experience through which we encounter God. It is God's self-disclosure. True, it comes to us mediated through the particulars of culture, through the incarnate experience of God, through religious symbols, and through sacred texts. But ultimately it is an experience where we encounter God. In that sense, it is no different than any other experience or encounter.

When we meet someone, we experience the whole of the meeting, not merely data about them or the words they speak. We might learn something through our conversation, but we also note how they look, their accent, their quirks, and their way of being. What we absorb from that meeting might be fragmentary; some things we will notice and other things we might forget. Nevertheless, from that meeting, we develop an impression of that person. That impression might be correct or incorrect. In time, we might even develop a relationship with the person, learn about their character and behavior, and establish a sense of trust. We may know something about the person, but we can never know that person fully. After all, we don't even know ourselves fully. But we come to know each other through relationship.

We experience our encounters with God in the same way. Because our experience of God is mediated through culture, fragmentary, and subject to misinterpretation, our language is always insufficient to accurately express the experience. Our biases and limitations always tend to distort our perception and understanding of God. Our family, community, church, and even scholars might have taught us about God. We, especially us theologians, might even have a nice repertoire of terms and concepts we use to speak about God. But at the heart of it all there is an experience, an encounter with God. It might be our own personal experience or it might be mediated through the symbols and traditions of our faith. The experience might have taken place millennia ago, recorded and interpreted through countless generations and cultures. But there was once an experience from which we, in time, came to deduce something about God.

We come to know God through our faith community, through our relationships, and through experience. We might not possess the full, unadulterated truth, but there is truth in our experience. And this truth, even if colored and distorted by the lenses of culture and the frailty of humanity, still comes from a primal encounter with the divine. The question of theological reflection, language, and epistemology is not whether there is an ultimate truth. Something real and true, some encounter or experience, is at the heart of our faith. The question is whether we can possess it, whether our human frailty and limits will allow us to get to such truth without any fragmentation or distortions. But we can still speak about God, even with our limited knowledge and biases. We can do so because we believe in God. Intellectual knowledge is not at the core of our encounter with God; faith is. It is not intellectual data or the fullness of knowledge that grounds our language about God. It is our experience and relationship with God. When we speak about God, we are not speaking of an abstract concept or a philosophical category. We are speaking about our God.

Second, while we or our ancestors might have had a valid experience of God, we still must contend with the fragmentary and limited nature of our language. When we try to put into words our encounter with God, we discover that our words are not sufficient to express the fullness of that experience.[8] Throughout Christian history, mystics have dealt with the inadequacy of language for expressing their experience with God. But it has never stopped them from attempting to speak about it. True, our language, words, expressions, and concepts will always be insufficient to fully grasp and express the nature of God. Whatever we could and do say about God is always in human terms.

Our language about God is fraught with dangers. If we ever took our words and concepts about God literally, we would be sorely mistaken. Our language and concepts about God can easily become fossilized, keeping us from growing and changing in our understanding of God.[9] Furthermore, even our ideas and doctrines can become idolatrous when we assume they adequately capture God. Idols need not be images made of stone, wood, and precious metals. They can also be images and constructs created by our mind and our philosophies.[10] Even more dangerously, as Justo González points out in his book *Mañana*, our idols not only lead us to a dead and cold god of rigid concepts and ideas, but they can also become instruments of socioeconomic oppression by protecting the cherished notions and ideals of a given culture.[11] Given the limits of our language for accurately expressing God's revelation and the dangers inherent in our words and concepts about God, how can we even dare to say anything regarding God?

Even though we only have limited and fragmentary knowledge about God, and even though our language about God might be inadequate for expressing the fullness of God, it is still possible and necessary to speak about God. Because we experience God as human beings, it should not surprise us that we speak about God through human terms. There is nothing unnatural about it. The Incarnation, central to Christian theology, shows us that God works through humanity. It also opens the way for speaking of God in human terms and recognizing that God speaks to us, not in abstractions, but through the particularity of concrete events and human beings.[12] When God speaks to us, God must inevitably relate to us in human terms, and it is through these terms that we come to understand God. Naturally, quite a bit might be lost in the translation and we ourselves might add to it, but at the core of revelation is the undeniable reality that our encounter with God occurs within a human context and occurs for humanity.

It is this fact, that God comes to us and that God is for us, that allows us and calls for us to speak about God. Karl Barth, the noted twentieth-century theologian, writes in his *Church Dogmatics* that in spite of the problems inherent in the inadequacy of our language for talking about God and the limitations of our knowledge of God, God justifies and sanctifies us, as well as our language, to enable us to speak meaningfully about God.[13] This does not mean that God makes it possible for our language and knowledge to be full expressions of divinity. But it does mean that what we know and say becomes sufficient for us to come to know God through faith. For Barth, knowledge of God is not simply an intellectual matter. It is an encounter that involves our entire self. We do not know God in terms, concepts, or information as an exercise of theoretical reason. We meet God. We enter into a relationship with God. Our language and concepts may be inadequate for us to fully grasp and speak about God. But God still allows us and encourages us to enter into such speech. God works through our cultures, through our language, through our experience, and through our history to enter into living relationships with us. When we speak about God, we are not merely speaking about an abstract philosophical concept. We are speaking about our God, the God we have come to know through our experience and our life, the God who acts and fellowships with us.

Thus, we can and should speak about God because we experience God in our lives and God sanctifies and sanctions our language about God. We are justified. Although we are not perfect, God accepts us as we are. By the same token, God justifies our language and knowledge about God, accepting it with all its limitations. Nevertheless, dangers still exist. This brings us to the third condition for speaking about God. Because we must contend with the limited and fragmentary nature of our language and knowledge of God, we must also engage in a constant process of discernment and theological reflection, examining our theologies, religious language, and practices.

Through this dynamic of reflection and examination, we can ferret out distortions and strive toward an enhanced understanding of God. But this is not with a given goal or mind-set other than the striving for a better understanding of God's self. We cannot escape our humanity. We cannot escape our context and culture to grasp the fullness of God. However, we can continue to speak about God while continually examining our theological language and concepts to make sure that we acknowledge our biases, identify the inevitable distortions that may seep into our theology, and recognize our limitations. In evaluating and examining our theology there is no single approach that suffices for all. Even the methods and criteria we use to examine our theology must be subject to revisions and analyses, for if we render them into absolutes we fall into the same trap of elevating our fragmented thoughts and constructs into absolutes. Thus, we must continually engage in dialogue and analysis, recognizing the tentativeness and limits of all our theological assertions, as well as recognizing the dangers inherent in assuming that we are the bearers and guardians of the ultimate truth about God.

To assume that we can be the purveyors of the ultimate truth would be to usurp God's place, to stand outside our finite being and grasp eternity. But this risk should not stop us from trying to understand God better, just as we seek to better know those we love. By engaging in dialogue with each other, we can gain a broader perspective and enrich our understanding of our faith and of our God. We can speak about God, as long as we recognize the fragmented and limited nature of theological language and avoid falling prey to the assumption and pretense of being the sole proprietors and purveyors of divine truth. Ultimately, in speaking about God, we must take to heart the admonition of Martin Luther that calls us to do all of our theology in humility, recognizing our limitations and failings, as well as the tentative nature of all theology.[14]

Whose Attributes?

Many of us are familiar with the divine attributes. We speak about God as being infinite, all-knowing (omniscient), all-powerful (omnipotent), and present everywhere (omnipresent) among many other things. All of these are characteristics that we attribute to God. But how did we come up with these attributes? Part of the answer is in the legacy of Greek philosophy that permeates Christianity. Christianity, from its beginning, attempted to make itself known to the surrounding cultures by appropriating symbols and terms familiar to these cultures and giving them a Christian meaning. Even the apostle Paul when preaching to the people of Athens made reference to the image of the unknown god (Acts 17:16-34). In attempting to understand their experience with God and to make their faith understandable to the Greco-Roman world, early Christian theologians turned to the philosophical language and cultural resources of the day. While some of these terms had limitations, they were tools that helped them understand and articulate their experience and their understanding of God. But as much as Christianity influenced the Greco-Roman world, the Greco-Roman world also influenced Christianity.[15] The terms stuck. Tradition preserved these cultural icons and philosophical constructs, at times elevating them to a status of dogma. In a sense, this was part of the strength of Christianity—its adaptability and ability to incorporate different cultural artifacts to convey its message, making Christianity from the very beginning a *mestizo-mulato* religion in its ability to negotiate the different cultural milieus of its context.

The attributes come partly from our attempts to delve into the mysteries of God through philosophy. They also reflect some of the characteristics of the cultural milieu of the time and our projection of what we think an ideal God would look like. The attributes can be grouped into two basic categories. The first category attributes to God the highest degree of an ideal characteristic that we think God should have, such as power or knowledge. This covers most of the "omnis" (that is, the prefix that means "all"), such an omnipotent, omniscient, and omnipresent. We value love, so we say God is all loving. We value might, so we say God is almighty. The other category negates a limitation of humanity, particularly those we deem as negative. We are finite. Hence, we say that God is infinite, without boundaries or end. We are subject to very human passions and whims, so we say God is impassible, not subject to passions and whims. We change, so we say God is immutable, or changeless.

Many of the attributes reflect logical necessities and philosophical presuppositions of the divine ideal. For instance, we understand God to be perfect, the highest good, and the most real. If this is the case, then it makes sense logically that God could not change, for any change would only lead to imperfection or to a lower nature. God must be immutable. However, if we analyze this attribute carefully, this perfectly reasonable logical necessity has unintended complications. First, while it might seem ideal for God to not change, then we are able to do something God cannot, change. In this sense, as human beings, we have an ability that God does not. Is this not a limitation placed on God? If this is the case, then God is not truly omnipotent and infinite, for there is something God cannot do, which in turn limits God.

Second, immutability assumes an essentialist understanding of reality, that is, that our very being is an essence or substance from which we derive our character and identity. If there is any change in our nature, then who we are changes. While this was a key philosophical premise of the time, there are many other alternatives to understanding what constitutes our being, including some philosophies that believe we are constantly in a state of becoming and others that understand being as relational in nature. While we might say that our basic character does not change, that does not mean that we do not change.

Third, the most problematic implication of the attribute of immutability is what it means for our faith. If God does not change, what difference do our prayers make? Naturally, for those who believe that everything is preordained, this may not pose a problem, but for those who do not, it is problematic. Our prayers may change us, but not God. If we cannot make God change, then why pray? I, for one, would like my prayers to make a difference. This is especially significant for minorities and those who live under oppressive structures. If there is no hope for change and our prayers make no difference, then we must remain under the oppressive structures. Even worse, if we apply a hermeneutic of suspicion to our analysis, we can see how such an attribute can be easily taken by those in power and used to preserve the status quo. After all, if we live a life of luxury and privilege, then it makes sense to assume that perfection implies that there should be no social change. Thus, Latino/a theologians, like González, raise a significant question: Could this idea of perfection as immutability be an attempt by privileged philosophers to justify their privilege and status quo?[16]

Of course, if we take the Bible seriously, we must contend with the many passages that show God as changing and relating in different ways to humanity. Maybe, given all these factors we should rethink how we understand immutability, so that we speak of God as immutable in God's love and being for us. Isaak August Dorner, nineteenth-century German historian and theologian, arrives at this same conclusion. After examining the history of divine immutability, Dorner concludes that the question of immutability has more to do with God's character and ethical nature than with some abstract ontological or metaphysical consideration that would, in his analysis, present problems for the doctrine of the trinity. Thus, according to him, God is not immutable in relation to the world, space, time, knowledge, or in what God wills for the world. Rather, it is God's ethical character and love that does not change.[17]

We can find similar difficulties if we analyze many of the other attributes. Omnipotence raises the troublesome question that if God is able to do anything and loves humanity, then why is there evil that appears to go unchecked? In light of the horrors of war, the Holocaust, September 11th, the fighting going on in the Middle East as I write these words, the ravages of famine and disease, and the destruction caused by natural disasters, why does God not intervene or at least ameliorate the suffering? Philosophically other questions are easily raised and absurd speculations made as to whether God can create logical impossibilities such as a square circle. Omnipotence cannot mean that anything goes. Contradictory things could not exist at the same time in a finite universe. A world or even a God without limits and self-determination would lead to chaos and true freedom would not exist for humanity or for God. As Karl Barth puts it: "God's freedom is not merely unlimited possibility or formal majesty and omnipotence, that is to say empty, naked sovereignty.... God Himself, if conceived of as unconditioned power, would be a demon and as such His own prisoner."[18]

The Bible speaks of God as almighty, but primarily in terms of God's dominion. The word, *pantokrator*, found in our creeds refers to God's rule over all, not to unbridled power to do anything.[19] Even Dorner, in analyzing divine immutability, came to the conclusion that omnipotence too must be qualified for us to understand God in terms of divine love, since love would require mutuality and freedom to respond on the part of the beloved.[20] Most biblical passages speak of God working through history and through people, working alongside humanity to make change, not overruling creaturely freedom. That God can do anything might be better understood in terms of God as the one for whom all things are possible. In this sense, the question is not one of overpowering, but of making new possibilities, creating new ways, empowering us to overcome adversity, and transforming the world through gentle persuasion, as a loving God would do.

The same can be said for attributing to God impassibility, that is, that God is without passions. It is perfectly reasonable to understand the need for an impassible God in the cultures of Greece and Rome, where the gods were subject to the same whims and passions of us mortals. This philosophical category that elevates God beyond our petty passions makes sense. In addition, it becomes quite useful for combating the monarchian modalist heresies that in preserving a strong monotheism argued that it was the same God who suffered in the cross, rejecting the trinitarian distinctions that were at the heart of Christianity. But the main problem with the heresy was its rejection of the Trinity, not the suffering of God. The God we find in the Bible is one who loves us and suffers with us, not a God who does not feel. A loving God cannot be an impassible, unfeeling God.

We can continue through the other attributes and find similar problems. Does omniscience mean knowing what we are going to do or what we might possibly do? The answer has serious implications to our freedom and to how we understand the future. For instance, if all our actions can be known, then the future must be predetermined and actual, not full of possibilities and choices. If this is the case, then we are not truly free, and if we are not truly free, then we cannot respond freely out of love. Infinity means that God has no limits, but this implies that anything goes and makes it difficult to know anything about God. It also begs the question: if God has no limits, there is something that God is not, limited. Hence, if God is not something, that is a limitation. Such flights of philosophical fancy and circular thoughts are inevitable when we try to get a handle on the attributes and on God. Ultimately, the attributes, while useful to some extent, can easily create problems for us if taken as absolute and accurate definitions of God. After all, they are not God's self-definition for us, but our attempt to define who we think God should be.

While the Bible provides us with many and varied accounts of human beings and their encounters with a living God, philosophical categories provide us with an idea of what we think God should be. And they are not always the same. Even worse, what we think we want in a god is not always what is best for us! Our ideal, who we think God should be, often pales in comparison with the reality of a living God who does not easily fit our categories and ruptures our preconceptions. Philosophy might give us a measure of sophistication. It might provide us with clean, abstract categories in which we can pre-package God, but these categories are our creations that we seek to impose upon God. These categories can easily become idolatrous, become instruments for preserving the status quo of oppressive hierarchies, or lead us to worship a dead god fashioned by our intellect. While we must not easily dismiss intellectual and philosophical inquiry into the nature of God, we must be careful not to fall prey to them, or try to fit God into philosophical categories instead of allowing them to serve as tools for our inquiry. Philosophy should be our servant, not a master that forces us to place the living reality of God in our carefully fashioned boxes or to nail God down on neatly crafted crosses.

In *Mañana*, González provides an excellent account that compares biblical references with the abstract philosophical notions that we use to speak about God. According to González, the Bible never attempts to penetrate into the mystery of God as God; instead, the Bible speaks of God in relation to us and to creation.[21] In other words, the Bible does not attempt to speak about God in philosophical categories; it speaks of God as our God. The language the Bible uses to speak about God is not a set of abstract projections of what we think God should be like. On the contrary, at times the Bible presents us with a picture of God as vulnerable, as affected and grieved by our rejection, as compassionate beyond reason, and as an exasperated parent. The God we encounter in the pages of the Bible is the God of human experience, the God who acts in and through history, who stands in solidarity with humanity. The biblical account is not an account of what we think God should be, but of how human beings have experienced God. It is this account, along with other human experiences and encounters with God through history, that should serve as our guide for understanding God.

It is quite easy to forget that these attributes and philosophical categories that we use to understand God are not universal truths or divine revelation, but culturally conditioned projections of human ideals upon our image of God. One of the critiques leveled against Christianity by Ludwig Feuerbach, a nineteenth-century philosopher, was that its understanding of God was merely a projection of our own ideals of humanity, a projection that blinded us from seeing the needs and potentials in humanity. The danger inherent in the attributes and in our attempts to speak about God is that we fashion a God out of our ideals, and in worshiping that God we forget about human needs and struggles—the very needs and struggles with which the biblical God seemed to be most concerned.

Conclusion

Human language about God is never exact. It is fraught with limitations and colored by cultural and socioeconomic hues. At times, we are tempted to believe that our doctrines and theologies are somehow right, orthodox, and the best window into God. Somehow, we got it right and others got it wrong. But in doing so, we forget that our language about God is just that— our language, our culture, our very human way of looking at God. At the same time we fall prey to a basic hubris that leads us to believe we somehow are superior because we have the inside track into God. We are the sacred holders and guardians of divine truth. Eventually, we succumb to temptation and begin to measure others with our yardstick of divine truth and, on occasions, even use the yardstick to beat them over the head.

Nevertheless, in making our language about God absolute, in assuming that our theologies are indeed the closest to the truth and that our theological language is correct, we are in effect creating an idol from our doctrines and limiting God to our attributes and to our way of thinking. We make God ours, rather than making ourselves God's. There is nothing wrong with speaking about God. There is also nothing wrong with doing theology or using philosophy to try to understand divine revelation and our experience with God. What we must be wary of is making any of these into an ultimate or absolute, for at that point, we close the door to dialogue and arrive at our conclusions. It is at that point that language about God ceases and idolatry begins.

Notes

1. According to Paul Tillich, revelation is always "for someone and for a group in a definite environment, under unique circumstances." *Biblical Religion and the Search for Ultimate Reality* (Chicago: University of Chicago Press, 1955), p. 4.

2. Once more, I allude to the excellent argument presented by Orlando Costas regarding the incarnation and contextualization in *Christ Outside the Gate: Mission Beyond Christendom* (Maryknoll: Orbis Press, 1982), pp. 5-12.

3. Paul Tillich, *Systematic Theology*, Vol. 1 (Chicago: University of Chicago Press, 1951), p. 124.

4. Justo González, in his book *Santa Biblia: The Bible Through Hispanic Eyes* (Nashville: Abingdon Press, 1996), speaks to the problem of human frailty in interpretation, a frailty that would affect our interpretation of even an inerrant text, including the hermeneutical problems inherent in interpreting any text and how our language and biases affect such interpretations, pp. 12-13.

5. Paul Tillich, *Biblical Religion*, p. 5.

6. Karl Barth addresses the limitations of language for capturing the fullness of God in his *Church Dogmatics*, G. W. Bromiley and T. F. Torrance, eds. (Edinburgh: T & T Clark, 1936, 1960), III/3, p. 293.

7. Ibid.

8. Karl Barth addresses the limitations of language for capturing the fullness of God in his *Church Dogmatics*, I/1 (Edinburgh: T & T Clark, 1936, 1955), pp. 149-50.

9. Howard S. Olson speaks of the dangers that the rigidity of language and doctrines brings to theology in his article "Theology as Linguistic Discipline," in *African Theological Journal* 13/2 (1984), p. 77.

10. Jean-Luc Marion expands the notion of idol to include our concepts and intellectual constructs in *God Without Being: Hors Texte*, Thomas A. Carlson, trans. (Chicago: University of Chicago Press, 1991), pp. 23-52. In addition, other theologians and philosophers have warned us of the same danger. See for instance Paul Tillich's assertion that the failure of the medium of revelation to point beyond itself constitutes idolatry, as well as his insistence that God can never be contained in any notion of existence, *Systematic Theology*, Vol. 1 (Chicago: University of Chicago Press, 1951), pp. 128, 205-10, 216. In addition, Justo L. González also articulates the same concern in *Mañana: Christian Theology from a Hispanic Perspective* (Nashville: Abingdon Press, 1990), p. 90.

11. González, *Mañana*, pp. 99-100.

12. González writes that the incarnation rejects any argument that would state that God cannot be spoken about in human terms. Ibid., p. 92.

13. Karl Barth, *Church Dogmatics*, I/1, pp. 51-73, 200-1, 262-72.

14. Preface to the Wittenberg Edition of his German writing, *Luther: Basic Theological Writings*, Timothy F. Lull, ed. (Minneapolis: Fortress Press, 1989), pp. 63-68.

15. González, *Mañana*, p. 96.

16. Ibid., p. 97.

17. Isaak August Dorner, *Divine Immutability: A Critical Reconsideration*. Trans. by Robert R. Williams and Claude Welch (Minneapolis: Fortress Press, 1994), see particularly pp. 165-66. However, his second and third essays in their entirety merit a close reading to fully appreciate his argument.

18. Karl Barth, "The Gift of Freedom," in *The Humanity of God* (Atlanta: John Knox, 1960), p. 71.

19. González, *Mañana*, p. 94.

20. Dorner, *Divine Immutability*, pp. 184-85.

21. González, *Mañana*, p. 92.

CHAPTER SIX

GOD FOR US

When Hispanics speak about who God is for us, we do not gravitate toward abstractions of God, such as the attributes we just discussed. As Latinos and Latinas, we tend to think of God as the living God of the Bible, who is at work in our lives.[1] We might be familiar with the philosophical jargon. But we speak of God as our God, because our understanding of God comes less from philosophical speculation and more from our readings of Scripture, our relationship with God, and our experiences. But I also suspect that it is not only Hispanic Americans who think about God in this manner. I suspect that most Christians think of God in concrete, relational, and experiential terms derived from Scriptures and from their own life. Most of us do not speak of an omnipotent, impassible, omniscient, and immutable God. We speak of God for us. Out of our experiences, readings of Scripture, and context we do speak about the God who is for us.

God As a Verb

At the center of God's self-revelation in the Scriptures is the Incarnation. As Christians, the Incarnation defines who and how God is for us. Throughout Christian history, one of the principal litmus tests of our faith has been encapsulated in the assertion that God became flesh for us in Christ. The Incarnation is a guide and a criterion for our understanding of our faith, experience, and humanity, but most significantly, it is essential for our understanding of God as Christians.

The first chapter of the Gospel of John speaks about the nature of God in christological terms in an interesting manner. When we read John's Gospel, we encounter that familiar phrase: "In the beginning was the Word, and the Word was with God, and the Word was God" (John 1:1 NIV). But when I read the same passage in Spanish, it reads slightly differently. It reads, "In the beginning was the Verb, and the Verb was with God, and the Verb was God." The Greek term that we translate into English as "word" is *logos*, a term full of rich meanings and potentials for interpretation. When translated into the Latin, the term becomes *verbum*, a term from which we get such words as "verbal" and "verb." While the earlier translator of the Bible into Spanish translated *logos* as word, later translators translated it as verb to distinguish the living Word from the written and spoken word, as well as to express God's act of becoming incarnate and God's active presence in Christ.[2]

Thus, when we speak and think about Christ and God in Spanish, we are speaking of the Verb who has become flesh. God for us is a God of action, who acts in history and in our lives, while also demanding action from us. Throughout the pages of the Bible we read of God not as a passive observer, but as an active agent of history who from the very beginning is creating, speaking, moving over the waters, and interacting with creation (Gen. 1:1–2:25). Throughout the Hebrew Scriptures and the New Testament, we meet a God who continually acts in history, interacting with us, judging and liberating us.

In a sentence, a verb is central, expressing action, content, and being itself. The verb connects the nouns and adjectives of a sentence in an act. While nouns name and adjectives qualify, verbs perform. Verbs express actions, commands, states of being, aspirations, and expectations. Mary Daly has argued that there is no reason to speak of God as a noun, a word, something that leads us to think of God as static, which kills a more personal and dynamic understanding of God as a Verb.[3] This is not a problem for those Latinos/as who speak and read the words of John's Gospel in Spanish. For us it is easy to imagine and understand God as the living Verb, a term that evokes rich new images of who God is for us and calling us to rethink our theology.[4]

Rather than static images of an unchanging and unmoved God, we envision a God who acts. When we understand God as a verb, our theology and our philosophy inevitably change. Our language about the being of God inevitably moves away from static substances and essences. The philosophical category of ontology becomes understood in terms of ontopraxis, where being and doing are one. Being is not an essence or a substance. Being is not a noun. Being is a verb. Being and acting must be taken together, must coincide one with the other. In theology, when we understand God as a Verb, we are drawn to speak of God's being and acting together.[5] Our understanding of revelation also changes. Divine revelation is not seen as information about God, but as divine action within history.[6] But most important our understanding of who God is changes, for we discover that we know who God is through what God does.

When Latinos/as understand God as a Verb through our readings of Scripture, religious rituals, symbols, and experiences, we are provided with a unique perspective into God that unleashes new and powerful imagery of a living and creative God. Our God is not a construct of our minds or a projection of our ideals and desires. Our God is active and creative, at work in our history and in our lives (Phil. 2:13). Our God is not far removed from us or indisposed. Our understanding of God is not in terms of a mere concept, but also as an activity. The God who was at work in the biblical times is still at work today. Thus, theology cannot be mere theory, it must also be praxis. Our faith must not be simply about belief, that is, intellectual assent to a set of presuppositions. Our faith must be about doing.

Understanding God as a Verb, as a God who acts in history and in our lives, is important to an oppressed people. Whether living in North America or in Latin America, the possibility that God is still actively working to change and transform our present human condition is both a source of hope and a necessity for anyone who is suffering, victimized, oppressed, or marginalized. The church must work tirelessly to destroy all immutable and impassible idols, whether made of stone or of philosophy, which preserve the status quo. Anyone who hopes for transformation and change also hopes in a God who is actively at work with us to bring forth change. For us, God is and must be a Verb.

God As Creative

According to the Bible, God's first action is to create (Gen. 1:1). But God's creative activity does not stop with creation.[7] Other passages speak of God's ongoing creation. In Isaiah, after a recollection of all the great things God has done, God tells Israel not to dwell on the past, but to look to the future because God is doing something new (Isa. 43:18-19). The motif of God's ongoing creative activity continues throughout the Bible, where all things, including ourselves are to be open to the continuing creative activity of God. Even in the end, God's creation continues with John's vision of a new heaven and a new earth (Rev. 21:1). Scripture, history, and experience reveal to us God's ongoing creativity and lead us to understand God as creative.

What does it mean to understand God as creative? Origen, a fourth-century theologian, believed that if God were creative, there must have always been some form of ongoing creation. Otherwise, God's nature would have changed. Origen believed that God must have always been a creator. If God had not always been so, the act of creating would have brought about a change in God thus making God mutable rather that immutable. While Origen supports his argument by appealing to God's immutability, there is another option. Because God is creative, then there must always be change and activity in God. Process theologians, for instance, see God as embodying possibility and defining creativity. This understanding of God as creative also affects how we understand God's infinity and omnipotence. Rather than understanding infinity as endless and undefined, we can speak of God's infinity as the ability to transcend limits and create new possibilities. In the same way, we can also understand omnipotence not as unbridled power, chaotic and limitless, but as God working in creation to provide us with new possibilities for being that do not limit creaturely freedom, but empower it. Even omniscience changes from knowing the future as an accomplished actuality to knowing all that is possible, while being open to the surprising power of a future not defined by the present. God's creativity also provides us with insights into divine providence as God's continual care for creation in opening new possibilities for life in spite of death and destruction.[8] God's grace to us comes as the gift of new possibilities for the future in the face of the closure of possibilities inherent in death, suffering, oppression, and marginalization.

To understand God as creative is significant for a battered and oppressed people in need of hope and new possibilities for life. God's ongoing creativity opens the possibility for hope—the possibility that the present need not define the future. Although present structures might seem to recreate and perpetuate themselves into the future, God's creative activity can surprise us in fashioning something unexpected and unimagined, making possible the impossible.[9] The potential we see in the present, whatever it may be, fades in the light of God's creative activity and fashioning of new possibility.

God As Love

In *Process and Reality*, Alfred North Whitehead notes three frequently used paradigms for understanding God: God as a divine ruler, fashioned after imperial rulers; God as the personification and legislator of morality; and

God as an ultimate philosophical principle. In contrast to these models, Whitehead offers a fourth option fashioned after what he terms "the Galilean origin of Christianity," a model that:

> Does not emphasize the ruling Caesar, or the ruthless moralist, or the unmoved mover. It dwells upon the tender elements in the world, which slowly and in quietness operate by love; and it finds purpose in the present immediacy of a kingdom not of this world. Love neither rules, nor is it unmoved; also it is a little oblivious as to morals.[10]

When we understand God through a paradigm of love, the attributes of impassibility and omnipotence quickly change. A God of love must feel and would work through persuasion rather than coercion, allowing for creatures that are free and able to respond out of love. Whether we understand God as all powerful or not, God's love and gift of freedom qualify God's power. Some theologians argue that God's power must necessarily be limited in itself while others argue that it is a self-limitation of God. But regardless of the reason, the result, from our perspective, is the same. God's power is inevitably qualified and limited by love.

Scripture gives us a glimpse into a God who deals with humanity with love and tenderness, patiently forgiving us, while extending extraordinary grace and mercy unto us. This portrait of God as loving is central to the Christian understanding of God and a common theme in the New Testament and early church. In the Gospel of John, for instance, love is a central motif, defining God's relationship to the world and Jesus' relationship to his disciples (John 3:16, 15:9-13). This motif is also central to the epistle of John, where we are told that love comes from God and that God's very being is constituted by love (1 John 4:7-8).

The theme of a loving God persists throughout Christian history and theology. For instance, in the early church, Augustine wrote that our very existence is possible only through God's love.[11] Even more, God is the source of the love that empowers us to love one another and serves as the basic paradigm for Augustine's understanding of God and the divine Trinity.[12] In the Middle Ages, Peter Abelard argued that the Incarnation itself reveals to us God's love; it shows us the extent of God's love in Jesus' willingness to stand in solidarity with humanity, facing death and calling us to love.[13] Even Abelard's contemporary and major detractor, Bernard of Clairvaux, agreed that Jesus' life and death revealed God's love for us.[14] More recently, an understanding of God as love plays a central role in Latin American liberation theologies and in Gustavo Gutiérrez's understanding of God's preferential option for the poor.[15]

While love is central to our understanding of God and ourselves, our understanding of love is always somewhat limited, partially shrouded in mystery, defined by abstractions, and clouded by emotional feelings.[16] Ultimately, love can be best understood through the actions that exemplify it. If we speak simply of God's love as an abstract notion, it lacks impact and action. Yet the self-giving, nurturing, and caring of love is seldom abstract in its manifestations, patience, and depth. Love is a bond that connects us, transforming both the one who loves and the beloved.[17] When we speak of God as love, we can no longer speak of God as detached, unmoved, and unaffected by humanity. God's self-giving love for us transforms us, but it also transforms God, for anyone who truly loves cannot simply remain unaffected by those one loves.

Understanding God as love is central for Latinos/as. Familial ties, caring for one another, define our culture and resonate with our understanding of God as love. Through our understanding of God's love as manifested in Scripture and in the Incarnation, we come to see God not as apathetic, but as one who lives in solidarity with our suffering, who is willing to risk rejection, abandonment, and death to stand at our side. Such a God can truly understand us and is worthy of our love. Rather than working through domination and control, like those who oppress us, we cherish the thought of a compassionate God who suffers with us and works through tenderness and persuasion to empower us and bring forth change.[18] Our faith in a God of love offers us the hope that this love will lead God to work for our betterment and comfort us in the midst of our suffering and struggle. Because God loves us, we are endowed with value and dignity as human beings who are indeed worthy of God's love.[19] Even when the world might reject us and look down upon us, we are still worthy because God loves us.

God As Power

Growing up in a Hispanic Baptist church in Miami, we sang the Spanish version of a well-known hymn, *"hay poder, poder, sin igual poder, en la sangre de Jesus"* (there is power, power, unequaled power, in the blood). We sang of God's power being able to move mountains. Knowing the power of God was comforting. However, we also knew in our life and experiences of the weakness and powerlessness that we felt as we tried to survive in the *barrio.* Understanding God as powerful is important to us, but it can never be a simple hierarchical understanding of power. While power might manifest itself in terms of force and compulsion, power is not simply an ability to use force and compulsion. Nor does it need to be destructive in nature. Paul Tillich, for instance, defines power as the ability to affirm one's being against non-being.[20] By this definition, power may involve force and compulsion, but not necessarily. Rather, power is the ability to be, to live, to exist, to make things happen in spite of nothingness, death, and destruction. But even in this definition, love and power cannot be separated.[21] Love qualifies power, but power is also necessary for love to exist. Power without love would be chaotic domination. Love without power would be mere submission.

God's love qualifies God's power. However, this does not mean that we believe in a powerless and impotent God. Faith in a powerful God is essential for those who suffer under the burden of oppression and injustice. It is also essential for those who are weak and powerless in our world to believe in a God of power who stands at their side. Otherwise, there would be little hope of change and liberation. But believing in a God of power is not the same as believing in unbridled omnipotence where anything goes, or absolute domination where freedom becomes inconsequential. If this were the case, then God would be inevitably aligned with those in power, with those who dominate others and perpetrate unspeakable acts of violence against the weak. Such an understanding of God's power would inevitably align God with those who exert power over us in the world. Either that, or God would be uncaring and unwilling to intercede on behalf of those who suffer, therefore condoning their suffering at the hands of the powerful. God, in either case, would be demonic, unworthy of our worship or love.

Typically, when we speak of power, we tend to speak of it in a hierarchical manner, in terms of a force exerted over something, and in terms of domination. But this is a limited understanding of power. True power cannot be merely the ability to dominate and exert control over others and over all circumstances; power must be understood in terms of self-giving, sharing, and empowerment. True power must be sufficient to share and give power to others without feeling diminished in any way. Such is God's power.

There are three ways we can speak about God's power without resorting to a hierarchical understanding of power or to unbridled omnipotence. We can speak of empowerment, possibility, and perseverance. The Bible speaks of God's power not just in terms of dominion, but also in terms of participation. Prophets spoke and acted in the power of the Spirit. At Pentecost, the power of the Holy Spirit is imparted upon the disciples (Acts 1:8), enabling them to reach out to others by speaking their language and creating unity while preserving the diversities of cultures. God's power comes to us as a vehicle of empowerment and enablement. God does not hoard power or lord it over us. God shares power with creation, thereby sustaining and empowering us. The ability to empower creation to act, to create, to share in God's power speaks of the wealth of God's power and self-giving. True power is being able to share power and empower others.

We can also speak of God's power in terms of possibility. God's creativity can open new possibilities for being when all possibilities seem to be exhausted. The power of the resurrection does not circumvent the reality of death. Rather, it opens a new possibility that denies death its finality. Divine power, understood in terms of possibility, is not power through domination, but power in spite of domination and its apparent finality. It is the power to overcome the finality of the status quo, of hopelessness and oppression, not by raw force, but through transformation. It is not destructive power or the power to capriciously do anything at all, but the realization that in God all things are possible. God's power as empowerment and as possibility come together in Paul's words to the Philippians, "I can do all things through Christ who strengthens me" (Phil. 4:13 NKJV).

Finally, we can also speak of divine power in terms of perseverance. God's ability to persevere beyond all human understanding allows God to surpass the finality of any human circumstance. God does not need to make things happen by fiat and raw power. God can outwait us. In human terms, loving persuasion appears inefficient as an agent of change. But we only need to see the stalactites and stalagmites in a cave to see how a single drop of water over time can change the look of things or how a flowing stream can in time carve out a mighty canyon. In God's patience, perseverance, and everlasting nature there is more power than any of us can ever imagine.

God As Life

Gustavo Gutiérrez, in his book *The God of Life*, argues that the Old Testament name for God, Yahweh, means more than "I am." God, as the one who is, is the source of existence and life. In that sense, Gutiérrez concludes, God is the God of life. Gutiérrez extends this argument beyond the Old Testament, finding in John's Gospel an affirmation of Jesus being life (John 14:6) and arguing for an understanding of life as communal in nature, so that "to live" means "to live with or for others."[22] The Scriptures often speak of God not only as the Living God, but also as a God of life. To understand God as the God of life means more than simply understanding God as the source of our existence and being. It means that in God there is life, and, as such, that God's very being stands in opposition to death, destruction, and all things that deny and rob us of life. To believe in a life-affirming God means that we too must affirm life. Through our affirmation of life, we affirm the very nature of God—of God as life.

The struggle for life becomes even more critical for those who live in marginalized communities, who must etch out their existence daily through hard and dehumanizing labor in fields and factories, deprived of the necessities of life. Our work and sweat in the fields and in the factories are literally an out-pouring of our lives. We invest our time, energy, and sweat into the fruit of our labors. The fruit of our labor sustains us and our family, but when others take a disproportionate bite of the fruit of our labor, they are taking a bite out of us, robbing us of life.[23] In this sense, just wages and living wage efforts are not mere economic issues; they are life and death issues. If we affirm God as life, then the issue also becomes a theological imperative.

Life and the affirmation of life are theological questions for Latinos/as. They emerge through our culture in different and various forms. Out of these forms the three most prominent are *la lucha* (the struggle), *fiesta,* and *lo cotidiano* (the daily). At times people mistakenly think that Spanish culture is fascinated with death. We celebrate the Day of the Dead and adorn our Cathedrals with graphic crucifixes depicting Jesus' death on the cross. But rather than displaying a morbid fascination with death, these practices are an affirmation of life. The Day of the Dead, for instance, affirms the lives of our ancestors and their continual participation in our life. In the same manner, the crucifixes we see in churches and in our culture affirm the struggle of life against death and ultimately the triumph of life over death.[24] As the Spanish philosopher and poet, Miguel de Unamuno so aptly put it: to live is to struggle.[25] This sentiment is echoed even more firmly in the work of Latina theologian Ada María Isasi-Díaz, who locates in the voices of marginalized Hispanic woman the notion of *la lucha* (the struggle) not as an expression of suffering, but as an affirmation of life.[26] In the everyday struggles of life, we acknowledge the presence of God through our life-affirming actions.

Like *la lucha,* the *fiesta* also stands as an affirmation of life. According to Latino theologian Roberto Goizueta, "The fiesta celebrates the *ultimate* goodness of life (even in the midst of suffering and, indeed, as the "subjunctive" denial of the ultimacy of death) it celebrates life as a gratuitous gift *that cannot be* destroyed by a dominant culture that, objectifying life, would destroy it."[27]

In this sense, the *fiesta* not only affirms life, but it actively stands in resistance to those who would seek to objectify or deny life. In the *fiesta,* there is an inherent recognition of God as the giver of life. Some Hispanic theologians even make reference to "El Dios fiestero," God as one who enjoys *fiestas,* in terms of the life-affirming aspect of deity. Even the Gospels portray Jesus as *fiestero* (Matt. 11:19). The *fiesta* is an affirmation of life in spite of suffering and death. It is more than a mere party; it carries an air of celebration, sacredness, and community that affirms the eternal dance of life.

While *la lucha* affirms life's ongoing struggle against death and the *fiesta* affirms the celebration of life in spite of death, a third notion, *lo cotidiano,* is a complex term that encompasses folk philosophy, creativity, and the active struggle of life.[28] It also can extend to ordinary and everyday practices that affirm and sustain life. In understanding God as life, the everyday acts that sustain and affirm life as we struggle to survive in a hostile world become places of theological reflection, rich in significance and religious depth. This is particularly true in *Mujerista* theology, where the everyday and shared experiences of women become a hermeneutical tool and a rich source of theological reflection. While there might be negative aspects to *lo cotidiano*, its emphasis is in the life-affirming aspect of lived experiences, struggles, and the "stuff" of life.[29]

While *lo cotidiano* has a particular use and meaning in *Mujerista* theology, there are other aspects of our everyday experience that strengthen our understanding of God as life. In the everyday aspects of life, especially in those activities through which we sustain life, whether it is through our work, caring, nurturing, cooking, mending, cleaning, bathing, and eating, there is an inherent spirituality. Ordinary aspects of our lives, such as work and family life, also bear a deep sense of spirituality that often goes unnoticed. Our work has an intentionality and creative nature that leaves a mark on us and our world. Through our work we sustain life, produce, and create—activities that can have a deep sense of spiritual presence. In our family life, the bonds of love and nurture sustain life. Our caring and life-sustaining activities are at the very core of our existence, and through them we affirm the life-giving reality of God.[30] In every aspect of life, as well as in the life-affirming activities of everyday existence, we catch a glimmer of God as the source of all life.

God As Liberator

Implicit in our understanding of God as love and life is an understanding of God as liberator. Both love and life, at their core, carry a tacit understanding that freedom is necessary for their existence. Life, devoid of freedom, loses its significance. Love, if coerced, ceases to be love. To understand God as love and as life requires that we also understand God as liberator, a central concept in Latin American theologies and Hispanic theologies. But this is not a new concept. In the Scriptures we cannot help being astonished with the numerous passages that depict God as liberator. The story of the Exodus from Egypt casts God, not Moses, in the role of the liberator (Exod. 3:7-10). The prophetic texts constantly call for justice and liberation from oppression. Even in the Gospels, Jesus defines his ministry in terms of liberation from captivity, oppression, and disease as he cites the words of the prophet Isaiah (Luke 4:18-19). To understand God as a liberator is not liberation theology, it is biblical theology. God works in history and in us to bring freedom from all the forces of oppression and domination that enslave us— God liberates us from sin and sinful structures.

The Feminine Face of God

In Genesis we read that God created humanity in the image of God, both male and female (Gen. 1:27). Barth, in addressing this passage, makes the controversial assertion that the image and likeness of humanity is one where we are placed in confrontation, juxtaposition, and conjunction with one another as male or female.[31] Other biblical scholars speak of this passage as asserting that humanity was created to be in community.[32] Even earlier, in the nineteenth century, Elizabeth Cady Stanton had used this verse from Genesis to argue that God was both male and female.[33] While we understand that God transcends the physical distinctions of gender, we must also recognize that being male and female are both included in God's image.

Our language about God is inevitably human language. When we speak of God as Father, we are basically making an analogy that compares God's relationship to us to a parent-child relationship.[34] It is not a statement about God's gender, but about God's relationship to us. However, when we fall prey to the dominance of patriarchal and male-dominated language, particularly in trinitarian language, we begin to associate God with the male gender, with all its traits and categories, doing damage to our understanding of God. As David S. Cunningham writes in an article on the Trinity, "We may never fully understand the subconscious effects of the overwhelming usage of masculine language, masculine metaphors, and masculine personal pronouns to refer to God."[35]

While we cannot limit certain characteristics such as strength, nurture, compassion, and tenderness solely to one gender or the other, we tend to associate some of these characteristics primarily with one sex or the other. When we use solely male imagery for God, we exclude the feminine characteristics from God, limiting our way of understanding God. Thus, it would be idolatrous to speak of God solely as male or female. Recognizing that in our different cultures and genders we embody and reflect different aspects of the divine image, it is important for us to also speak of the feminine face of God, and not limit ourselves strictly to male language, characteristics, and imagery.

While some of us might choose to speak of God as our Father, we must not reject the maternal character and feminine imagery of God. Understandably, some people gravitate to New Testament imagery of Father and Son, but we should also not forget that the New Testament also gives us maternal images of God and Christ, as Jesus' lament over Jerusalem illustrates: "Jerusalem, Jerusalem, . . . how many times have I tried to gather your children, as a mother hen gathers her chicks under her wings" (Matt. 23:37; Luke 13:34). Some of the characteristics we tend to associate with maternal nature, such as nurture, creativity, care, and love should not be removed from our understanding of God.

Other biblical images, particularly in the Hebrew Bible, personify Wisdom as a woman (Prov. 8–9; Matt. 11:19). For instance, Proverbs 8:22-30 portrays Wisdom as feminine and as being with God since the beginning. It also portrays Wisdom as participating in God's creation, often in ways similar to that of the *logos*, God's word—both imagery and functions of which would later be associated with Jesus in the New Testament. Regardless of whether we interpret these passages as allegories or metaphors, it is important that we contend with the feminine presence in the way we understand God.

Many Hispanics do not necessarily think of God in feminine terms. We are a culture that bears the marks of sexist characteristics and patriarchal structures, to the extent of having contributed words such as *macho* and *machismo* to the English-speaking world. At the same time, there are strong matriarchal ties that bind our communities and families, serving as the driving force behind many families and churches. The role of women in Hispanic churches is significant—even when it goes unrecognized, as is often the case—and essential to the survival of many congregations and parishes. Affirming the feminine characteristics present in God helps us acknowledge and affirm the value and contributions of women in the church and society to a greater extent.

As humans, we also crave certain levels of connection and intimacy with God that often are absent from male-dominated models of deity, such as tenderness, emotional accessibility, comfort, and nurture—characteristics that rightly or wrongly we tend to associate with feminine traits. The fourteenth-century mystic Julian of Norwich writes that in God we find both Father and Mother, identifying in the Trinity the property of motherhood, which she connects with Jesus who in her words is our Mother, Brother, and Savior.[36] It is also important for Christianity to recover maternal characteristics of the divine to liberate it from oppressive mythic language. Most recently, Mark Taylor has suggested a recovery of the maternal metaphor in our christological language and our Christian praxis to recover a mythic language that recognizes the sacred in women and their maternal powers.[37] At times, we need a heavenly Mother as much as we need a heavenly Father. As a society we tend to place an inordinate value on traditional family models, yet when it comes to God, we seem to be satisfied with a single parent! To take this analogy one step further, just as a single parent often must be both mother and father to the child regardless of his or her gender, God also must be both a Mother and Father to us.

There are two areas where the feminine face of God might emerge in Latino/a cultures. One is through the presence of the Holy Spirit, and the other is through the Virgin. While most people do not think of the Holy Spirit in terms of a particular gender, there are some who do associate the Holy Spirit with female characteristics, particularly in terms of the immediacy, intimacy, passion, and love evoked by the Spirit. Once a woman in a Hispanic congregation confided in me that she identified more with the Holy Spirit because she had always thought of the Spirit in feminine terms. Her thoughts were not new or unique to Christianity. Elxai, an Ebionite and an exponent of Judaizing Christianity with Gnostic tendencies, believed that the Holy Spirit was feminine.[38] While the Ebionites were viewed as heretical for their adoptionist views regarding Jesus, it does show that the association of the Spirit with femininity is not a recent development.

More recently, Jung Young Lee connects the Spirit to the Asian concept of ch'i, developing an understanding of the Spirit as female in its sustenance of life and the womb of the world, also associating the Spirit with love, compassion, and other maternal characteristics.[39] His identification of the Spirit with feminine and maternal traits leads him to state that it is the Spirit that in conjunction with Mary is the true mother of Jesus and that the failure of the church to recognize the feminine aspect of God was what would lead to the divinization of Mary.[40]

It is entirely possible that in Protestant churches that reject the elevation of Mary to a quasi-deity, the Spirit assumes some of the feminine characteristics of God. Just as the Latina woman confided in me her views about the Spirit as feminine, I will venture to say that many others also think of the Holy Spirit as the feminine face of God. The life-sustaining, affirming, and creative power of the Spirit may justify such claims, at least in understanding that God's relationship to us is as both Mother and Father. As Leonardo Boff argues in *Cry of the Earth, Cry of the Poor*, the Spirit is feminine in both Hebrew and Syriac, and is typically associated with life processes that evoke feminine characteristics.[41]

The second way in which Hispanics seek to connect to the female aspect of divinity is through the Virgin. The image of the blessed Virgin takes many forms depending on the culture. In Cuba, it is Our Lady of Charity. In Puerto Rico, it is the Virgin of Monserrat. In Mexico, it is the Virgin of Guadalupe. While primarily found in Catholic settings, the connection with the Virgin is such a strong and powerful cultural symbol that in some instances, images of the Virgin of Guadalupe are found in Protestant churches, including a United Methodist church I visited in Washington, D.C., as well as in some Protestant churches in the Southwest.

The importance of the Virgin to Latinos/as is multifold. In many instances she serves as a motherly mediator between humanity and God, relating to us with compassion and tenderness. In her encounter with Juan Diego she referred to herself as the merciful mother and mother of all nations and to him as her son and child.[42] To some Latinos/as, Guadalupe is a feminine aspect of God. As Virgilio Elizondo writes, the Virgin "stimulates new ways to think about God—for instance, she challenged the patriarchal Christianity of that time with the reality of the femininity of God."[43] The Virgin balances our male-dominated God language, providing us with a feminine face for God.

Two other significant elements of the accounts of the Virgin in Hispanic culture are the way she appears to us and to whom she appears. In the Guadalupe account, the Virgin appears to Juan Diego, a poor mestizo worker, as a mestiza, a woman of mixed Native and Iberian heritage. Mestizos were the product of the violent conquest of the Americas, often the product of rape. They were seen as inferior and were generally marginalized and oppressed by the dominant powers of society. That the Virgin appears to one of these lowly persons and identifies with him to the extent of appearing as a mestiza gives us significant and powerful theological insights into God's identification with those who are violated, oppressed, and marginalized. The Virgin not only embodies the liminal place between the cultures as a bridge, but also their marginalization, oppression, violence, and rape.[44] Even if we did not consider Guadalupe to be a feminine expression of God, we cannot discount the theological significance of this account.

The Guadalupe story is not the sole story of the Virgin identifying with the poor, marginalized, and conquered people. Cuban accounts of Our Lady of Charity (*La Caridad del Cobre*) parallel the story of Guadalupe. It is an African slave, Moreno, and two Amerindians that find the statue of the Virgin that would later be credited with miracles, some witnessed by the three of them. In addition, the event transpires in a poor community of copper miners. Once again, the story originates among the marginalized and depicts the Virgin as walking in solidarity with them, in the same manner that the Bible speaks of Jesus walking with the poor and the outcasts of his time.[45]

Whether these stories depict actual events, are used as evangelistic tools, or are popular creations—as is often debated—they do provide a corrective to our male-dominated God language. They are sources for theological reflection that lead us to reconsider idolatrous images of God and to envision God beyond our narrow understanding. Male-dominated language about God can easily become in league with views of power as domination and control, traits we often associate with male imagery. At the same time, feminine-oriented language can express the persuasive power of love, compassion in identifying with the oppressed, the forgiveness of grace, and concern for dignity and life. Thus, it should not surprise us that these feminine ways of imaging God often also bear the marks of liberation.

God As Trinity

Our basic understanding of God as triune comes not so much from philosophical interpretations—those would come later—but from the way people experience God. At its core, the doctrine of the Trinity comes out of human experience, which fits well with Hispanic theology and its emphasis on experience and Scripture. The Incarnation forced us to locate God in humanity and to reconcile this new insight with traditional monotheism. People had experienced God both as human and transcendent, as flesh and as Spirit. Biblical language referred to God in three different ways. But we were left to understand these claims. Some, later deemed heretical, sought to preserve the unity of God by not recognizing the differences, such as Monarchian Modalism. Others denied the full divinity to one or the other, as occurred with Arianism. By far one of the best-known and accepted ways of speaking about the Trinity came from Tertullian, who talked about the Trinity in terms of three persons and one substance, using illustrations that compared the Trinity to such things as the Sun, sunrays, and the warmth of the rays.

Today, we continue to develop our language regarding the Trinity. Instead of abstract and static notions of substance, we at times speak of fields, such as those found in scientific and mathematical theories, or activity and relationships. The way we understand persons has also changed in two thousand years, with new and more complex meanings coming from psychology and philosophy. Basically, to understand the Trinity, there are two options. We can try to peer into the very being and nature of God (ontological Trinity) or try to comprehend how God has related to us and worked through human history (economic Trinity).[46] However, I will venture to say that for Latinos/as, it is more important to know how God relates to us and works through our history. It is through this knowledge of who God is for us—and that God is for us—that we can know who God is.

The Trinity As Iconoclastic

Trinitarian language forces us to recognize the limits of human language in speaking about God and prevents us from rendering any definition of God into an absolute. The Trinity is iconoclastic, breaking apart our tendency toward static and idolatrous language about God. If we think of God as the transcendent and infinite creator, we are also forced to think of God as a human being, incarnate in Christ, subject to suffering and death. If we think of God as human, we are forced to think of God also as the divine Spirit that pervades all creation. If we think of God as an immanent Spirit indwelling all creation, we are reminded that God also transcends all. Eventually, we come full circle. Trinitarian language serves as a constant reminder that our language about God is never sufficient to express the totality of God. There is always more to God than what we can grasp. The Trinity severs our tendency toward idolatry by making any single way of understanding God problematic without the others, leading us to recognize the diversity that is present in God's nature as manifested in the Trinity. The same can be said for the way we speak about God and do our theology. To try to give priority to any theology or to make any perspective normative is idolatrous. There is a place at the theological table for all perspectives, including Latino/a perspectives.

The Trinity As Relationship

The Trinity serves as a model to emulate both personally and communally. The Trinity is about relationship, about empowerment, about accompaniment, and even about economic justice. First, the Trinity reveals something about God. It reveals that God exists in relationship. This relationship not only exists between the persons of the Trinity, but also with us. That we can speak of a triune God tells us something about God: God comes to us and seeks to be in relationship with us.[47] To Latinos/as and other marginalized groups, knowing that God loves us, comes to us, and seeks to live in relationship with us is essential. For us, the ties of community, connection, and accompaniment are vital. We understand our world as interconnected. Our relationships help define us. Thus, knowing that God is communal in nature resonates with our worldview. Even more, it is important for us to know that God seeks us out and stands in solidarity with us. God not only understands suffering and death, but God also has not abandoned us. It is important for us to know that God has not left us alone; that God accompanies us in our life journey, through our struggle and our suffering.[48] The doctrine of the Trinity exemplifies how God accompanies us in Jesus and in the Spirit. Through them we know that we do not walk alone. We know God walks with us and that we belong to a greater community than our own barrios and people.

The Trinity As Immanent Sacramentality

Alfred North Whitehead wrote that before it became mired in philosophical speculation about divine absolutes, the Trinity was one of the most innovative contributions of Christianity to philosophy. Its strength lies in its emphasis on God's direct immanence in the world.[49] Understanding divine immanence like this resonates with Latinos/as who see all of creation as being imbued with divine presence and sacramentality.[50] The world is not a mere material and mechanical thing; it is God's creation, a living creation filled with God's Spirit. We should not mistake this with pantheism, where all things are God. Rather, it is a realization that all creation bears the mark of the Creator and that God's presence suffuses all of reality.[51] The doctrine of the Trinity brings God out of the sky and out of the realm of abstract speculation, making God near and dear to us, without negating God's transcendence. Thus, the doctrine of the Trinity resonates with our understanding of God's Spirit who pervades all creation and God's Son, Jesus, who accompanies us in our struggle.

The Trinity and Economy

Usually, when we speak of the economic Trinity, we are referring to God's action in history, the way God has come to us, in contrast to the ontological Trinity. However, there is another way of understanding the Trinity that carries political and socioeconomic ramifications. In *Mañana*, Justo González builds upon Karl Barth's definition of God as being for others, arguing that the Trinity shows us a God of love whose essence is sharing.[52] But understanding God as one who loves and shares leads us to very concrete socioeconomic consequences. When we speak of the Trinity in terms of its giving and sharing, we are also making a socioeconomic statement. If God shares and lives in community, why is it that we don't? González builds upon the work of Christopher Mwoleka the Bishop of Tanzania, who argues that maybe the Trinity is a model to imitate, not a mystery to solve, calling us to live in community with one another, sharing with one another.[53]

Of course, such concerns with socioeconomic issues are not novel ideas presented by Bishop Mwoleka and González. As early as the book of Acts, we are told that after Pentecost, the Christian community lived as a true community, selling their possessions, giving to the poor, sharing with one another, and holding all things in common (Acts 2:44-47). While our economy has been built upon the hoarding of capital, the Trinity reveals to us a model for being like God, where sharing and love become the norm. In addition, while many are often driven by greed and an unbridled thirst for power, the trinitarian model of God calls us to empower one another.

The Trinity As Diversity

As Latinos/as we realize that even within our cultures there is broad racial, social, and cultural diversity. How are we to reconcile this diversity with being made in the image of God? At times, people gravitate toward arguments that create hierarchies that say one group is closer to God's image than others. Hence, they feel justified in lording their perceived perfection over others whom they treat as inferior. However, the doctrine of the Trinity provides us with a different answer. God exists in the diversity of three different persons who are equally God. In the same manner, there is not one culture or people who bear the image of God. We all do. It is only in our diversity that we are able to bear the image of a God who embodies diversity. We are diverse because God exists in diversity.

In the United States, God's affirmation of diversity is important in this age where xenophobia often dominates our national ethos as we close our borders out of fear and seek to find unity by forcing sameness through English-only movements, acculturation, assimilation, and the hegemony of the "melting-pot" myth. While we fear what is different and try to make it fit into our categories and standards by assimilation or by its elimination, God celebrates difference and diversity. The danger inherent in the denial of the Trinity, as occurred in Monarchian heresies, is in the enforcement of unity in terms of a singular dominant identity and a denial of plurality and diversity.[54] The story of Babel in Genesis speaks to the dangers of assumed unity through sameness, the danger of hubris (false pride), domination, and the desire to usurp God's place. As they sought to reach heaven, God confused their language and hence they had no other quality to maintain their unity. The story of Pentecost affirms the opposite. The coming of the Spirit fosters and affirms diversity, allowing people to hear the gospel in their own tongues. Yet, the affirmation of diversity does not destroy their unity.

God As Spirit

Because Latinos/as have a strong sense of God's Spirit as pervading all creation, pneumatology, the doctrine of the Holy Spirit, takes on added significance for us. In Hispanic communities, Pentecostal congregations are rapidly growing, and Charismatic movements are sweeping through many Hispanic

Protestant and Catholic churches alike. The attraction of Pentecostal and Charismatic movements is due to a variety of reasons. Some factors are socioeconomic. Pentecostals often have a greater level of engagement with the poor, in part due to their style of worship, music, passion, and expressiveness, as well as their autonomous character—which empower them to be self-governing. But for marginalized and oppressed people, there is also certain attractiveness in understanding the work of the Holy Spirit as empowering them and giving them a voice as instruments of God.[55] Eldin Villafañe cites various reasons for Pentecostalism's ability to thrive among Hispanic congregations and the poor, including its ability to offer healing to people experiencing health and spiritual crisis due to poverty. He also cites its primal spirituality, including glossolalia, which gives voice to the poor, affirms the value of all as vehicles for the divine, and provides a sign of God's presence in their midst. Coupled with piety, the possibility of miracles, and its eschatological hope, Pentecostalism provides many venues of empowerment and hope for a disenfranchised people.[56]

The significance of the work of the Holy Spirit in our communities merits serious consideration. We cannot speak of the doctrine of the Trinity within a Hispanic context without addressing pneumatology. In his book, *The Spirit, Pathos, and Liberation,* Samuel Solivan develops a Hispanic Pentecostal theology rooted in pneumatology. He also introduces the term orthopathos (right feeling) as an intermediary between orthodoxy (right doctrine) and orthopraxis (right action), providing through this term a space for feeling to enter into theology as a epistemological resource, a way of knowing. This term introduces feeling and passion into our believing, thinking, and acting. At the same time, it moves us away from apathetic and impassible ways of understanding God, allowing us to see suffering as a place of revelation and moving us toward compassion.[57] In the face of the poor and the suffering we can find God and be moved to compassion (feeling with them) and liberative action, but it is the Holy Spirit who is present in both—suffering with the one who suffers and empowering our love and compassion toward liberation.[58]

It is important to us who have often been depersonalized or treated as nonpersons to encounter the Spirit as personal, empowering our own sense of personhood.[59] Rather than a disembodied force, it is the most intimate and personal nature of God that binds us in God's love to one another. It is through the Spirit that we have life and enter into communion with God.[60] It is the Spirit that binds us to God and to one another.

Who God is for us is partially rooted in history and Scripture, but it is also the product of our cultures, hopes, and aspirations. While Scripture and human experience shape some concepts of God, speculation and philosophy shape others. As theologians, ministers, and laity, we must enter into dialogue with different perspectives and wisely discern the value of each, recognizing that we can never fully capture the fullness of God in human terms, nor do we need to. In the Incarnation God has already done that for us.

Notes

1. Ismael García writes that "Hispanic Americans are neither moved nor prone to speak about God in abstract terms," instead we tend to think of God in terms of the biblical God and from our understanding of ourselves. *Dignidad: Ethics Through Hispanic Eyes* (Nashville: Abingdon Press, 1997), p. 122.

2. For a more detailed account of how this translation came to be see chapter 4 of my book *Jesus Is My Uncle: Christology from a Hispanic Perspective* (Nashville: Abingdon Press, 1999), pp. 85-106, particularly pp. 89-94.

3. Mary Daly, "God Is a Verb," *Ms.* 3 (December 1974), p. 97.

4. This paragraph summarizes an argument that I develop to a greater extent in *Jesus Is My Uncle*, pp. 103-6.

5. The argument for understanding God as act is not new, nor limited to a translation that renders *logos* as Verb. Process philosophy makes a connection between being and becoming. Eberhard Jüngel speaks of the Trinity in terms of God's being as grounded in becoming and continual activity in *The Doctrine of the Trinity*, trans. by Horton Harris (Edinburgh: Scottish Academic Press, 1973) and later in *God as the Mystery of the World*, trans. by Darrel L. Guder (Edinburgh: T & T Clark, 1983), leading him to a creative, dynamic, and relational view of God that is a viable alternative to static substance language. Other arguments also provide us with dynamic and relational ways of understanding God's being in dynamic and active terms.

6. Jürgen Moltmann has a similar argument, connecting revelation to history in terms of God's promise. *Theology of Hope* (New York: Harper & Row, 1967), pp. 112-17.

7. Christopher Morse argues this same point in *Not Every Spirit: A Dogmatic of Christian Disbelief* (Valley Forge: Trinity Press International, 1994), p. 221.

8. For more on this topic see my article "In Harms Way: Theological Reflections on Disasters," in *Quarterly Review* (Spring, 1997), pp. 1-17.

9. Eberhard Jüngel speaks of God's infinity as the ability to create possibility out of impossibility, hence differentiating the future as potential that is inherent in actuality and the future as creative possibility. "The World as Possibility and Actuality," in *Theological Essays*, trans. by J. B. Webster (Edinburgh: T & T Clark, 1989), pp. 111-12.

10. Alfred North Whitehead, *Process and Reality*, corrected edition, ed. by David Ray Griffin and Donald W. Sherburne (New York: Free Press, 1978), p. 343.

11. Augustine, *On Christian Doctrine*, in *The Nicene and Post-Nicene Fathers*, first series, vol. 3, ed. by Philip Schaff (Albany, Ore.: Ages Software, 1997), Sermon 1, II.

12. Augustine, *Enchiridion*, 31.117, p. 96 and *On the Trinity*, 9.1.1., p. 234, in *The Nicene and Post-Nicene Fathers*.

13. Peter Abelard, *Exposition of the Epistle to the Romans*, 2.1-3, in *A Scholastic Miscellany: Anselm to Ockham*, Eugene Fairweather, ed. and trans. (Philadelphia: Westminster Press, 1956).

14. Bernard of Clairvaux, *On Loving God* (Albany, Ore.: Ages Digital Library, 1997), p. 20.

15. Gustavo Gutiérrez, *The God of Life*, trans. by Matthew J. O'Conne (Maryknoll: Orbis Press, 1991), pp. 9-16, 94.

16. Paul Tillich argues that love cannot be simply understood as emotion. Rather, it

must be understood ontologically, in terms of the structure of being and the desire to reunite with what is estranged. *Love, Power, and Justice: Ontological Analysis and Ethical Applications* (New York: Oxford University Press, 1960), pp. 24-25.

17. For more on the understanding of God's nature as transformed by God's love, see Eberhard Jüngel, *God as the Mystery of the World*, pp. 300-384. I also develop this further in my dissertation, *Infinity in Finitude: The Trinity in Process Theism and Eberhard Jüngel* (Charlottesville: University of Virginia, 1994), pp. 248-63.

18. I make this argument in *Jesus Is My Uncle*, pp. 44-46.

19. Ismael García examines the ethical implications of being loved by God and how it vests us with dignity and worth in his book *Dignidad: Ethics Through Hispanic Eyes* (Nashville: Abingdon Press, 1997), pp. 154-57.

20. Paul Tillich, *Love, Power, and Justice*, pp. 48-53.

21. Ibid.

22. Gustavo Gutierrez, *The God of Life*, pp. 12-13.

23. Enrique Dussel, *Praxis Latinoamericana y filosofía de liberación* (Bogota: Editorial Nueva America, 1983), pp. 153-54.

24. Virgilio Elizondo, *Galilean Journey: The Mexican-American Promise* (Maryknoll: Orbis Press, 1983), pp. 41-43.

25. Miguel de Unamuno, *The Agony of Christianity* (New York: Ungar Publishing Company, 1960), p. 20.

26. Ada María Isasi-Díaz, *En la lucha/In the Struggle: A Hispanic Woman's Liberation Theology* (Minneapolis: Fortress Press, 1993), pp. 168-69.

27. Roberto S. Goizueta, "Fiesta: Life in the Subjunctive," in *From the Heart of the People: Latino/a Explorations in Catholic Systematic Theology*, ed. by Orlando O. Espín and Miguel Díaz (Maryknoll: Orbis Press, 1999), p. 96.

28. See Ada María Isasi-Díaz's article "Lo Cotidiano: A Key Element of Mujerista Theology," *Journal of Hispanic/Latino Theology* 10/1 (August 2002), pp. 8-10.

29. Ada María Isasi-Díaz, *Mujerista Thelogy* (Maryknoll: Orbis Press, 1996), pp. 66-71.

30. Martin Heidegger, in *Being and Time*, trans. by John Macquarrie and Edward Robinson (New York: Harper and Row, 1962), pp. 349-62, connects caring with *Dasein*, the being that is there, that is, the human being. Caring is at the source of our existence, which can be connected to Being itself, the source of all being, which we can understand in terms of God. In this sense, the very activities that affirm life manifested in the everyday existence of humanity and through our care are reflections of being and an affirmation of life. This can allow us to begin to understand God in terms of life.

31. Karl Barth, *Church Dogmatics*, volume III, section 1, p. 195.

32. For instance, see Claus Westermann's commentary, *Genesis: 1–11: A Commentary*, trans. by John J. Scullion (London: SPCK, 1984), p. 160.

33. Elizabeth Cady Stanton, *The Woman's Bible* (Seattle: Coalition Task Force on Women and Religion, 1895, 1987), pp. 14-25.

34. Gregory of Nyssa's argument against the Arians resided in that the Father and Son primarily expressed a relationship, not an essence or a nature. While this argument is developed through many of his works, see for example *Against Eunomius*, book III, Sect. 4, in *The Nicene and Post-Nicene Fathers*, trans. by William Moore and Henry Austin Wilson (Grand Rapids: Eerdmans, 1988), pp. 144-46.

35. David S. Cunningham, "The Holy Trinity: The Very Heart of Christian Ministry," in *Quarterly Review*, 22/2 (Summer 2002), p. 130.

36. Julian of Norwich, *Julian of Norwich: Showings*, ed. and trans. by Edmund Colledge, James Walsh, and Jean Leclercq (New York: Paulist Press, 1978), pp. 279-97.

37. Mark Kline Taylor, *Remembering Esperanza: A Cultural-Political Theology for North American Praxis* (Maryknoll: Orbis Press, 1990), pp. 194-95.

38. See Justo González, *A History of Christian Thought: From the Beginnings to the Council of Chalcedon*, revised edition (Nashville: Abingdon Press, 1970), pp. 125-26.

39. Jung Young Lee, *The Trinity in Asian Perspective* (Nashville: Abingdon Press, 1996), pp. 95-111.

40. Ibid., p. 106.

41. Leonardo Boff, *Cry of the Earth, Cry of the Poor,* trans. by Phillip Berryman (Maryknoll: Orbis Press, 1997), pp. 166-73.

42. See Virgilio Elizondo's translation of the *Nican Mopohua* in *Guadalupe: Mother of the New Creation* (Maryknoll: Orbis Press, 1997), pp. 7-8.

43. Ibid., p. 124.

44. Some scholars have argued that the historical Mary was a rape victim in the hands of a Roman soldier, a common occurrence in occupied lands, which led to Jesus' birth. Thus, Mary's identification with the violated and subjugated *mestizos/as* and Jesus as *mestizo* would not be surprising. See Elizabeth Schüssler Fiorenza, *Jesus: Miriam's Son, Sophia's Prophet* (New York: Continuum, 1995), pp. 182-86.

45. See Miguel H. Diaz's account and interpretation of the story of *La Caridad* in his article "*Dime con quién andas y te diré quién eres* (Tell me with whom you walk, and I will tell you who you are): We Walk with Our Lady of Charity" in *From the Hearts of the People*, pp. 155-57.

46. This argument is not just a product of Hispanic theology. Karl Barth argues that the fundamental error which dominated the doctrine of God was in beginning the doctrine with a doctrine of the Trinity forged from formal logic rather than revelation and God's coming into history. *Church Dogmatics*, Vol. 2, part 1, trans. by T. H. L. Parker, W. B. Johnston, Harold Knight, and J. L. M. Haire (Edinburgh: T & T Clark, 1957), p. 261.

47. According to Barth, God's revelation and act in history, exemplified in the Trinity, shows us that God is one who comes to us in love, seeking our reconciliation and seeking to be in relationship with humanity. Ibid., pp. 257-62.

48. Roberto Goizueta, *Caminemos con Jesús: Toward a Hispanic/Latino Theology of Accompaniment* (Maryknoll: Orbis Press, 1995), pp. 205-11.

49. Alfred North Whitehead, *Adventure of Ideas* (New York: Free Press, 1967), pp. 168-69.

50. Roberto Goizueta writes that Hispanics see the world as interrelated and suffused with Spirit in *Caminemos con Jesús*, p. 9.

51. Leonardo Boff writes that the whole of creation is the body of the Trinity, while the Spirit works to transform the universe, Christ to liberate it, both bringing it into reconciliation with God the Father and with the Trinity. *Trinity and Society*, p. 230.

52. González, *Mañana*, p. 115.

53. Ibid., pp. 113-14.

54. See Leonardo Boff, *Trinity and Society*, pp. 20-21.

55. Samuel Solivan, *The Spirit, Pathos and Liberation: Toward an Hispanic Pentecostal Theology* (Sheffield: Sheffield Academic Press, 1998), pp. 30-32.

56. Eldin Villafañe, "Spirit without Borders: Pentecostalism in the Americas," in *Apuntes*, 22/4 (Winter 2002), pp. 128-35.

57. Samuel Solivan, *The Spirit, Pathos and Liberation: Toward an Hispanic Pentecostal Theology*, pp. 60-61.

58. Ibid., pp. 101-3.

59. Samuel Solivan, "The Holy Spirit: A Pentecostal Hispanic Perspective," in *Teología en Conjunto: A Collaborative Hispanic Protestant Theology* (Louisville: Westminster Press, 1997), p. 53.

60. The creation accounts speak of God's Spirit *(ruah)* as moving over the waters of chaos at the very beginning of creation. In Genesis 2:7, it is God's breath *(ruah)* entering into us that gives us life. In this sense, our own spirits are a gift of God's Spirit, part of the divine image in us.

CHAPTER SEVEN

JESUCRISTO

Jesucristo, *Jesucristo*, we sing and clamor to the name. *Jesucristo*—Jesus the Christ—in Spanish the two words come together, inseparable from each another. It is almost as if in that one phrase the entire christological problem is encapsulated and resolved. Jesus, the human being born of Mary into a particular history, context, and culture, comes together with the title, the Christ, the Messiah, the anointed of God. The words seem to convey an innate understanding that we cannot take one without the other—that we cannot understand who Jesus is apart from Jesus' work as the Christ. What Jesus does defines who Jesus is for us. While originally neither of the words christ nor messiah implied a divine nature, these titles now speak of a particular relationship to God. They are the opening to understanding Jesus' role in human history and in God's plan, and as such, they are an opening into our experience of Jesus as divine. *Jesucristo* expresses, in a sense, the very essence of Christology, the coming together of humanity and divinity in a way never before encountered.

Christ Through Culture

Hispanic Christologies don't begin with philosophical speculation. They begin with human experience, and in particular, with the experiences of the Latinos/as. Through Jesus we experience God's love in our lives and in our cultures. We meet Jesus through our churches, pastors, and priests. We meet Jesus in the lives of others and in our own lives. We meet Jesus through our cultures, not in spite of them. Both Christology and the Incarnation serve as prime examples of the intersection of faith and culture, a topic that merits some attention in trying to understand how Christology and theology as a whole can and must be understood in the light of our cultures.

When H. Richard Niebuhr wrote *Christ and Culture*, he offered five paradigms for Christ's relationship to culture: Christ against culture, Christ of culture, Christ above culture, Christ and culture in paradox, and finally Christ as the transformer of culture.[1] Most likely, he would place the Hispanic understanding of Christ within the paradigm of the Christ of culture, where Christ becomes accommodated to culture because cultural expressions mediate Christianity and often become the vehicles and filters for understanding our faith. However, I will venture to say that this is not the case—that while many of Niebuhr's paradigms are indeed valuable ways for understanding the relationship of Christianity to culture, there is a sixth paradigm: Christ through culture.

Throughout the earlier chapters, I have argued that both Christ and Christianity are always found in a given context and culture. As Orlando Costas writes:

> It does not take much effort to show how theology—from the patristic writings to the present—has been situational through and through. Indeed it has been generally bound to the experiences and categories of western culture. . . . Biblical contextualization is rooted in the fact that the God of revelation can only be known in history. Such a revelation comes to specific peoples in concrete situations by means of particular cultural symbols and categories.[2]

Costas's argument draws its strength from the Incarnation, which places the highest expression of God's self-revelation within a specific cultural and historical context. Thus, can anyone who takes the Incarnation seriously truly believe that we can separate either Christ or Christianity from its cultural and historical matrix?

At the same time, we cannot reduce Christ and Christianity to a mere product of culture. The Incarnation occurs within the context and history of a particular culture, but it is not merely a product of that culture. In the same manner, Christianity developed within the contexts of history and cultures throughout the ages. To a certain extent, all of us recognize that there is a prophetic element in God's revelation and in the work of the church that hopes toward a transformation of the world and its many cultures. To some extent, we must agree with Niebuhr's fifth paradigm, Christ transforming culture. We do want Christ and Christianity to exert a prophetic voice in culture in the hopes of a transformation. Liberation theologies, in their eschatological aim for the reign of God on earth, work toward the transformation of culture.

However, in Niebuhr's paradigm, culture takes on a somewhat universal definition, even if it takes on various expressions. Culture becomes a synonym for civilization, defined in terms of the artifacts of humanity—artifacts such as language, ideas, beliefs, customs, social organizations, inherited artifacts, technical processes, and values.[3] The universal presupposition in Niebuhr's definition of culture is most evident in that culture is singular rather than plural. Through most of his definition, culture appears monolithic, rather than pluralistic. Only toward the end does he acknowledge that there are diverse elements and interests, often conflicting, within a culture.[4] But this pluralism tends to be placed more within culture, rather than acknowledging the diversity of cultures. Niebuhr's definition of culture is in terms of "high culture"—the high achievements of humanity rather than the organic reality of a people. In other words, he defines culture primarily by the arts, philosophy, sciences, and other intellectual and artistic expressions. Culture, in this definition, is the realm of the theater, the symphony, the museum, and the academy. In contrast, low culture—a hierarchical imposition that sees it as a lesser cultural expression—is the realm of the worker, the artisan, the folkloric, the dialects, and such. As an academic, it is perfectly reasonable to understand Niebuhr's definition of culture in terms of high culture. After all, Niebuhr does acknowledge one important element for our understanding of Christology and theology as a whole—that no one can escape culture and the conditions it imposes on our perspective and worldview.[5]

Paul Tillich also recognizes the intricate connection that exists between culture and faith. In his *Systematic Theology*, he defines culture as "that which takes care of something, keeps it alive, and makes it grow."[6] In crafting this definition, Tillich understands culture almost in agrarian terminology, that is, in terms of cultivation. For him, culture is both a reactive *praxis* and a receptive *theoria*.[7] It is not limited to artistic expressions or theoretical insights. Culture is what cultivates and cares for the human spirit, civilization, and society along with all the things that emerge out of that process of cultivation, including language and technology, making the term more inclusive in nature. Tillich still falls prey to the same trap of associating culture with high culture in his writings, but his definition opens the door for including such practices as popular religion, which cultivates and cares for the human spirit, and folk and grassroots cultural expressions. Tillich's broader definition of culture allows us to expand its use and application to broader cultural expressions.

Tillich also argues that all theological enterprises and aspects of human spirituality are irreducibly embedded in cultural vehicles such as language, so that divine revelation and theological reflection both occur within a cultural matrix.[8] If revelation comes through culture, then Christ, as God's ultimate revelation, must also come through culture. By understanding Christ through culture, we acknowledge two things. First, Jesus is not a mere creation of culture. He is born into a culture. His life, teachings, and actions occur within the context of a culture. But they cannot be reduced to that culture nor can we assume that they are irrelevant beyond it. If the values and artifacts of one culture were incommensurate and irrelevant to other cultures, then we would not be able to enjoy Mozart, Greek tragedies, Zen gardens, Arabic numerals, and chocolate, among many other things. Second, God's revelation does not occur apart from culture. While the two are not identical, they are connected. Culture serves as the vehicle and means through which we come to know divine revelation, Christ, and Christianity. The task of the theologian is not to surgically remove and abstract one from the other, but to discern how it is that Christ and revelation come to us through a given culture.

We know Christ through our experiences and through our culture. Human beings have no other recourse or access to knowledge of God apart from them. But the Christ that comes through culture and through our experiences is neither the Christ of culture nor a distortion made to conform to our cultural context. Rather, there is a parallel between the life and ministry of Jesus of Nazareth that correlates to our experience and situation.[9] The New Testament accounts represent who Jesus was for those closest to him, and those accounts serve as our guide in trying to understand Jesus and discern how Christ comes to us through our cultures and our experiences. Thus, we have a legitimate claim in trying to understand who Jesus is through our culture and experiences. At Caesarea Philippi, Jesus asked two questions of his disciples: "Who do people say that the Son of Man is?" and "Who do you say that I am?" (Matt. 16:13-15). In this account, we see the acknowledgment of the many ways that people can understand who Jesus is, but also a call to answer the question for ourselves. We are called to discern who Jesus is and what he means to us. At the same time, we must also be able to discern how and where Jesus comes through culture to meet us.

In the Name of Jesus

While not all Latinos/as speak Spanish, for those of us who do and were raised in Spanish-speaking churches, *Jesucristo* or *Cristo* are the preferred ways to speak of Jesus. After all, Jesus is a common name in Hispanic cultures, as common as Maria, José, and the names of other biblical protagonists. Jesus was the name of one of my uncles. It was also the name of a deacon in my church, a neighbor, and several classmates at school. When well-meaning evangelists who were not raised in a Spanish-speaking culture would come through the neighborhood and ask us if we knew Jesus, they were often surprised when we would tell them, "Yes, he lives in that house over there."[10]

Naming our children Jesus probably originated in the Iberian Peninsula, where Muslims, Jews, and Christians coexisted for centuries. In a world inhabited by people bearing such names as Mohammed and Moses, bearing the name of Jesus was as much an expression of religious identity as it was a practice of honoring the name. So it should not surprise us that many Latinos are named Jesus. What should surprise us is that this is not the case in Anglo culture. In a way, whether we name our children Jesus or make it taboo is telling of how we understand Christology. When we say "Jesus" in Spanish out of surprise or fright, it is almost as a prayer and by no means taboo. We even say it when someone sneezes in the same manner that we say "bless you" in English.

But saying the name "Jesus" in English during similar circumstances often is considered cursing, the taking of God's name in vain, and in that is the key to the distinction. Underlying the taboos against speaking Jesus' name are cultural perceptions of Jesus as God. English-speaking cultures consider Jesus' name to be sacred, hence they consider certain ways of using it desecrates and profanes the name. This leads us to another tacit cultural perception of Jesus that places more emphasis on his divine nature and transcendence than upon his humanity and immanence. This perspective can erect a barrier between humanity and God, instead of bridging that distance. In effect, it removes Jesus' name out of ordinary language and usage, and places it within the context of the sacred, separate from the mundane.

However, this effectively removes God from the ordinary and everyday aspects of our lives as well. God transcends the world, but does not inhabit it. As a result, we remove God from creation and deny its sacred nature. This may even reflect a form of Gnosticism that devalues the material world and places it at odds with the divine. Emphasizing the divine to this extent can deny the human in Christ and the value of the Incarnation. Without the incarnate reality of Jesus entering human history and taking on human flesh, God remains at a distance. Isn't the point of the Incarnation to show us God in human form?

We can relate to Jesus not because he is God, but because he is human. Rather than removing Jesus and God from human language, the Incarnation should lead us to recognize the presence of the divine in our midst. It should bring God into humanity, not remove Jesus from it. The God who has suffered with us can truly understand our suffering. At the feet of the crucified, we can find solace and hope in the presence of death. Latino/a culture places Jesus right in the middle of our lives. We recognize Jesus' divinity, but we also celebrate his humanity. He inhabits sacred space, but he is also present in the secular, mediating and collapsing the gap between the two.

Latinos/as do consider Jesus' name sacred, but we also take it as a sacrament. In our use of Jesus' name, we acknowledge his sacramental presence in human life. God is not far from us. God is very near and dear to us. The people that bear Jesus' name serve as a constant reminder of Jesus' humanity and presence in our midst, reminding us that humanity bears the image of God and that whatever we do to each other, we do to God (Matt. 25:34-45). It reminds us that Jesus is subjectively present in our acts of love and objectively present in the lives of those who suffer under the indignities of sin and oppression. Jesus, as incarnate, bridges the gap between divine transcendence and imminence, between the sacred and the secular, reconciling the two in one person.

Whether language reflects or affects the cultural reality of how we understand Jesus and Christology is hard to tell. It is probably a bit of both. As the product of culture, language reflects our worldview, and as such, also reflects our way of understanding how God relates to the world. For instance, whether we translate the term *logos* in its reference to Christ either as "word" as in English, or "verb" as in Spanish, the terminology makes a difference in the way we understand God. While both are valid translations of *logos*—after all, a verb is a word—the term "word" places the emphasis on concept, definition, and even stasis. On the other hand, "verb" places the emphasis on action. Thus, for one, Christ is a concept, for the other, an action. Christ is God's self-expression on one hand, God's act on the other. One culture can emphasize God's revelation in Christ in terms of a self-disclosure of concepts, information, or data. For the other, God's revelation in Christ comes through action. Both ways of looking at it relate God to the world and speak of God's self-communication, but they lead to different perceptions about God. They lead to different understandings of faith—one conceptual, and the other active. This is not to say that one is better than the other, only that we should consider both. By understanding God through different cultures and languages, as well as through their nuances and unique perspectives, we can enrich both our faith and our understanding of God.

Another linguistic use that affects our understanding of Christology is the word *incarnation.* The English word has its roots in Latin, a language more closely related to Spanish than to English. Unlike the translation of *logos* as word or verb, incarnation in Spanish is *encarnación*. Here the nuances of the word emerge not from the use of two different meanings, but from the context and connections each word has to its respective language. In English, incarnation has a very direct meaning as a philosophical or literary term that signifies something manifested in human form or flesh. Most of the cognates or related words in English tend to have slightly negative connotations, such as carnal, carnage, carrion, or carnivore. Other words are neutral, like carnation or carnival, but lack any connotation to the original meaning of the word in Latin. These negative connotations almost evoke in us a picture of the Incarnation as God's entrance into something foreign, base, and unspiritual that can easily lead to a dualism that devalues our earthly realities of life as flesh and blood creatures. In the same way that Jesus gets removed from common parlance and placed in a sacred space that limits the use of the name, a wedge is driven between the spiritual and the material, placing greater value on the former and less value on the latter.

However, in Spanish, *encarnación* evokes other connections, in the same way that the original Latin term would have evoked.[11] While the nuance of the term might escape theologians in the twenty-first century, it surely did not escape the first theologians that crafted the terms. In Spanish, *encarnación* is both closely related and a cognate of *carne*, the Spanish word for flesh and meat. When we think of the Incarnation in Spanish, we cannot help thinking of the flesh on our bones and the meat that we eat. It is a word that connects with life and evokes a more visceral reaction. We are familiar with terms like *chile con carne* but seldom think of them as somehow connected to the incarnation. But in Spanish, the relationship is more evident. The Incarnation cannot be separated from the realities of life as flesh and blood. It is difficult to say whether it is our culture's affinity for life or the nature of our language—probably a little bit of both—that makes us more aware of the connections to the flesh and to our embodied life.

When we think of God becoming incarnate, it is not difficult to make a connection with the meat *(carne)* being sold in the marketplace and butcher shop *(carnicería)*. The food that we eat, the animals that are slaughtered to nourish us, the giving and taking of life that are all part of the conditions of existence become entangled with the meaning of the incarnation. The work and the sweat of the people who till the ground and prepare the food that feeds us become bound together with God's entrance into the flesh. The spiritual converges with the material world. Jesus becomes enfleshed in the Incarnation. Our living, working, eating, and suffering all become sacred spaces where we can encounter God. The space between the spiritual and the material worlds collapses. The Incarnation places God in the middle of human life. God does not enter into human flesh in the Incarnation, God is already found there. Jesus is not the entrance of God into human flesh in a dualistic sense; Jesus is the embodiment of God.[12]

In certain Spanish-speaking cultures, the word *carnal* has an idiomatic use that does not carry the negative connotations of its English-language counterpart. Rather, in such idiomatic usage, the word means "brother," literally, someone of the same flesh, used to refer to someone who is a close friend.[13] When we read passages that speak of Jesus as the firstborn of many brothers and sisters (Rom. 8:29), it makes perfect sense to us. In Jesus humanity and divinity come together affirming that we are all brothers and sisters in Christ. Thus, it should not come as a surprise that in many Hispanic evangelical and protestant churches, it is common to call each other brothers and sisters.

More than the semantics of language, the Incarnation itself contextualizes God in the midst of human history. In the Incarnation, God's revelation does not take place as a disembodied word spoken from heavenly heights or through the voice of a prophet. The Incarnation reveals God through flesh and blood. God's word becomes flesh for us. God's revelation occurs through a concrete reality embodied in the fullness of humanity. As Tertullian argues against Marcion, how can the crucifixion and resurrection hold true if "Christ did not truly have what it takes to be crucified, to die, to be buried, and to be raised— that is, this flesh of ours, suffused with blood, built up on bones, woven through with sinews, intertwined with veins?"[14] In the Incarnation, God becomes flesh for us, taking on human flesh and all the conditions particular to it. This invests all of humanity, including our bodily existence, with spirituality and sacredness. Athanasius, the fourth-century Bishop of Alexandria, for instance, believed that the flesh is corrupt only as the result of our sins. Hence, without God's full presence in human body and spirit, humanity could not be restored to its full state as the bearers of God's image.[15] God does not save the human spirit disembodied from the flesh. God enters human history in a concrete fashion as flesh and blood, saving human beings as a whole.[16]

The Incarnation vests all of creation with sacredness, spirituality, and value. The material world and the flesh do not stand in opposition to God.[17] Rather, they are the places where we find God. The physical realities of the flesh are important to God. The Scriptures clearly call us to feed the hungry, give drink to those who are thirsty, care for the sick, and free the imprisoned (Matt. 25:31-46).Being spiritual does not mean ignoring these and other physical concerns for loftier spiritual ideals. On the contrary, being spiritual means we need to take the very needs of the flesh and blood existence of humanity seriously. Salvation is not merely something reserved for a world or life to come; it is for this world as well.

For Latinos/as the physical realities of our embodied life are quite important. We feel our aching bones after a hard day's work. Words alone do not satisfy us, for we also crave physical contact, a warm embrace, and the feel of a touch making each other's presence concretely real. We celebrate life, with all its heartaches, and enjoy the food that nourishes our bodies. We are physical and do not see the physical world as inferior to the spiritual. Life embodied in flesh and blood is very real to us. We may not be alone in feeling this way and I suspect that these notions are indeed not limited to Hispanics. But because we are aware of the realities of the flesh, the *carne*, we cannot ignore the physical needs of our brothers and sisters who suffer hunger, abuse, and neglect. The Incarnation and our understanding of reality make it impossible for us to separate the spiritual and the physical world. Both are part of God's reign and intricately interconnected with each other.

Who Jesus Is

When we think of Jesus today, we have the benefit of two millennia of theological and philosophical speculation. We have the biblical accounts, the resurrection narratives, and the teaching of the church to tell us about Jesus. But just for a moment, we should put ourselves in the place of the early disciples. To understand Christology fully, we must begin on the dusty roads of Judea and the windy shores of Galilee. It is in those places that we first meet Jesus of Nazareth. When the first followers of Jesus met him, he probably did not seem any different to them than anyone else. He was a flesh and blood human being, the son of Joseph and Mary.[18] There was no halo to signify his deity nor did he glow in the dark! However, through his words and deeds, his followers came to see in him a divine presence, a revelation of God in human flesh that told them that somehow he was more than a prophet. How then were they to reconcile their understanding of God with the divine presence they experienced through Jesus?

Christological and trinitarian problems revolve around questions of relationship. Scripture speaks of Jesus as human, but it also speaks of him as divine. While the trinitarian problem focused on the relationship between Jesus' divinity and the God of the Hebrew Bible, the christological questions focus on trying to understand how divinity and humanity could coexist in the person of Jesus. Traditionally, Christology covers two themes, the person and the work of Christ. The person of Christ speaks to the identity and seeks to answer the question of who Jesus is, as well as how the human and the divine come together in him. The work of Christ seeks to answer the question of what Jesus does and how that is significant for us. A third, and less commonly used, question revolves around the states of Christ, following the kenotic (emptying) hymn of Philippians 2:5-11, which traces Christ's equality with God, the emptying or divesting of divinity to descend into the world and the exaltation after the resurrection.

When we look at the debates as we try to understand who Jesus is, we can trace a line along a vertical axis. We can also draw a line along a horizontal axis, placing the person of Christ at one end and the work of Christ at the other. At the top of the vertical line we can place high Christologies, that is, those Christologies that understand Jesus as divine almost to the exclusion of all humanity. Here we can put such Christologies as those espoused by the different forms of Gnostic and Docetic teachings, some which even argued that Jesus' body was a mere phantasm, an illusion, and that his suffering at the cross was just acting! Philosophically, these theological assertions made Christology easy and more philosophically palatable by removing Jesus from the messy fleshy realities of the material world. Thus, then, they did not have to contend with a God who changes, suffers, and gets tangled up with what they considered to be the inferior nature of physical reality that the Greek philosophers sought to escape. But, by denying Jesus' humanity, they deny the reality of the Incarnation and its significance. Of course, if we applied a bit of a hermeneutics of suspicion, we find that such a spiritualizing of Jesus made it easier to allow for the status quo to go unchecked and removed the responsibility of transforming society and meeting the physical needs of those who suffer in the world.[19] It was, by all means, a safer position to take.[20]

At the bottom of the line we can place low Christologies, those Christologies that understand Jesus primarily as human, almost to the exclusion of the divine. These are Christologies that speak primarily of Jesus' prophetic role or forms of Adoptionism, the view that Jesus was adopted by God or simply filled with the Holy Spirit. While this approach to Christology acknowledges Jesus' humanity and all it signifies, it still denies the Incarnation and keeps God separate from humanity. In a sense, it is still able to safeguard the impassible God who does not suffer and thus fulfills the Greek philosophical ideals of divinity. While God can inhabit human flesh through the Holy Spirit and even adopt a human being, humanity and divinity are still alien to one another. We can also apply a bit of hermeneutics of suspicion to these Christologies and see in them a touch of the "local boy does good" or "anyone can make it" myths. As Justo González points out in *Mañana*, this is an oppressive myth that assumes that those in higher classes got there through hard work and that those who have little are lazy or could accomplish anything through hard work, without acknowledging all the oppressive barriers that stand in their way to success.[21] Inherent in both extremes of Gnosticism and Adoptionism is a shared assumption that humanity and divinity are incompatible realities.

In part, christological controversies in the early church occurred because rather than allowing Jesus to define both divinity and humanity for us, we allowed our preconceptions regarding humanity and divinity to guide our attempts at understanding Jesus. Who we thought God should be, often guided by Greek philosophy, and our assumptions about humanity, along with the use of categories of static substances became the determinants for understanding Jesus. Hence, we did not allow God's revelation in Jesus to shape our understanding of divinity and humanity. Instead, we tried to understand Jesus by our own preconceived ideas of what divinity and humanity were.

The same assumptions were present in other attempts to understand how the two natures, the human and the divine, were present in Christ. The debates between the Antiochene school and the Alexandrine school were indicative of these problems and of our propensity toward quasi-docetic views. The Antiochenes, centered in the city of Antioch, argued for the importance of the full humanity of Christ. At the same time, they tended to protect the impassibility of the divine, often keeping the human and the divine completely separate. For example, Nestorius, Patriarch of Constantinople, had tried to resolve the issue by keeping each nature apart to the extent that he was accused of dissolving the unity of the two natures. This did not sit well for those of the Alexandrine school, centered in the city of Alexandria, who felt the union of the two natures was important for our salvation, often at the expense of the fullness of humanity. For instance, Apollinarius, associated with the Alexandrine school, sought to save the unity of the two natures by arguing that the divine logos was the spirit that animated and guided the human body of Jesus. Some, like Eutyches, even emphasized the unity to such an extent that the two natures mixed into one single nature with the divine overshadowing the human.

In the fifth century, over 400 years after Jesus, the church finally found a resolution. The Council of Chalcedon affirmed the full presence of both natures in Christ, without any mixture or confusion between them. Both divine and human natures are fully present in one actual individual or person (hypostasis). By stating that Jesus is both fully human and fully divine, of the same substance or essence as God (homoousia), without mixture or error, the council was able to broker a compromise and set the rule for speaking about Christ.

But all three, the Council of Chalcedon and the two schools involved in the controversy, held one common assumption. They assumed that the two natures were incongruous or radically different from the other. As a result, all three made Jesus radically different from us. In addition, they also tended to elevate the spiritual over the physical. When the Council of Chalcedon met to resolve the christological controversy, the language available to them came from philosophy and defined both humanity and divinity in terms of static substances. As a result, the discontinuity between the human and the divine became more pronounced.[22] In addition, Chalcedon did not resolve the question of the relationship between divinity and humanity in Christ. It only set the grammar or rule for christological language. It showed us how we needed to speak about Christ, as both fully human and fully divine, setting the ground rules for christological language and the boundaries for Christology. But, it did not resolve the question of how both humanity and divinity can be fully present in Christ.

Liberation theologian Jon Sobrino in *Jesus the Liberator*, argues that we cannot affirm Jesus' divinity at the expense of his humanity. Instead, we should affirm their commonality and begin with those characteristics that both God and humanity share, such as love and compassion.[23] Scripture provides sufficient evidence to indicate that Christ is significant not because there is a radical discontinuity with human existence, but because of the fullness of God's presence in him.[24] The divine and the human do not need to stand in opposition or discontinuity in Jesus, for humanity is not discontinuous with God.

If we take seriously that we were created in God's image, then it should not surprise us that God can become present through humanity. Jesus is not unique because his nature is radically different from ours. What makes Jesus unique is the extent of God's presence in him. The Incarnation is not only a venue for the full revelation of God, but also the revelation of what authentic humanity should be.[25] The Incarnation makes the contrast between divinity and humanity an untenable position.[26] Rather than placing humanity and divinity at opposite ends of the axis, as many Christologies do, we should look at them as complementary of each other; for the nature of humanity as created by God is to bear the divine image. The incarnation is not the anomaly, it is the rule, and the present state of humanity is the anomaly.

The Mestizo-Mulato *Christ*

Chalcedon did not resolve the question of how divinity and humanity can both be fully present in the person of Jesus, and we still must contend with the question and its implications. Today, we have different options for understanding divinity and humanity—options that go beyond static substance and philosophical paradigms. For instance, when we consider that we were created in the image of God and focus on characteristics we hold in common, such as love, the coexistence of divinity and humanity in the particularities of one person are not inconceivable.

Our cultures themselves can offer us alternative paradigms for understanding the person of Jesus. The borderland existence of Hispanics, for instance, can offer us unique insights into how divinity and humanity can exist fully in one person. Since we ourselves often embody two or more cultures, races, and languages, to say that Jesus is both human and divine does not present us with a dilemma. We know viscerally what it is like to fully embody the tensions of disparate realities that may seem incongruous with one another. In a sense, the Incarnation is the ultimate act of *mestizaje* and *mulatez* joining together humanity and divinity in one act.

It would be simplistic to speak of *mestizaje* or *mulatez* as a mixture, although both terms come from root words that mean just that. More specifically, the terms mean a hybrid. When José Vasconcelos uses the term *mestizaje* in his treatise *La raza cósmica* (the cosmic race), he uses it to mean a mixing of cultures and races, both culturally and biologically.[27] For him, this mixture was essential in accomplishing his vision for a future where humanity would achieve an aesthetic unity of a cosmic race and a cosmic culture defined not by the dominance of one race or culture, but by the incorporation of the many traits into a new humanity. In articulating this vision, Vasconcelos hoped to accomplish two things.[28] First, he hoped to put an end to violence, racial oppression, and nationalism through this vision of a bridge people that would embody the traits of all humanity. Second, he hoped to lift the *mestiza/o*, whom society saw as inferior because of a mixed heritage, to a new status as the embodiment of the future of humanity.

This vision for a new humanity is not too far from the message preached by Jesus almost two thousand years earlier. In the Incarnation, disparate realities are brought together. We are called to eradicate violence and love one another not simply because we embody a common humanity, but because we embody a common sacredness instantiated by the presence of God. Just as Vasconcelos hoped to reconcile disparate races into a new humanity that embodied all, the Incarnation reconciled divinity and humanity by bringing them together fully. *Mestizaje* and *mulatez* provide us with a new imagery that helps us understand an aspect of the incarnation, not through philosophical abstractions such as substance, but through culture. It provides us a glimpse into what the church is called to be.

In both *mestizaje* and the Incarnation two realities come together to create a new humanity—one racially and culturally, the other theologically—which embodies the future and hope of humanity. However, for some the inherent danger of this imagery is in the nature of mixture. Chalcedon rejects Eutyches's view that two natures mix to create something new for fear that the divine aspects would obscure the human. But is this necessarily the case? First, if we consider humanity and divinity as incongruous, static substances, it might well be the case. But, if we consider humanity as created in the image of God and focus on the continuity instead of the discontinuity, then it may indeed be possible to say that the divinity present in Jesus *fulfills* his humanity, instead of obscuring or overwhelming it.

Second, despite Docetist and Gnostic heresies that claimed that Jesus' humanity was merely an appearance, there is no indication in the experience of the people who came in contact with Jesus that would lead us to believe that divinity had indeed overwhelmed humanity. As I am fond of telling my students, Jesus did not glow in the dark. He doubted and struggled with his ultimate destiny. He ate, cried, and died like any of us. For all practical purposes Jesus appeared, behaved, and suffered as a human being. His actions and message might have revealed his divinity, but in terms of human experience there was no indication that divinity dominated his humanity.

Finally, to say that divinity would overcome Jesus' humanity presupposes certain notions about divinity and humanity that need not be the case, notions of divine power and glory that overwhelm and dominate humanity. If divinity could not be present in creation without overwhelming it, then creation is devoid of divinity and sacredness, again perpetuating a dualistic and hierarchical view of reality. God would be fully transcendent and never immanent. Furthermore, how could the two natures coexist in one body without one overwhelming the other even if there is no mixture? In the same manner, we can even ask how the Holy Spirit can be present in us without overpowering and overwhelming us. Even if the power and glory of God would overwhelm humanity in Jesus, the kenotic passages in the New Testament imply that the Incarnation involved a divestment of divine glory and power, an emptying out that made the mutual presence of humanity and divinity possible. Hence, the imagery evoked by *mestizaje-mulatez* should not be readily dismissed either semantically or doctrinally without serious consideration.

An additional consideration is that most Hispanic theologians do not use *mestizaje* to mean a simple mixture. Virgilio Elizondo, who introduces the term into the theological arena, does not see it as a simple mixture, similar to the melting-pot metaphor that is popular in the U.S. Rather, it is a coming together of two identities and two cultures.[29] They come together to form a new reality that is not a mere amalgam of the two, but the mutual presence of qualities from both. The *mestizo* is both an insider and an outsider to both cultures, enabling him or her to understand both cultures even better at times than those who belong to one or the other.[30]

Those of us who live at the juncture of cultures, at the borderlands of races and societies, are keenly aware of the uniqueness of the cultures and races we embody. We know our skin tone comes from great-grandma's side of the family, that the curly hair comes from our father's side, and our features come from such and such a heritage. We know when we are speaking English or Spanish. We know where each part of our culture comes from. We are not porridge where all the ingredients are mixed together into a blended and sometimes unsavory mess. We are a savory stew, or as Miguel De La Torre likes to say, an *ajiaco,* where the different vegetables and meats come together to enrich one another without losing their uniqueness. *Mestizaje-mulatez* joins different realities together, but it does not dissolve them. It keeps them in tension. In the same way, the Incarnation brings humanity and divinity together, creating a new reality that does not eradicate their own uniqueness.

We cannot reduce the paradigm of *mestizaje-mulatez* just to the races and cultures of the *mestizo/a* and the *mulato/a*, although most Hispanics embody these realities to some extent. Nor can we reduce it to the Indigenous, African, Arabic, and Jewish heritages that blended with the European in the Iberian Peninsula. The *mestizaje-mulatez* encompasses also our reality in the U.S., the different cultures we inhabit, the languages we speak, and much more. It is a reality that places us at the threshold between cultures, languages, and races. It is the paradigm we encounter in the Incarnation, where diversity comes together in the life of God.

I choose to continue to use the *mestizo/a-mulato/a* paradigm over those of hibridity or biculturalism for one simple reason. The *mestizo/a-mulato/a* brings another theological dimension to the table. The words carry a pejorative edge. Historically, the *mestizo* and the *mulata* have been subject to oppression, diminished because of their mixed heritage, and treated as inferior.[31] Arguing that in recent years *mestizo/a* has lost its pejorative edge, Latina theologian Loida Martell-Otero uses the word *sata* and *sato* (mongrel) for the same purpose. This term, often used for animals of mixed breed, still maintains the pejorative edge that *mestizaje* once held, bearing the elements of rejection and pain of those who are social outcasts. By lifting them up, God transforms the lowly into saints, making them instruments of salvation.[32] Interestingly enough, Martell-Otero uses a play on words to accentuate this transformation from lowly to chosen that might escape those who do not speak Spanish: By adding the letter "n" to *satos* you get *santos*, the Spanish word for saints. Those who are rejected by society are the very ones that God chooses and sanctifies.

According to Elizondo, Jesus' birth in Galilee, a place at the borderlands, meant that Jesus lived in a place where cultures met.[33] The inhabitants of Galilee had an accent that could be recognized as different from the elite in Jerusalem, where they were looked down upon (Matt. 26:73; John 1:46). Thus, the geographical and physical location of the Incarnation made sense. Jesus' *mestizaje* is not simply spiritual, but also actual, adding another layer to how Latinos/as identify with Jesus, who like them also lived on the borderland of cultures. Even further, Jesus' flight with his family into Egypt to avoid slaughter at the hands of Herod also resonates with many Latinos/as. Like

Jesus, many Latinos/as have fled their homes, going as immigrants to foreign lands due to economic and political repression.

The Incarnation lifts up the lowly and the rejected, giving them new value because God comes to the world as one of the rejected and oppressed, at the same time giving us a direction for where to find God's revelation—at the borderlands. By using the paradigm of *mestizaje-mulatez* we assert that Jesus identifies with the oppressed and the marginalized, locating the presence of God in their midst. Unlike an abstraction, such as hybridity, *mestizaje-mulatez* as a metaphor and cultural symbol places flesh and blood on the Incarnation, preventing us from disembodying it. It particularizes it and opens the door for understanding reconciliation as more than a spiritual concept. It also brings races and cultures into relationship with one another, incorporating them into the life of God. The *mestizo, mulato,* and *sato* Jesus embodies reconciliation not just spiritually, but also physically.

Who Jesus Is for Us

We can try to understand who Jesus is for us through identity and cultural symbols, but that is not enough. In a sense, Hispanic Christologies bring together the person and the work of Christ. We speak of Jesus as being divine, not because of some essence that exudes divinity; we speak of Jesus as being divine because of what Jesus does. Jesus is the incarnate Verb, God's action in humanity. Thus, if we apply the concept of ontopraxis to Christology, we realize that we know Jesus through what Jesus does. It is through his ministry, death, and resurrection that we recognize Jesus as divine. According to Justo González, it is God's love—God's giving and being for others—that reveals the fullness of divinity in Jesus, as well as God's humanity.[34]

In speaking of revelation in terms of encounter, Daniel Migliore writes that "while verbal communication is valuable, we should not underestimate the importance of personal self-disclosure through action."[35] It is through action that we know the character and essence of a person. But I would venture to go a bit further. The very term *being* is a verb. Our action and our being are intricately connected. We are both the product of the actions of others and of our own actions. To be is pure activity. Thus, we can speak of Jesus as being God through cultural symbols and philosophical paradigms. But we can also speak of Jesus as being God because of what Jesus does. Jesus' message, love, service, self-giving, life, death, and saving action are all insights into his divinity and into who he is for us. It is through his actions and his work that we best see his divinity and his humanity exemplified.

Notes

1. H. Richard Niebuhr, *Christ and Culture* (New York: Harper & Row, 1951).

2. Orlando E. Costas, *Christ Outside the Gates: Mission Beyond Christendom* (Maryknoll: Orbis Press, 1982), p. 5.

3. Niebuhr, *Christ and Culture*, p. 32.

4. Ibid., pp. 38-39.

5. Ibid., p. 39.

6. Paul Tillich, *Systematic Theology*, Vol. III (Chicago: University of Chicago Press, 1963), p. 57.

7. Ibid.

8. For more on this topic see my article, "Tillich's Theology of Culture and Hispanic American Theology," in the *North American Paul Tillich Society Newsletter* (1999), from which much of this argument comes.

9. See Costas's argument on this topic in *Christ Outside the Gates*, pp. 15-16.

10. For more on this topic please see my book, *Jesus Is My Uncle: Christology from a Hispanic Perspective* (Nashville: Abingdon Press, 1999), pp. 15-16. In addition, please note that some of the themes presented in this chapter also appear in that book, although I also address some new implications and applications here.

11. The Latin term from which incarnation comes has its roots in *caro* (meat or flesh) and its genitive form *carnis*. The term *incarno* where we get the term *incarnation* can convey many rich meanings, including the taking of flesh, causing flesh to grow, and embodiment. Ibid., pp. 74-75.

12. Ibid., pp. 75-76.

13. Several Hispanic writers note this connection of carnal to brother in relating to the Incarnation. For instance see Caleb Rosado's article "The Church, the City, and the Compassionate Christ," in *Apuntes* 2 (Summer 1989), p. 31. Also Eliseo Pérez Alvarez cites Rosado's article to address a similar issue in his essay "Hispanic/Latino Christology Beyond the Borders," in *Teología en Conjunto: A Collaborative Hispanic-Protestant Theology*, ed. by José David Rodríguez and Loida Martell-Otero (Louisville: Westminster John Knox, 1997), p. 35.

14. Tertullian, "On the Flesh of Christ," 5.5, in *The Christological Controversy*, Richard A. Norris, trans. and ed. (Philadelphia: Fortress Press, 1980), p. 70.

15. Athanasius, "On the Incarnation," *Christology of the Later Fathers*, Edward R. Handy, ed. (Philadelphia: Westminster Press, 1954), pp. 71-84.

16. Gregory Nazianzus writes that Christ must assume all aspects of humanity to bring salvation to all of humanity. If Adam fell as a whole, then the whole must be saved.

17. As Tertullian writes, "if these things are part of the human being whom God redeemed, will you render what he redeemed shameful to him? He would not have redeemed what he did not love.... He restores our flesh so that it is free from trouble; he cleanses it when leprous, gives sight to it when blind, heals it when paralyzed, purifies it when it is demon-possessed, raises it when it has died. Does he then blush to be born in it?" "On the Flesh of Christ," 5.4, *The Christological Controversy*, p. 68.

18. Costas writes that "The New Testament teaches that Jesus was a thorough human being. He was a Jew, the son of a modest family, who grew up in an insignificant town in the province farthest from the capital and the most culturally backward. He spoke with a Galilean accent, had a limited formal education, and was a carpenter by trade. He was

aware that he belonged to a 'unique people,' although one humiliated for centuries by foreigners." *Christ Outside the Gate*, p. 6.

19. See Justo L. González's argument in *Desde el siglo y hasta el siglo: esbozos teológicos para el siglo XXI* (Mexico City: A.E.T.H. and Ediciones STPM, 1997), p. 26.

20. Justo L. González writes that "there is comfort in believing that whatever happens in this world has no ultimate significance, and that for that reason one is not to be concerned about the evil one sees in the world." *Mañana: Christian Theology from a Hispanic Perspective* (Nashville: Abingdon Press, 1990), p. 141.

21. Ibid., p. 144.

22. Ibid., p. 150.

23. Jon Sobrino, *Jesus the Liberator: A Historical-Theological Reading of Jesus of Nazareth*, rev. ed., Paul Burns and Francis McDonagh, trans. (Maryknoll: Orbis Press, 1993), pp. 75-80.

24. See Aloys Grillmeier on this topic in *Christ in Christian Tradition: From the Apostolic Age to Chalcedon*, vol. 1, John Bowden, trans. (Atlanta: John Knox Press, 1964, 1975), pp. 24-25.

25. Costas, *Christ Outside the Gates*, p. 12.

26. Karl Barth makes this claim in his *Church Dogmatics*, vol. IV/1, G. W. Bromiley and T. F. Torrance, eds. (Edinburgh: T &T Clark, 1957), p. 186. This passage is also cited by González in *Mañana*, p. 151.

27. José Vasconcelos, *La raza cósmica/ The Cosmic Race*, Didier T. Jaén, trans. (Baltimore: Johns Hopkins University Press, 1925, 1997), pp. 26-27.

28. Ibid., pp. 38-40.

29. Virgilio Elizondo, *Galilean Journey: The Mexican American Promise* (Maryknoll: Orbis Press, 1983), p. 23.

30. Ibid., p. 18.

31. Ibid., p. 100.

32. Loida I. Martell-Otero, "Of Satos and Saints: Salvation from the Periphery," *Perspectivas*, Summer 2001 (Princeton: Hispanic Theological Initiative), pp. 8-9.

33. Virgilio Elizondo, *Galilean Journey*, pp. 43-47.

34. Justo González, *Mañana*, pp. 153-54.

35. Daniel L. Migliore, *Faith Seeking Understanding: An Introduction to Christian Theology* (Grand Rapids: Eerdmans, 1991), p. 31.

CHAPTER EIGHT

JESUS SAVES: SALVATION AND THE WORK OF CHRIST

When I was in seminary, I remember a cartoon that appeared in the satirical evangelical magazine *The Wittenberg Door*. It depicted a lifeguard sitting on his chair and donning a *sombrero* at the beach. On his chair was a sign that read "Jesus Saves: Jesus Garcia, lifeguard." In a sense, the cartoon captured the essence of the cultural differences in our use of Jesus' name and the essence of the work of Christ. But how exactly does Jesus save? And how do different cultures understand this aspect of Jesus' work? In the previous chapter, I made the argument that Christology can be divided into two areas: the person of Christ and the work of Christ. But for most liberation theologies, these two areas cannot be kept separate; soteriology and Christology must coincide and lead into one another.[1] Hence, I also made the argument that for Hispanic Christologies, the work and the person of Christ actually come together, so that you know who Jesus is by what Jesus does. Jesus' actions revealed his divinity. But what is it that Jesus does? If you were to ask most Latinos/as the answer would be a resounding "Jesus saves." We cannot reduce Jesus' work to a simplistic view of salvation such as the atonement, but Jesus' work does have a salvific significance. Thus, I have chosen to put together soteriology, the doctrine of salvation, and the work of Christ, although, for me, they are aspects of Christology.

Salvation implies several things. It implies salvation from something, by something, to something. How you understand salvation might vary based on how you understand what it is that you are saved from, how you are saved, and for what you are saved. Are we saved from death to eternal life? Or are we saved from oppressive structures to liberation? The answers and views of salvation that emerge from those premises might be quite different. Each premise that we change also changes the outcome. Here, I am more concerned with the means of salvation in terms of how it is that we are saved in relation to the work of Christ. Although I touch on the "from what we are saved" and the "to what we are saved" occasionally, I am reserving the bulk of the discussion of the "from what" for the chapter on the human predicament and the bulk of the discussion of the "for what" for the chapter on eschatology. However, a full understanding of salvation entails all three questions. As you may know, the Hebrew understanding of salvation is holistic in nature and encompasses more than any simple view might imply.[2] Thus, Jesus' work is salvific in more than one way. His love, his message, and his life, death, and resurrection all manifest different aspects of our salvation.

We are not simply saved spiritually; we are saved in our physical reality as well. Salvation is not merely about the afterlife, it is also about this life. If sin pervades all parts of creation, all human structures, and the whole of our existence, then salvation must transform not just the individual, but all of creation and all human structures that perpetuate evil. Salvation is not just an event. While it is an historical event, it is also a continuing process as God, together with the church, continues to transform the structures of the world into a new creation.

The Person and Work of Christ

The work of Christ cannot be set apart from his identity as God, an identity manifested through his life, message, and love. It is through what Jesus does that we can truly understand him as the Christ and as God. As Jon Sobrino writes in *Jesus the Liberator*, "Jesus' practice is what gives us the best chance of understanding and organizing all the elements that make him up: the events of his life, his teaching, his inner attitudes, his fate and his most intimate dimension, his person."[3] This means that it is what Jesus does that defines who Jesus is. But how are we to recover what Jesus did without becoming entangled in the quagmires of the search for the historical Jesus?

Although we cannot escape the lenses of faith through which we see and understand Jesus, there are some characteristics to his practices that come across through the tradition, characteristics such as his concern for the poor, the weak, and those living at the margins of society, as well as his compassion and confrontation of the oppressive structures of his time. Although our faith has often detached Jesus from his humanity and earthly ministry, shrouding him in a quasi-Docetic aura of divinity and power, it is essential for theology to recover the concerns that were at the root of Jesus' message and ministry—concerns that were formative of the early Christian church and resonate with minorities today.

To understand the work of Christ and its significance for us, we could look at many different aspects of Jesus' life, recognizing that we can never fully disavow ourselves from our perception of him as divine. But we do know that his message and ministry affected the people closest to him, and it comes through the accounts we find in the Bible. Thus, we can look at Jesus' message. We can look at his death and resurrection. We might even look at the love and caring he exemplified in order to understand who he was and what he means for us. Particularly, the way in which liberation theology and Latino/a theology has sought to recover Jesus' message is to understand how it defines who he is, his saving work, and his significance for us today.

A classical paradigm for understanding the work of Christ offered by John Calvin is referred to as the *triplex munis*, or triple office, of Christ as King, Christ as Priest, and Christ as Prophet.[4] While this paradigm, like any other, is artificial and problematic at times, it can be useful in structuring our discussion of the message and ministry of Christ. Hence, I chose this paradigm, as artificial as it may be, as a framework for analyzing Christ's work. These three offices or roles can also fit on a vertical axis, with the office of King emphasizing a higher Christology and prophet being closer to a lower Christology. In many instances, that is what some have indeed done. But this hierarchical structure need not be the case always, especially when we understand the work of Christ in the broader context of the meaning of salvation.

Jesus the Prophet

When we speak of Jesus' work as a prophet, we cannot limit the discussion solely to his proclamation. Since Jesus reveals God to us, we can understand his whole life as prophetic in nature. The content of Jesus' prophetic message and the nature of his actions also place him in continuity with the prophetic tradition of the Bible in other significant ways. Jesus, through his ministry, advocated a level of social change that went counter to the established norms of society in his age and included a radical call for justice, as well as the inclusion and empowerment of social outcasts within that society.[5]

Jesus' ministry and preaching demonstrate a deep concern for the oppressed and the marginalized in his society—a concern often overshadowed in churches today by luxurious buildings, elaborate programs, and extravagant worship services. Jesus' call for justice for the oppressed, the poor, and the outcasts marks his prophetic ministry, which resonates with many Latinos/as. This call for justice is not mere words either; it is exemplified in Jesus' actions. Jesus' work on behalf of the oppressed and others living at the margins of society parallels the experiences and thirst for justice of many Latinos/as. For this very reason, liberation theologians tend to emphasize Jesus' role as a prophet above others. While in some instances this emphasis might lead to a low Christology—one that stresses Jesus' humanity over his divinity—the emphasis is understandable, since this important part of Jesus' ministry validates our own calls for social reforms, empowers the outcasts of society, and frees the poor from inhuman conditions.

Jesus' ministry and prophetic voice help us see that salvation is not merely a spiritual concern. Salvation liberates us from all aspects of sin, both of our personal guilt and of the sinful structures that oppress and victimize us (Luke 4:18-19; Matt. 25:31-45). A holistic view of salvation requires that salvation begin here and now transforming our present social conditions, so that the transformation brought forth by Christ is not solely at an individual level as many churches, even Hispanic churches, emphasize. All of creation and the whole of our present social order must also be part of the transformation. Jesus' prophetic demand as attested to by the New Testament and the early Christian church affirms life and liberation, while calling us to struggle against all forms of injustice, exploitation, enslavement, and death.

Jesus as Priest: Atonement, Sacrifice, Reconciliation, and the Cross

Liberation theologies often place a greater emphasis on Jesus' prophetic role—his call for justice, teaching, and preaching with its emphasis on liberation from the structures of evil. However, the emphasis on Jesus' prophetic work does not mean that we can deny Jesus' priestly and kingly roles either. The work of the priest involves the offering of sacrifice, which becomes embodied through Jesus' life as he sacrificially gives to others throughout his ministry and eventually gives his life at the cross. In giving to others, even giving his life, Jesus reveals to us God's nature and love, showing us how to live by giving freely of ourselves to one another. The power of the cross is crucial to the Christian faith and critical to our salvation. But what occurs at the cross is still open to debate. Did Jesus have to die to bring us salvation? And how exactly did his death bring us salvation?

Jesus Paid It All: Theories of the Atonement

Throughout Christian history the debate has raged as different theories of the Atonement, the reconciliation between God and humanity and expiation of our sin, would come to light. Generally, as the subtitle of this section might indicate, most, but not all, of these views of the Atonement understood Jesus' death as a payment for our sin. One of the earliest views proposed was what came to be known as the ransom theory. According to this view, Adam's sin made us slaves to sin and to Satan. In order to rescue us, a price, or ransom, had to be paid to the devil to secure our freedom. Jesus' death was that payment, but through the resurrection, God triumphs over the devil by paying the ransom while also cheating him of the final triumph of Jesus' death. Another view, the recapitulation (re-heading) theory attributed to Irenaeus of Lyon, places the emphasis on the actual incarnation itself and its ability to restore humanity. By restoring what humanity was intended to be, the image of God marred by our sin, Jesus restores humanity's rightful place in creation and our fellowship with God.[6] Even the apostle Paul in Romans 5:12-23 similarly argues that through the life of one person, the whole of humanity becomes justified and restored.

In the eleventh century, Anselm of Canterbury presents another model for understanding how Jesus' death brings about our salvation. According to him, humanity's sin is against God and offends God's honor. This offense demands restitution for the injured party, God, through the shedding of blood. But the offense is so grave that humanity alone cannot pay the price; after all, the offense is not against a mere mortal, but against God. Hence, someone who is both God and human must pay the price and die on our behalf to satisfy our debt against God. Jesus, being both God and human, can satisfy this injurious debt. While it may seem barbaric that God would demand the shedding of blood to satisfy God's wrath and honor, we must not forget that for Anselm, it is God who also takes on the responsibility of fulfilling this debt and paying the ultimate price.

In the twelfth century, Peter Abelard developed another model of the Atonement that provides us with an alternative to Anselm's theory. Abelard rejects Anselm's model as being barbaric and problematic for Christianity. Instead of emphasizing the need to pay a price Abelard places the emphasis on the revelatory power of God's love—a love exemplified through the whole of Jesus' life. According to Abelard, Jesus' life shows us the depth of God's love through the works of his ministry and God's willingness to stand in solidarity with us even through death. Jesus' life and death provide us with an example to follow, while also evoking in us a loving response to such a great demonstration of divine love.[7] In recognition of God's love for us, we respond by loving God in return.

While this sampling of theories regarding the Atonement helps us see the various ways theologians through the ages have sought to understand the meaning of Jesus' life and death, they also demonstrate how culture can affect our theological interpretation. For instance, during a time where people often sold themselves into slavery and had to be ransomed from it, the ransom theory made good sense. Philosophical views derived from Plato held that the actions of one person, the archetype, in turn affected all of human nature. This in turn supported the idea that one person's sin could affect all humanity and one person's faithfulness could justify and restore it. Anselm, living in a time where duels were fought to satisfy injuries to one's honor, could easily understand how sin could damage God's honor and how this debt would have had to be satisfied through the shedding of blood. Even in Abelard's theory, we can still see the effects of the theologian's context in the development of his theology. It should not surprise us that Abelard, whose tragic love for his student, Heloise, led to dire consequences and a life of unfulfilled love, would develop a theory of the Atonement based on love and sacrifice. In all these instances, cultural norms, philosophies, personal experiences, and values serve as hermeneutical instruments that assist the theologian in interpreting and illustrating in a culturally relevant manner what occurred at the cross.

In addition to the influence of culture, when we apply a hermeneutics of suspicion to these theories, we can see echoes of how power structures can use them to oppress others. Some theories of the Atonement assume that the problems faced by humanity are due to a debt we owe God; others assume that they are the result of our ignorance about God.[8] These views seem to echo how some people understand the causes of poverty. Some say that people live in poverty because of their indolence and vice (sin)—that they brought it upon themselves. Others assume that with better education (revelation) and work programs poverty can be overcome. In both instances, the blame is placed on the individual, while ignoring the structural dimensions of sin and oppression that are embedded in society. Both also ignore the role power plays in legislating remedies for the poor and marginalized that fail to empower them or to allow them to speak with their own voices.[9] This is the flip side of the Atonement theories. Those in power can use the theories to claim that our oppression comes because of our sin and debt to God (Anselm) or because we do not love God enough (Abelard).

To these theories, we can add many more. We can talk about justification, the theory that states that Jesus' life in obedience to God justifies the rest of humanity. We can talk about appropriation, the theory that says that Jesus took on, or appropriated, all our sins on the cross, like a cosmic vacuum cleaner, as well as the punishment that is the result of our sins. We can speak of substitution, Jesus taking our place at the cross and enduring the punishment we deserved. We can even say that through Jesus' life, death, and resurrection, Jesus was able to triumph not just over sin, but over death itself. All of these views, along with the ones discussed earlier, are present in our churches today. We see them in the songs and hymns we sing. Often, these views are mixed with one another as people speak of justification, ransom, and other views together and interchangeably. But this still does not resolve the question of how Jesus brings about our salvation and the significance of his death and resurrection.

For some scholars, theories of the Atonement understood simply in terms of a sacrifice become problematic. For instance, Mark L. Taylor argues that Jesus' execution is not a salvific event. What is salvific is the whole of what takes place around the cross, such as Jesus' confrontation of the political and religious authorities, as well as the movements that continued after his death as part of his reconciling work.[10] John McIntyre also warns of separating the Atonement from the Incarnation, stating that the whole of Jesus' life is salvific in nature.[11] In this same vein, Latina theologian Loida Martell-Otero, drawing in part from Irenaeus, argues that it is not the cross that saves us, but the whole work of Jesus' life—the Incarnation, who he was, his ministry, his death, and resurrection—that is salvific. Hence, it is not the crucifixion itself that saves us, but the Incarnation, which initiates God's work of reconciliation that becomes manifest through his whole life.[12] The cross of suffering and death is not salvific apart from God's presence in Christ at the cross. Nor can the cross be salvific without the Incarnation—the life, ministry, and resurrection of Jesus. We know Jesus is God not through a singular event, but through the whole of his life. Just as we cannot separate the person and the work of Christ, we cannot separate the whole of his life from salvation. For Latino/a theology, the whole of Jesus' work and life is salvific, from his birth to his resurrection.

Jesus as Priest and Reconciler

The role of the priest cannot be reduced solely to the sacrificial aspects of priesthood. The sacrifices taken on their own are merely a perpetuation of violence inflicted out of vengeance. The role of the priest also involves reconciliation. However, by reconciliation I do not mean an abstract notion that leads to an idyllic vision of peace and passivity.[13] After all, peace and reconciliation are not the same as passivity. Often, they require confrontation, resistance, and restitution. They must be more than spiritual realities. They must also take on social and historical dimensions.

As priest, Jesus functions as a mediator between humanity and God. This work of reconciliation brings God and humanity together not just in a spiritual sense, but in a very real sense as the two realities become fully present and embodied in one life.[14] In Christ, the divine and the human come together in one reality; they are no longer in opposition to one another. Physically, there is another aspect to the reconciliation brought about by the incarnation. When we recognize Jesus' Galilean identity as a *mestizo-mulato*, we see the embodied promise of reconciliation that is part of the *mestizo-mulato* identity. By embodying the tension of not only divinity and humanity, but also of the borderlands of cultures, the hope for reconciliation not just between humanity and God, but also among all people becomes real. Serving as a bridge between people and cultures, the *mestizo-mulato* embodies the hope for reconciliation between cultures and races long divided by prejudice, hatred, and violence.[15] This does not necessarily mean that all *mestizos* and *mulatos* are automatically idyllic vehicles of reconciliation. It simply means that they hold a key to reconciliation because they have, united in themselves, different cultures, races, and people.

Reconciliation is important to us and to our liberation in many ways. By bringing God and humanity together, we find forgiveness and the hope for our salvation. But reconciliation cannot be merely a spiritual relationship between God and humanity. Reconciliation must also bring together human beings who are divided by race, prejudice, hatred, economic inequality, and violence. In recognizing Jesus as priest and reconciler, we recognize our own complicity in sin and our own guilt. Reconciliation cannot occur without reparations or forgiveness. Reconciliation must be concrete, reflected in our actions and in our social structures.

While the oppressed, the marginalized, and the poor might receive preferential attention by God and are victimized to a greater extent, we must not confuse this with innocence. The poor commit violence against others. The outcast of society still sin. None of us is immune. God's concern for them comes out of God's love in light of their disproportionate suffering. Nevertheless, all of us are in need of reconciliation with God and with one another. There is another factor involved in our need for reconciliation. The sense of anger and pain that accompanies the plight of the poor and marginalized must also be healed through reconciliation. Resentment, hatred, vengeance, and retribution can still keep people prisoner even long after they are set free from physical oppression and discrimination. The lessons learned in South Africa in the work of the Truth and Reconciliation Committee serve as evidence of this need. After the violence and oppression brought forth by *apartheid* in South Africa, there was a need for national healing. Such healing could not occur by perpetuating more violence and revenge. Thus, the work of the committee took shape through three sub-committees: one focusing on amnesty, one on reparations and rehabilitation, and one on human rights violations. Blanket amnesty without uncovering the truth and seeking restoration cannot work. In the same manner, liberation requires reconciliation, not only with God, but with each other, as well as with those who oppress us. Recognizing Jesus' work as priest serves as a constant reminder to us of the need for reconciliation with God and with one another.

Jesus Knows: Accompaniment, Suffering, and Revelation

my sorrow

"Nobody knows, the trouble I've seen, nobody knows but Jesus," the words of an old African American spiritual declare. The same song can be sung in our churches. Thus, the significance of the cross comes from the recognition of God's accompaniment of humanity. Jesus' life and work resonate with our struggles and suffering. Our suffering, our struggle, and even our death find meaning in the life of Jesus, for in Christ we know that God understands. God understands us because God has been one of us. The power of the incarnation and of the cross, I will venture to say, comes primarily from what it reveals to us about ourselves as well as about God.

Jesus' life reveals what true humanity should be. His words and deeds reveal to us God's work for justice, God's presence in humanity, and particularly, God's presence in the midst of suffering humanity. In the faces of the poor, the suffering, the outcasts, God objectively reveals Godself to us as one who suffers in solidarity with us. According to Melito of Sardis, Jesus' suffering was prefigured in the suffering of innocents, prophets, and anointed men and women throughout the Bible.[16] In the same manner that Jesus' suffering was prefigured in them, we can say that Jesus' suffering is postfigured in the suffering of innocents, the violated, the oppressed, and the exploited who are living in the margins of society today. We find this idea—that Jesus is uniquely present in the places and in the lives of those who suffer and die—as a recurrent theme in liberation theology and Latino/a theologies. This prompts Latino theologian Harold Recinos to claim that Jesus is present in the junkie dying alone on a rooftop in the barrio and in the lives of those subjected to institutionalized violence throughout the world.[17]

The Power of the Cross

Liberation theologians tell us that we encounter God's presence in the poor, the rejected, the exploited, and the suffering people of our world. The cross stands as a symbol of God's solidarity with the least of society, because we find God incarnate in their midst, enduring their fate. Throughout the ages, those in power have claimed to have God on their side. Even today, many politicians and leaders make the claim that their work is to oppose evil or to defend our way of life—a way they would claim is sanctioned by God. But the cross provides us with a different way of interpreting with whom God identifies. God has not taken the side of those who are in power and who bear the imprimatur of the authorities. If we were to look for where God might be found, it is not in the palaces or in the halls of Congress. Instead, we find God in those who live in poverty, who are outcasts, who are violated and exploited by the established structures of society. While many have tried to understand God in terms of power, dominion, and glory, terms that also tend to align God in our imagination with those in our society who yield power over others, the cross subverts that view, identifying God with those who are rejected, abandoned, and exploited by society—the poor, the weak, the outcasts.[18]

Throughout history, many rulers have sought and claimed divine authority by virtue of an appeal to their power. The argument they make is that their power and status comes from God, making a facile correlation between their claim of power and their understanding of God's power and authority. The cross unmasks these claims as lies. Power, dominance, and political authority are not necessarily aligned with God. At the cross we see these powers as the source of Jesus' death. By locating God at Jesus' cross, we are also locating God in a surprising new place—in the midst of human weakness and suffering. At the feet of the crucified we recognize that God understands our suffering, our rejection, our pain and our abandonment. The cross binds our suffering, rejection, and death to the living God. In Christ, God accompanies us and enters into community with us.[19] The cross helps us recognize that God has not abandoned us. On the contrary, God accompanies us and hurts as we do. The crucifixion empowers us to confront those in power and unmask their contention that they are the legitimate conveyors of God's presence. Ultimately, it also forces those in power to recognize that indeed, what they do to the least of society—the poor, the weak, the marginal—they also do unto God.

At the cross, Jesus brings the fullness of human pain and anguish into God's life. Jesus reveals God's love for us at the cross by risking rejection, submitting to the violence of human power, and standing in solidarity with all others who are rejected, dehumanized, and victimized by the ravages of human sin.[20] We find power and liberation by recognizing through the cross that God understands us fully, even our pain and suffering, and is willing to stand with us in solidarity. We are neither abandoned nor alone. God gives meaning to our lives and to our deaths.

Second, the power of the cross also comes from its power to reveal. While Jesus' life reveals what humanity should be, the cross reveals what humanity has become. It unmasks our pretense of goodness and forces us to confront the depth of our sin and violence against one another. The cross forces us to see how institutionalized violence and political oppression bring death and suffering to even those who are innocent. It shows us how easily we are willing to torture and kill one another for the sake of misguided religious values and self-interest. It forces us to face the sin and violence we continually perpetuate against one another. Jesus does not die for our sins as a substitute; Jesus dies because of our sins, as a direct result of our violence and sinful actions.

The French thinker René Girard speaks of the cross in terms of the scapegoat effect, where a victim becomes the bearer of mimetic violence by the masses. This victim of violence brings forth reconciliation by bearing the brunt of the violence that individuals would perpetuate against one another, thus diffusing their urge toward violence. According to Girard, the roots of this violence lie in our propensity for imitation (mimesis). Human beings learn through imitation. The problem with imitation comes with desire. When the one being imitated and the imitator both desire the same thing, competition and strife occur. Their desire for the same object leads to rivalry, frustration, and eventually to violence.[21] Because we tend to imitate, we also imitate violence, which leads to more violence. In addition, when the imitator-disciple becomes too much like the model-master or threatens to surpass them, resentment inevitably occurs.[22] Minorities can easily identify with this aspect of mimetic violence. While we are trying to mimic dominant society, we are accepted. But whenever we threaten equality or threaten to surpass members of the dominant society, we are immediately viewed with suspicion, discredited, and put in our place—at times through violent means.

Mimetic violence has another problematic effect when it becomes institutionalized and driven by collective violence. The frustrations and violence of the community against each other become focused on one individual who represents, even if innocent, the evils and frustration of the whole society.[23] There are many instances in human history that exemplify this scapegoat phenomenon, such as violence committed against the Jews who were blamed for the plague in Europe or the burning of women believed to be witches responsible for illnesses and misfortunes in the community.[24] In most instances, the scapegoat is usually someone who lives at the margins of the society and who lacks power—hence the Jews or women being the ones blamed. Latinos/as who live at the edge of society, as well as other minorities, can relate well with this interpretation of the cross, for we often bear the blame for the ills of society and become the subjects of collective violence, often perpetuated by the authorities. The cross serves to unmask this violence we level against each other while also providing us an alternative model for imitation—service and sacrificial love—in the person of Jesus rather than in the violence of society.[25]

Finally, the cross locates God's presence not in power and glory, but in the places where people suffer and die—in the poor, in the marginalized, in the outcasts of society, and in the victims of systemic violence. The cross provides us with an alternative way of understanding God's power and a different perspective on where we must look to find God. Rather than seeking God in the majesty of the heavens, in the thrones of power, and in national fervor, we must look for God in the lowly places and persons of society. But the cross not only forces us to look at ourselves to reveal our sinfulness, it also reveals to us the extent of God's love, in that while we were still sinners, Christ died for us. Finally, the cross liberates us by affirming that we are not abandoned or rejected by God when we too encounter our own crosses. Nor does our suffering and death occur in vain, for at the cross, God vests our own crosses with meaning and the hope of life in spite of death.

Jesus Loves Me

God's love, revealed to us through Jesus, is an important part of our faith. But love means nothing in the abstract. Love must be concrete; it must become incarnate. Jesus demonstrated this love for others through his calls for justice, through his compassion for those who hungered and hurt, and through his willingness to give freely to others. Jesus does not use power to dominate others, he uses it to heal and give life. Even in his judgment over sinners, Jesus offers forgiveness. While Abelard's theory of the Atonement could be distorted toward oppression, as we saw above, there is a certain resonance between Abelard's view and our own walk through life. To know that Jesus stands in solidarity with us, even to the extent of suffering death and humiliation, is important to Hispanics and other minorities. According to Abelard, Jesus' life and death revealed to us the extent of God's love, and this resonates with our experience. The God who became flesh and blood, suffering with us and dying on the cross, concretely reveals in history God's love for us. We know that God loves us through the compassion, mercy, and care we experience. But the incarnation reveals this love to a greater extent and in a more specific manner: God stands in solidarity with us.

According to Justo González, Jesus' divinity comes through love—a love that manifests itself in being-for-others. This love not only reveals his full divinity, but also his full humanity.[26] While the suffering of the cross reveals to us the depth of our sinfulness, Jesus' love for us not only reveals something about God, it also reveals something about us. It reveals how we should be and what we were called to be as human beings. But this love also exacts a judgment upon us. In knowing what we are supposed to be, we also become aware of what we are not. Because God loves humanity and because we too are called to participate in that love, we must work with God to transform the social structures and conditions that dehumanize people and rob people of life. We are called to be Godlike in our love for one another, even though that love is often clouded by bigotry, prejudice, and hatred for those who are different from us.

Jesus Is Lord and King

While we could easily remain fixated in Jesus' role as prophet and priest, we must not forget Jesus' role as Lord and King. For many minority theologies, this may not seem like a palatable option, for it appears to validate many of the values of those who oppress us, including patriarchy and political domination. That is why some Latina theologians, such as Ada María Isasi-Díaz prefer the term kin-dom, which expresses the relational aspect of God's reign and moves away from domination and male-dominated imagery. But Jesus' role as "king" or "lord" is important to Hispanics, as it should be to other oppressed groups, not because it identifies him with patriarchy and domination, but because it subverts them. Jesus' prophetic message, loving compassion, and tragic death might reveal God's love for humanity and what the world should be like in light of such love, but they do little to guarantee the ultimate triumph of this vision of what the world could be. To understand Jesus' role as Lord provides all of us with the hope that indeed change can be brought about and that victory over the powers of evil can be achieved.

Dominant power structures, political interests, and patriarchal structures can easily manipulate the imagery of Jesus as King to suit their enterprises. History has many examples to offer. European royalty often held their positions of power under the guise of a divine imprimatur on their reign known as the Divine Right of Kings. Male imagery associated with the symbol can easily be taken as normative and divinely ordained. But the potential for abuse that plagues this symbolic role should not lead us to abandon it. When

Christianity refers to Jesus as King, Lord, or even as Messiah, its significance does not come from his identification with dominant power structures, the same structures that led to his death, but from their subversion. As Letty Russel has argued in her works, seeing Jesus as both Lord and Servant subverts the tendency to contrast them or make them a dualism by presenting us with the scandalous notion of a Lord who is a Servant, thus rupturing our understanding of both.[27] Rather than finding God's power manifested through glory and dominance, at the cross we find God identifying with the lowly and the victimized, denying the powerful their claims that God is on their side. When we find God at the cross we also find that the ultimate power of domination and violence—the power to dehumanize and deny the image of God in us—is a lie.

In proclaiming Jesus as Lord, we are proclaiming a new understanding of power that transforms society through love, compassion, and humility instead of by sheer force, violence, and subjugation. The very proclamation of Christ as Lord becomes an affront to the power structures that crucified him, denying them their power to have the final word. The symbolism asserts a new paradigm for power and condemns the present power structures. As Virgilio Elizondo writes in *Galilean Journey*, "Humiliated by the world, Jesus was now exalted by God. If his name had been ridiculed by society, it was now extolled by God above all other names."[28]

However, the story does not end at the cross. The resurrection affirms the ultimate power of God's love over the structures of evil, and affirms God's ultimate triumph not by avoiding evil or circumventing death, but by confronting them. Through the resurrection God vindicates Jesus' message, life, and struggle against the powers of evil. What the resurrection affirms are not facile escapist attitudes that promise us a prosperous life and heavenly rewards, as some churches may seem to preach. Taken together, the cross and the resurrection promise us that life and love will triumph over death and hatred by confronting them and enduring in spite of them. Death is no longer the final word that defeats us and keeps us prisoners of fear. Our existence matters to God, even when it is demeaned at the hands of self-serving interest and corrupt power structures. God guarantees that our life and our struggles are not in vain. The promise of life in spite of death emboldens and empowers us to live and to confront evil. Death does not end God's boundless possibilities and grace. In spite of death, God grants us new possibilities for life.[29]

Like the incarnation, the resurrection also affirms our earthly and physical existence. Some scholars and Christian groups might be tempted to speak of the resurrection as spiritual to render it more palatable to our scientific worldview. But this is no different from Gnostic and Docetic interpretations that foster a dualism that devalues the material world in favor of a loftier spiritual reality. It is an escapist ploy that denies the sacredness of the world and the whole of creation, freeing us from any responsibility for transforming our present reality. I cannot speak for all Hispanics, but I will venture to say that the majority of us believe in a physical resurrection. Not because we have a precritical and unsophisticated literal view of the Bible, but because we intuit the reality that the resurrection affirms, the value of our bodily existence, and the need to transform the present structure of society. Furthermore, the resurrection shows us that we are not mere spirits trapped in a physical body, but both spiritual and physical beings.

While the physicality of the resurrection might not be a simplistic resuscitation of our present body, something that the biblical text itself does not seem to support, as we shall see later in the chapter on eschatology, there is a bodily reality to the resurrection, even if it is a different reality from our present one. Our existence is not in a disembodied spiritual state. It is particular and concrete, able to affect and interact with its surroundings. The resurrection serves as a seal and foretaste of things to come. It seals the victory over death and over sin, affirming that in spite of death and hatred, life and love will prevail. It also affirms that our struggle against evil will not be futile and meaningless. Our existence is not banal; it matters to God. The resurrection reveals that God was indeed at work in Jesus and that his message is also God's message. It is the inauguration of God's reign.

Finally, the resurrection points to the communal nature of our struggle. We cannot overcome the power of evils alone as a Hollywood hero might; we need others and we need God. The New Testament speaks both of Jesus being raised from the dead by God (Acts 2:32, 3:15, 4:10; Rom. 4:25) and as having risen from the dead (Matt. 28:6; Mark 16:21). The German theologian Jürgen Moltmann writes that in the resurrection, Jesus both rises and is risen, so that God's activity and Jesus' act coincide.[30] In this respect, the resurrection manifests God's work as a collaborative work. Alone we cannot overcome the powers of evil. We need God. Ultimately, when we speak of Jesus as Lord or King, we acknowledge God's ultimate triumph over the powers of evil and recognize God's ultimate dominion over creation. But we also subvert secular power structures by denying them their ultimate victory and bringing into question their validity.

The Sacraments and Jesus' Continual Work

The work of Christ is the work of salvation in its broadest sense. It reveals Jesus' divinity to its fullest. Jesus manifests God's saving work through his life.

159

God's activity coincides with Jesus' life, death, and resurrection. God's act, love, and will coincides with humanity in Jesus. Through Jesus' prophetic message, sacrificial love, and selfless giving, Jesus reconciles and saves us. But while his work initiates the reign of God and our salvation, the work continues through the church and people of faith.

As a Baptist, it may seem difficult for me to write about sacraments, particularly in terms of means of grace or God's continuing salvific work. But as a Latino theologian, it is important to address the topic. It is important because many Hispanics have a sacramental theology. By this, I mean two things. First, many Hispanics are Catholic or belong to Protestant churches that have sacramental theologies. In this sense, it is essential to acknowledge the role this plays in Hispanic theology. Second, Hispanics, for the most part, do have a sacramental view of reality and the world that pervades everything and that imbues most aspects of reality with sacredness and divine presence, the sacraments included. Hence, whether they see Baptism or the Eucharist as a sacrament or an ordinance, they still relate to them in a sacramental manner. Furthermore, the significance of baptism and communion (Eucharist) are important to the church as part of Jesus' ongoing work. In both baptism and communion, we bind ourselves as a community of faith, participating together in Jesus' death and resurrection, reaffirming our role in the ongoing work of God. By partaking in these common rituals and sacraments of the church, we acknowledge our ongoing participation in the struggle of life and love over the powers of death and hatred.

The sacraments bring us together as a community of faith affirming our common struggle and fostering our identity. Baptism initiates us in the community of faith, as well as in the struggle against evil. Whether we are celebrating the life of an infant or the new life of an adult, we are affirming life and the ultimate triumph of God over evil. Whether we understand it as a means of grace or an acknowledgment of grace already received, God's sacramental presence is real in both the community and the act. What does this mean? First, while the ways we understand the significance and manner in which God is present might vary theologically, the act or ritual acknowledges the reality of this presence. Second, in that moment, the community and the sacrament reveal the real presence of God. For example, Martin Luther's understanding of the sacraments revolves around his understanding of God's, and by extension, Jesus' omnipresence. Thus, according to Luther, we can say that Jesus is really present in the sacraments, particularly in the Eucharist. This is one way we might understand the presence of God in the sacraments. Taking this example, my point is that while we might always understand Christ as God present everywhere, the sacrament acknowledges, reveals, and affirms that understanding in a particular act. Hence, the sacrament affirms and reveals the sacramental presence of God uniquely, locating it in that specific community, place, and time.

The sacraments also serve a symbolic and didactic purpose. Baptism's use of water can symbolize burial and resurrection. It can also symbolize the cleansing of sin or even the waters of childbirth. It can even symbolize the refreshment and life-giving qualities of water, forcing us to think not only of a spiritual reality, but also of our embodied reality. Likewise, the bread and the wine of the Eucharist refresh our spirit, serve as symbols of the brokenness of Christ's body and the shedding of his blood on our behalf, and remind us of the struggle of life against death and evil. But the bread and wine also refresh and nourish our bodies as much as our soul, reminding us of our embodied realities and basic human need for food and drink.

The material reality of the sacraments forces us to go beyond a simple spiritual interpretation of them. They compel us to recognize our physical realities. Just as in the incarnation, God's presence occurs through a material medium that counters our dualistic tendencies and brings together the physical and the spiritual. When we eat of the bread and drink of the wine, we must acknowledge the physical realities and needs of humanity. The Eucharist reminds us of more than Jesus' sacrifice; it also reminds us of the epic struggle of good against evil, life against death. And it reminds us that there is a very real physical dimension to that struggle. God is present in the food that we eat and the wine we drink. We are not simply nourished spiritually by God; we are also nourished physically. Even more, we are also nourished physically by those, many of them Hispanic migrant workers, who toiled in the fields to cultivate the wheat and the grapes from which the elements of the Eucharist are made. In partaking of the sacraments, we are partaking of their sweat and labor. We are consuming the life they have poured out into the production of the bread and the wine. In consuming the sacraments, we are not only partaking of eternal life in Christ, we are also partaking of the life and sacrifice of those who toil to bring food and wine to our tables.[31]

What Would Jesus Do?

In recent years, the phrase, "What would Jesus do?" has become popularized in American churches and evangelical circles, symbolized by WWJD inscribed on bracelets, bookmarks, and T-shirts. The intent of the phrase might be a noble ethical reminder to ask ourselves what we think Jesus would do if he were in this situation. But the phrase has some implications that have often gone unexamined. First, it implies that we actually know what it is that Jesus would do if faced with that situation. Of course, in most cases we read into the phrase the same things we read into Jesus. We interpret what Jesus would do in terms of our own cultural values, which often do not reflect Jesus' prophetic message, calls for justice, and concern for the oppressed and marginalized. The assumptions are even more dangerous when we assume that our interpretations are indeed what Jesus would do, hence identifying God's will with our actions, ethics, and values. Thus, we can claim a divine seal of approval for ourselves and condemnation for others.

There is another disturbing implication in this popular phrase. The implication becomes more evident if we complete the sentence: What would Jesus do if he were here? Implicit in the phrase is the assumption that Jesus is not here. Again, there is an implicit dualism that places divine activity and Christ's presence outside of the world. The unintended implication is that Jesus is not here and is not active in our lives and in our world. In effect, it de-sacralizes and de-sacramentalizes the world.

Rather than asking what Jesus would do, we might be better served in asking what Jesus is doing and where. When we consider that God's work continues today through us and through the work of the Holy Spirit in our lives, in the church, and in the world, we are called to the recognition that Jesus' work does indeed continue today. If we look closely at the stories of the New Testament we can gain a deeper insight into where Jesus is today and what Jesus is doing in the world. In the New Testament accounts, Jesus dwelt among the poor, among those living in the margins of society. Jesus was said to live in the company of sinners, to be present where there was human suffering, to bring healing to their lives. Today, it is in those very same places that we must look to see Jesus. We must look to the poor and to those living in the margins of society. That is where the Holy Spirit is at work today. It is there that we find Jesus actively present today.

Notes

1. See Jon Sobrino, *Christology at the Crossroads* (Maryknoll: Orbis Books, 1978), p. 9. Jaquelyn Grant agrees with the need for feminist and womanist Christologies to maintain the inseparability of Christology and Soteriology, quoting Sobrino in her book *White Women's Christ and Black Women's Jesus: Feminist Christology and Womanist Response* (Atlanta: Scholars Press, 1989), p. 89.

2. Loida I. Martell-Otero provides a good overview of the different Hebrew understandings of salvation in her article, "Of Satos and Saints: Salvation from the Periphery," *Perspectivas*, Summer 2001 (Princeton: Hispanic Theological Initiative), p. 18. These rich Hebrew images of salvation include deliverance, forgiveness, turning back, restoration, healing, to set free, rescue, and wholeness.

3. Jon Sobrino, *Jesus the Liberator: A Historical-Theological View*, Paul Burns and Francis McDonagh, trans. (Maryknoll: Orbis Press, 1993), p. 53.

4. John Calvin's discussion of Jesus' triple office in *Institutes of the Christian Religion*, Henry Beveridge, trans. (Grand Rapids, Mich.: Eerdmans, 1989), bk. II, chap. 16, pp. 433-52.

5. For more detailed information on this, see Marcus J. Borg, *Jesus in Contemporary Scholarship* (Valley Forge: Trinity Press International, 1994), pp. 26, 112-16, 151-52.

6. Irenaeus of Lyon, *Against Heresies*, 3.18.1-2, in *The Ante-Nicene Fathers*, vol. 1, A. Roberts and J. Donaldson, eds. (Albany, Ore.: Ages Software, 1997).

7. Peter Abelard, *Exposition of the Epistle to the Romans*, 2.1-3, in *A Scholastic Miscellany: Anselm to Ockham*, Eugene Fairweather, ed. and trans. (Philadelphia: Westminster Press, 1956).

8. Justo González, *Mañana: Christian Theology from a Hispanic Perspective* (Nashville: Abingdon Press, 1990), pp. 154-55.

9. Clodovis Boff, "Epistemology and Method of the Theology of Liberation," in *Mysterium Liberationis: Fundamental Concepts of Liberation Theology*, ed. by Ignacio Ellacuría and Jon Sobrino (Maryknoll: Orbis Press, 1993), pp. 74-84.

10. Mark L. Taylor, *The Executed God: The Way of the Cross Is Lockdown America* (Minneapolis: Fortress Press, 2001), p. 108.

11. John McIntyre, *Theology After the Storm: Reflections on the Upheavals in Modern Theology and Culture* (Grand Rapids: Eerdmans, 1997), p. 148.

12. Martell-Otero, "Of Satos and Saints," pp. 19-26.

13. Jon Sobrino warns of the danger of reconciliation as a "sublime abstraction" in *Jesus the Liberator*, pp. 15-16.

14. See Orlando E. Costas's discussion on reconciliation and communion in *Christ Outside the Gates: Mission Beyond Christendom* (Maryknoll: Orbis Press, 1982), pp. 30-33.

15. This is the model presented by Virgilio Elizondo, who argues that Jesus' Galilean birth placed him at the borderland of cultures within a people rejected by both the Romans and the Jews. This in turn is parallel to the Mexican-American who also exists in the borderland of cultures, hence able to serve as a bridge between the cultures. *Galilean Journey: The Mexican American Promise* (Maryknoll: Orbis Press, 1983), pp. 101-2.

16. Melito of Sardis, "A Homily of the Passover," in *The Christological Controversy*, Richard A. Norris and William Rusch, eds. (Philadelphia: Fortress Press, 1980), pp. 37-43.

17. Harold J. Recinos, in *Jesus Weeps: Global Encounters at Our Doorstep* (Nashville: Abingdon Press, 1992), pp. 22, 40, and later in *Who Comes in the Name of the Lord: Jesus at the Margins* (Nashville: Abingdon Press, 1997), pp. 59-71.

18. For instance, Martin Luther argues against what he calls a "theology of glory" and in favor of a "theology of the cross," that is a theology grounded in the "back" and visible things of God, things such as the weakness and suffering of God manifested at the cross. Hence, according to him, God cannot be found in glory and power, but in suffering and in the cross. "Heidelberg Disputation," pp. 19-22, in *Martin Luther: Basic Theological Writings*, Timothy F. Lull, ed. (Minneapolis: Fortress Press, 1989), pp. 42-44.

19. See Roberto S. Goizueta's, *Caminemos con Jesús: Toward a Hispanic/Latino Theology of Accompaniment* (Maryknoll: Orbis Press, 1995), pp. 205-11.

20. Recinos, *Who Comes in the Name of the Lord?* p. 73.

21. René Girard, *The Girard Reader*, James William, ed. (New York: Crossroads, 1996), p. 9.

22. René Girard, *Things Hidden Since the Foundation of the World* (Stanford: Stanford University Press, 1987), pp. 290-91.

23. Girard, *The Girard Reader,* pp. 10-14, 166.

24. René Girard, *The Scapegoat,* Yvonne Freccero, trans. (Baltimore: Johns Hopkins University Press, 1986), pp. 2-4.

25. James G. Williams makes this argument in relation to Girard in "René Girard without the Cross? Religion and the Mimetic Theory," *Anthropoetics II,* no. 1 (June 1996), pp. 3-5.

26. Justo González, *Mañana,* pp. 153-52.

27. Letty Russel, *The Future of Partnership* (Philadelphia: Westminster Press, 1979), pp. 67-68.

28. Virgilio Elizondo, *Galilean Journey,* p. 115.

29. See, for instance, Eberhard Jüngel's article "The Word as Possibility and Actuality: The Ontological Doctrine of Justification," in *Theological Essays,* J. B. Webster, trans. (Edinburgh: T & T Clark, 1989), pp. 95-123. The key to my argument, which builds upon Jüngel's article and Whitehead's process philosophy, lies in understanding the difference between potential, inherent in our actuality, and possibility as God's provision of grace, which is not inherent in our actuality. Death might appear as the end of our potentiality and the closure of any new possibility, but the resurrection provides us with the hope of a new possibility for life in spite of death.

30. Jürgen Moltmann, *The Way of Jesus Christ: Christology in Messianic Dimensions,* Margaret Kohl, trans. (San Francisco: Harper Collins, 1990), p. 248.

31. See Enrique Dussel's analysis of the topic and the relationship of the work we produce to our sustenance, which I extend to the Eucharist in *Praxis Latinoamericana y filosofía de la liberación* (Bogota: Editorial Nueva America, 1983), pp. 140, 153-55.

CHAPTER NINE

THE HUMAN PREDICAMENT

M*ira al pobre cristiano,* "Look at that poor Christian" my grandmother said as a man in dirty ragged clothes pushing an old shopping cart walked past her house. As I tell the story in *Jesus Is My Uncle,* I speak of my frustration as a young and naïve Baptist minister that my grandmother would call this man a Christian. After all, how could we know if he had ever made a personal profession of faith in Christ? It was not until later that I came to a deeper sense of awareness of the wisdom in my grandmother's words.[1] The expression is common in Spanish. What frustrated me was that the expression seemed to be used almost synonymously with "human being." But what I had missed is that the term "Christian" is usually qualified by the term "poor." The term is not synonymous with humanity per se; it is synonymous with "suffering humanity."

While I am not aware of the exact origins of this expression, many of the Romance languages do use "Christian" as an equivalent to "humanity." But, it is important to note that most of these languages do indeed use it primarily to refer to the poor, the handicapped, the deformed, or the defenseless individuals in the society.[2] The reason for using it to refer to these people who live at the margins of society was in part to remind us that in spite of their affliction and social location, these people are nevertheless human beings, and not just human beings, but Christians, baptized into the same church and loved by the same God. The term reminds us that the lowly, the poor, and the powerless of society are still made in God's image and loved by God. Indeed, if we consider that Jesus is present objectively in the poor, suffering, and weak members of society, then they are Christlike in that they represent Christ, making them Christians in a deeper sense of the word. Hence, we need to treat them with love, compassion, and dignity. We need to treat them as we would treat Christ.

I begin this chapter with this story because it is telling in many ways of the human predicament. We are created to bear the image of God. But we live in a fallen world and recognize that we do not always live up to what we were meant to be. Structures of sin and injustice deface human beings, create suffering, and bring death. The man in the story is homeless, carrying his meager possessions in an old shopping cart. My grandmother's response is one of compassion and recognition of his common humanity—a humanity defined by identification with Christ. In the human predicament we find the fallenness of sin, the ability to act with compassion, and our common humanity in the image of God we bear. To understand the human predicament, particularly from the cultural perspective of Latinos/as, we first must understand the nature of sin and evil that defines so many of our experiences.

Sin and Evil from a Latino/a Perspective[3]

John Calvin argues in *Institutes of the Christian Religion* that our questions on how God can use the wicked, or even permit evil, without somehow incurring blame come from the limitations of our carnal mind's ability to grasp the fullness of God's work and nature.[4] Since our limited nature, corrupted by sin, is insufficient to peer into the mysteries of God, some might argue that we should not try to address the problem but accept it as a mystery. However, as Paul Tillich writes, "You must not avoid the question by retiring behind the term 'mystery.' Of course there is mystery—divine mystery—and, in contrast to it, the mystery of evil. But it belongs to the insights demanded of you that you put the mystery in its right place, and explain what can and must be explained."[5]

To merely accept the existence of evil and put our trust in God is not an option for Latino/a theology. On the contrary, such arguments can easily become instruments for oppression and for promoting passivity. This can occur in several ways. We might be told, as a student in one of my classes once argued, that we are simply to accept our lot in life and glorify God through our suffering. This is fine for someone living in privilege, since this argument in effect justifies the suffering of the oppressed and the privilege of the powerful as part of God's plan. It can even imply that those of us who suffer and face oppression somehow deserve our situation due to our inherent depravity. These arguments also can become oppressive through a glorification of suffering that can easily lead to passivity, acceptance, and inaction, keeping us subdued under the bondage of oppression—a danger that Latina theologians, such as Ada María Isasi-Díaz and Nancy Pineda-Madrid, warn us about.[6] Suffering is not the same as evil. We might suffer due to many causes, such as unrequited love or frustration, which are not necessarily evil. But evil does cause suffering that is not part of God's will.

How we speak about evil can even serve to justify oppression and violence against those who are different by portraying them as evil and deserving of their treatment. In times of war, our enemies are demonized as the evil ones. By denying their humanity and portraying them as evil, it makes it easier for us to wage war upon them, for they are no longer fully human in our eyes. In some cases, we may even project onto other people and cultures our value judgments and perceptions so that by seeing others as evil we can in contrast see ourselves as good and superior.[7] Even the way we try to answer theologically the problem of evil can serve as a tool for oppression or hide our complicity in evil structures and their effects.

At times, theologians like Irenaeus and Augustine have argued that the pain and suffering we experience as the result of evil helps us grow, love God, and develop a sense of morality.[8] Of course, while we can learn and grow from our encounters with such evils, it does not mitigate the pain and suffering we incur by its ravages. This argument is particularly problematic for those who often suffer the ravages of evil to a greater extent, as is the case for many Latinos/as, especially when these arguments serve to justify our suffering and poverty at the hand of oppressive social structures.

Latino/a Theology and the Problem of Evil

Theologically, the problem of evil can be summarized thus: If God is willing to prevent evil but unable, then God cannot be omnipotent; if God is able but unwilling to prevent evil, then God cannot be a loving God. Generally, theologians answer this problem by either qualifying divine power, the existence of evil, or divine love. Theologians also distinguish between natural evils—such as disasters and disease—and moral evil, which is attributed to human agency. How we understand natural evil is telling of our presuppositions. For instance, we can say that natural evil is either a punishment for our sins or a result of our sins. But to say that natural evils are a punishment for sin is problematic, since the victims of disasters and diseases are not necessarily worse sinners than those spared. Often it is the young, the poor, and the elderly who suffer the worst from such tragedies. Even if we all share some blame due to our sin, the Bible, as we see in Job, warns against believing that calamities befall us simply as a punishment for sin.[9] Even worse, facile answers can easily lead us to blame the victims, without admitting that other causes might be in play.

When we speak of natural evils, seldom do we note how the socioeconomic dimensions of sin can aggravate them. At times, sin and ignorance put us in harm's way as we intrude farther into the natural domains. By building homes in floodplains and fire-prone areas, we exceed our boundaries and wreck the environment.[10] But socioeconomic conditions and sin also affect us. To enhance profit, we cut corners that lead to pollution and that expose people to toxins. Greed leads to poor building construction and disregard for safety. Those who live in poverty often must place their lives in peril by living in poorly constructed homes or in dangerous locations. They are also more susceptible to disease, malnutrition, and epidemics.[11] Latinos/as and others living at the margins of society are more vulnerable to natural evil due to the socioeconomic structures that place them at greater risk. Thus, we can say that these calamities are a result of our sin and the sin of others, not as a punishment, but as their inevitable consequence.

Love, Omnipotence, and the Problem of Evil

Some theologians try to resolve the problem of evil by qualifying divine power, either as a self-imposed limitation to allow for creaturely freedom or as a necessary limitation of God's nature.[12] My contention with both of these positions is that regardless of whether God is limited by nature or by choice, our experience is the same. We still suffer the ravages of evil and sin. While most theologians favor qualifying God's power to explain the presence of evil, I think the answer is in God's love. By this, I do not mean that God does not love us enough. Rather God's power cannot be understood as separate from God's love. I believe the same can be said about evil. We cannot understand evil apart from God's love. The qualification of divine power, the presence of freedom, and the existence of evil are all grounded in the abundance of God's love.

Being capable of loving God and each other requires us to be able to choose freely and to respond to one another out of love and compassion. For love to exist, freedom to respond must exist. By allowing all creatures to respond freely, God also risks the possibility of rejection, along with the possibility for hate and violence, the opposite of love, to occur. God's omnipotence and dominion over creation are circumscribed by love. God would not overpower creation nor impose God's will upon it. Instead, a loving God would work through persuasion and provide new possibilities to rectify the destructiveness of evil. The possibility and presence of evil exist because of God's abundant love for all creation.

It is also important to note that God's loving vulnerability is not the same as impotence. Through love and grace, God provides new possibilities for us to act and to exist in spite of the ravages of sin and evil. God's power works through the endurance of love, persuasion, and creative grace to open new venues and possibilities for us in spite of evil. While persuasion and creative grace might seem to be slow and weak vehicles for transformation, they are surprisingly able to effect change while empowering us. Lightning, with all its power and force, might elicit awe in us, but its power to transform the landscape fades in comparison to the power of a gentle trickle of water that through millenia can form rivers and carve mighty canyons. Such is the power of God's love. God's subtle whispers turn into the voices of prophets and stir the whirlwinds of history to bring forth change. The subtle introduction of ideas, persuasions, and creative grace slowly but surely brings change.

Freedom and the Seduction of Evil[13]

What is it about sin and evil that draws us to it like a moth to a flame? Why do we choose evil instead of love? I believe the answer lies in the nature of power and freedom accorded to humanity by virtue of our being made in the image and likeness of God.[14] We assert our freedom and our power by opposing God, for in our imaginings we believe that only in rebellion, in asserting our will against God's can we find freedom and power.[15] But this simply confuses freedom with independence, power with dominion. Independence assumes a lack of dependency, a self-sufficiency that does not need any relationship.[16] Under such assumptions, we interpret power as control or dominion, a mastery of self and others so that relationships to others are under our control. By becoming independent, we sever our relationships with others and destroy community.

However, both Scriptures and our theology imply that God, as one who loves us, exists in community. The doctrine of the Trinity also implies that God exists in community. If we are made in God's image, it makes sense that we too should be communal in nature. Human life is communal in nature. As Gutiérrez writes in *The God of Life*, "As understood in the Bible, 'to live' always means 'to live with,' 'to live for,' 'To be present to others,' in other words, life implies communion. Death is utter isolation."[17] Thus, if life is being in community, and sin is a move toward independence and isolation that ruptures community, then it makes sense that the wages of sin are death (Rom. 6:23). Death is not a punishment for sin; it is the inevitable result of sin.

Freedom, on the other hand, is an ability to choose. In making our choices, we decide between different alternatives, yet our choices by their very nature always occur in relationship to another. Freedom implies that we depend on something or someone beyond ourselves.[18] Freedom depends on choices, possibilities that lie outside us, often beyond our control. Hence, we exist in relationship to others. Nor can we understand power as self-sufficiency or as asserting control over others. Rather, it is the ability to give freely to others. This form of power is what lies at the root of love, which at its very heart is the freedom to be in a relationship with others.[19] Freedom empowers us to respond to the needs of others, to rush to their aid even at our own peril, and to give bountifully to others out of care and love. However, when we sever relationships and assert control over others, as often occurs in oppressive systems, we sin against others and against God.

Sin, Moral Evil, and Lo Malo

Augustine writes in *The City of God* that "things solely good, therefore, can in some circumstances exist; things solely evil, never, for even those natures which are vitiated by an evil will, so far indeed as they are vitiated, are evil, but in so far as they are natures they are good."[20] Basically, what Augustine is saying is that evil does not exist apart from its embodiment in the will of a creature. A creature that does evil, by virtue of being created by God, is not evil in nature, but rather in its perversion and action. This leads Augustine to conclude that evil is actually the privation or absence of good, without any real being. It is destructive in that it turns us away from God who is the source of goodness and being. Evil is no more than a movement away from God and toward nothingness, a negation of existence and all that is real and good. In taking this stance, Augustine does not deny our experience of evil. Instead, he denies the existence of something that is inherently evil in itself. Evil is a corruption of creation. It is not a substance or a deity; it is an act and a consequence. It is the turning away from the creator, the God of life, toward the nothingness of death and destruction.

We tend to speak of evil as an abstract, disembodied force that pervades the universe, or as localized in a spiritual being, such as the devil, that personifies and instigates evil. However, Spanish has no such word as evil. The words we do use, such as *mal* (badness), *malo* (bad one), *malvado* (wicked one), or *maldad* (wickedness or mischief), tend to speak to a sense of maliciousness that locates "evil" within a person or act. These words also tend to view evil in terms of its consequences. Something, or someone, is evil because the consequences of its actions are bad for us. We may speak of a disaster, illness, or accident as bad, but not as evil. It is not so much that there is natural evil, but that there are things in nature that are bad for us. When we look at the problem of evil in this way, it changes our perspective and makes it easier for us to understand how limitations, ignorance, and vulnerability to the forces of nature could easily lead to bad consequences for us without necessarily making these forces evil. When we speak about *mal* instead of evil, the definition of evil shifts from that of a disembodied force or abstract reality to a reality embodied in concrete beings and acts that have very real consequences that are bad for us.

Evil exists only as far as it is done, but it also breeds more evil, becoming systemic in nature and scope, often having consequences far beyond the original intent of its perpetrator and affecting all of creation.[21] The evil we commit has ramifications beyond the act, affecting our relationships with others and creating a web of relationships defined by our act and its consequences. These consequences have historical and economic vectors that alter the very nature of our society and world. In time, evil becomes inherent and embodied within the very fabric of society and life, affecting all of creation. Evil perpetuates evil, and *lo malo* (the bad), in time, easily perpetuates itself, becoming *peor* (worse) as our actions and their consequences become institutionalized within our society and our economic practices. Those who toil under the burden of injustice, poverty, and discrimination can attest to the actuality of evil taking structural dimensions that cause oppression, suffering, poverty, and death.

Sin and evil affect more than the individual perpetrator of sin. Sin is relational. Sin is not an act done in isolation; it affects the whole of the community. The Bible often states that when we sin, we sin against God and against others (2 Chr. 6:22-26; Ps. 51:4).[22] As Ada María Isasi-Díaz writes, "Sin, while personal, is not private, for it is something that affects our communities negatively."[23] We might think of sin as a spiritual problem between us and God, but the truth is that sin is always and inevitably a communal problem. Our sin affects not just us, but also those around us, particularly those victimized by our acts. Sin ultimately destroys our relationships with God and with others. In time, through habitual acts, power structures, and social conventions, our sinful acts become entrenched in the very fabric of society—in politics, economics, and social structures. As the late Latino theologian and missiologist Orlando Costas writes: "Sin is structural as well as personal. It is structural in the sense that it answers to the 'logic' behind collective behavior. Society is not the sum total of its members; it is composed of a complex network of interpersonal, cultural, and institutional relationships."[24]

Let me illustrate. If I steal your land from you by deceit or coercion, through my sin I gain the benefit of your land and possessions, while you are deprived of them. You might be forced to work for someone else to survive, while I might enjoy the benefits of my ill-acquired land. This places me in an advantage over you. In time, this advantage can lead me to obtain a stronger position in society than you. My children would then inherit the land I stole from you, while your children inherit poverty. As my power grows, my children might lobby the government for laws that will protect my ill-acquired land and status. Through our use of power, we rob people of their life and livelihood, and create oppressive structures, poverty, and social alienation.[25] Like a pebble on a still pond, one sinful act has ramifications that affect the whole fabric of society. Throw more pebbles in the pond and it becomes chaotic!

Gustavo Gutiérrez, in his groundbreaking book, A *Theology of Liberation*, addresses both the personal and sociohistorical dimensions of sin as they become manifest not in abstract notions but in concrete and particular instances of exploitation, injustice, subjugation, enslavement, and socioeconomic repression. But what Gutiérrez does is not truly new. Actually, it is a return to biblical principles that are at the heart of our faith, as indicated by his copious use of Scriptures in his writing. The desire for justice and the struggle against oppression are not novel theological ideas, but the fruit of God's love for humanity.[26] To the slate of economic oppression and exploitation that serve as hallmarks of Latin American liberation theology, Latino/a theologians add other issues such as cultural oppression, racism, and sexism.

For instance, racial stereotypes lead dominant classes to view Latinos/as with suspicion, regardless of their socioeconomic status. Like most minorities, we are not given some of the considerations that members of the dominant race might receive—such as the presumption of innocence, respect, access to housing, and other basic freedoms. While many institutions might boast the presence of diversity, true inclusion does not occur. For example, the opinions of members of the dominant society are given more weight than those of minorities. Media and sociocultural stereotypes reduce us to a common sameness that obscures our uniqueness. We internalize negative stereotypes in time, slowly eroding our own sense of empowerment and self-value. Our cultural values, language, and traditions are denigrated, dismissed, or suppressed, adding to our loss of self. For women, the situation is even worse because they feel the double impact of gender bias and stereotypes on top of the racial and cultural biases that oppress us and deny our worth as human beings.[27]

Regardless of how we understand the nature of sin and evil, our ultimate response should be to confront evil in all its manifestations. Escapists' theologies that defer the end of these structures to an afterlife or end of the world scenario are not an option for those who live under these structures. Nor should it be an option for anyone. Instead, we must confront the power of sin and evil in the world, revealing it for what it is. As David Traverzo Galarza writes, "From a Latino perspective, an understanding of sin also includes the battle against it and all its manifestations."[28] To this end, Latino/a theology calls us to engage in what Orlando Costas calls an integrative approach to evangelism. This approach looks beyond a mere spiritual understanding of sin and salvation, and takes a holistic approach that looks at the whole person and the social condition in which that person lives. It seeks to create new systems and institutions that can empower social transformation and confront the evil entrenched in socioeconomic structures. Ultimately, it calls us to both reflection and action, recognizing that in Christ's death and resurrection we can see that evil "does not have the last word."[29]

Virgilio Elizondo also calls us to confront all the powers of evil that exploit, deface, and oppress humanity. In what he terms the "Jerusalem Principle," Elizondo examines the confrontation between Jesus and the power structures of his day as told in the New Testament accounts.[30] Through his examination of *mestizaje*, Elizondo argues that Jesus identifies with those living at the margins of society and under oppressive conditions. However, what Elizondo calls the "Galilee principle," identifying with the oppressed and marginalized, is not enough. God also calls us to confront power structures that condone, perpetuate, and cause oppression. By confronting these dehumanizing and oppressive structures, we risk death. But by confronting them we unmask the sin and evil that hide behind these structures of power, making possible not only our liberation, but also that of the oppressors who, as Martin Luther King, Jr. said, are also in need of liberation from the sin and evil that possess them.[31]

In confronting the power structures that cause oppression, we are confronting people who, seduced by power, sin, and evil, are also in need of liberation. Thus, we cannot be guided by anger, hatred, vengeance, or violence, for these can only cultivate more sin and evil, *lo malo*. Instead, we must be guided by love. By confronting evil with love, we unmask it for what it is—hatred, violence, and destruction. Love requires us to act on behalf of those who suffer under the burden of the sin and evil committed by others and to confront the perpetrators of evil and oppression with love. Our human predicament calls us to confront *lo malo*, both within and without. But we must also face the question of what it means to be human in the first place, what it is that we were intended to be by God.

The Image of God in Us

While sin, evil, and oppression deface humanity and rob us of dignity, our present predicament is not what was intended for us. In Genesis's account of creation (Gen. 1:26-27), we read that humanity was created in the image and likeness of God. Later, the account of Genesis 2–3 tells of God's Spirit breathing life into humanity, making humanity a living soul. While the two Genesis creation accounts come from different sources and traditions, there is a common thread. Both make reference to humanity as being in the likeness and image of God either directly or indirectly. From the creation accounts we can deduce that an intricate connection exists between God and humanity. Our lives are intricately connected with God. In John 10:34-35, Jesus cites Psalm 82 to assert the right for a human being to claim a familial connection with God. These passages also affirm the possibility of the Incarnation occurring. As the Gospel of John indicates, if those to whom the word of God has come can be called gods, then we should not be surprised at the possibility of Jesus being the Son of God (John 10:36).

Most of us would agree that the human condition as it now exists, with a few gleaming exceptions, seems to bear more resemblance to the demonic than the divine. For the most part, while the majority of theologians seem to believe that through our sin we have lost or effaced the image of God in humanity, it is clear that the majority would also agree that humanity was indeed intended to bear the divine image. However, whether diminished or lost, there is little consensus on what the divine image is. Traditionally, many theologians have sought to locate the image of God in humanity in terms of an essence, capacity, or quality. Some have equated the divine image in humanity with reason, a capacity that distinguishes us from most of the rest of creation. This should come as no surprise, since the Greek term *logos*, which in its most common use means reason or word, has also been used to refer to Christ in John's Gospel. While we have not lost our capacity to reason, theologians who associate the image of God with our reasoning ability would say that sin has corrupted it, so that only a vestige of it remains.

However, the danger of associating the image of God with any essence or characteristic in humanity, including rationality, is in how easily it can lead to a rationale for oppressing others. Those who look different or whom we portray as lacking particular characteristics can easily be cast as inferior, as

174

lacking humanity, and as not bearing the image of God, while we elevate our own status to one of being more godly. Such rationale has been at fault in many dark periods of our histories. The subjugation of the native inhabitants of the Americas and the enslavement of the Africans was often justified by elaborate theological arguments that denied them equal status as human beings or lesser status as bearers of the image of God.[32]

Thus, to speak of the image of God as an essence or capacity we possess, whether it is physical, intellectual, or spiritual can be problematic and potentially dangerous. On the other hand, ontopraxis connects our being and our actions. If we connect who we are with what we do, then the image of God might be found in our actions and our relationships. I coined the term onto-praxis to forge a connection between being and action that is often absent from theology. Action, a component of praxis, involves both our process of deciding and our doing.[33] Even inaction reflects a negative decision. Every decision we make and every action we take affects who we are. Where I decide to go, what I decide to study, and the profession I engage in all make a difference in who I am and how I interact with others. Our actions can even make a difference in whether we live or die, hence influencing our being in a more dramatic fashion. The choices we make combined with the choices of others, along with our actions, make us who we are.

In this respect, there are three ways in which we can speak of human beings as bearing the image of God. First, we can speak of it in terms of a possibility or potential inherent in every human being. By this, I mean that the image of God in humanity is not an essential quality that can be located, but rather a potentiality.[34] Rather than an actuality, human beings have the potential for mediating the presence of God. In other words, it is possible that we might encounter God in a human being. The advantage of this argument is that it does not exclude any human being from bearing this possibility, which might be made actual at any moment, even when we fail to recognize it. Hence, we must treat everyone as if God is present in them.

This is not an alien concept for Christianity. After all, we believe that God resides in us through the indwelling of the Spirit. But the indwelling of the Spirit is not a given, for the Spirit is not bound to us. It may come and depart from us. Some might even limit the indwelling of the Spirit to those who believe or express their faith in a particular fashion. Another advantage of speaking of the image of God as a possibility is that it makes it more difficult to reduce the image of God to a given quality. How God becomes present in us might manifest itself in different ways. To recognize that all human beings can possibly bear God's image ultimately means that we cannot dismiss the possibility present in each other and must treat each other with the respect and recognition that we might accord to God.

Two more specific ways in which God's image might be present in us is in suffering and love. From the New Testament to today's liberation theologies, we see God as being uniquely identified and present in human suffering. The New Testament parable of the sheep and the goats tells us of those who encounter Christ in the sick, the captive, the hungry, and the thirsty (Matt. 25:31-46). Liberation theologies, taking this motif seriously, argue that God is present in the poor, identifying with them and with both the ills and generosity that they might receive. Thus, we can say in this sense that God's image in us is found in the faces of all who suffer and die as victims of violence, oppression, and apathy.

Another possibility for understanding God's presence in humanity is in the actions of those who mediate God's love to others. Through words and deeds, these people become an incarnate and palpable presence of God in humanity. We find this divine image in the lives of saints, both acknowledged and unrecognized. In our recent past, we might point to people such as Mother Teresa, Martin Luther King Jr., and Oscar Romero—people who, while not always perfect, were able to mediate God's liberating presence and the love of God to others in sacrificial ways. But we not only find it in saints, we also find it in the small gestures and magnanimous actions of many whom we might never come to know. Again, this is not a given essence, but a possibility manifested in us. Through our actions we can embody the divine presence to others, so that just as in Christ we come to know God not through an essence or substance, but through what is done.[35]

Identity and the Image of God

Who we are is an important question that theologians often touch only in tangent to other discussions. In looking at sin, for instance, we address the question of who we are in a negative sense. We know that we are not who we should be. On the other hand, when we speak of the image of God, we also address the question of our identity—who we are intended to be. For Latinos/as, identity is a significant issue, essential to theological anthropology. In particular, our identity is deeply connected with our culture and our ethnic understanding.[36] But our identity is also a complex issue that must be unpacked.

First, our identity is neither an essence nor a simple characteristic. In many ways we claim multiple identities that cannot be simply located. A milieu of relationships shapes our identity and defines our own particularity and location by differentiations and identifications that make us this rather than that. Identity is not a rigid reality. It is an intricate web of relationships and multiple contexts that help us define who we are at a particular time and place. As Miroslav Volf writes:

> We are who we are not because we are separate from the others who are next to us, but because we are *both* separate *and* connected, *both* distinct *and* related; the boundaries that mark our identities are both barriers and bridges: . . . Identity is a result of the distinction from the other *and* the internalization of the relationship to the other; it arises out of the complex history of "differentiation" in which both the self and the other take part by negotiating their identities in interaction with one another.[37]

Identity is not a fixed essence. It is a complex of relationships that differentiate and connect us. We might be parents and children, depending on the relationship we are focusing upon. We can be Americans and Latinos/as, or neither. Our relationships, context, and even our actions help to define us.[38] These relationships become increasingly complex for those of us who live within the bounds of different cultures, relating to cultures that do not always fully accept us and that often seek to erase components of our cultural and ethnic identity—such as our language and traditions.[39]

Living at the borderlands of cultures, identity becomes an issue that most Latinos/as must contend with. In most instances we are neither here nor there, caught in the hyphen of different racial and cultural identities. We are in the in-between of being Mexican-American, Cuban-American, and Hispanic-American, not being one or the other, nor accepted by either group. We are not accepted in our countries of origin any longer, but we do not quite belong to this country either. This sad truth was brought home to me upon returning to my native Cuba for a conference after thirty-two years. Often, I was approached by street vendors with the common greeting in broken English, "Welcome to Cuba my friend; where are you from?" I would proudly tell them in Spanish that I was from Cuba, to which they promptly replied, "You may think you are from here, but you are not." I was born there, but I no longer belonged. Yet, I did not always feel welcome in the United States, where as Virgilio Elizondo so aptly puts it, "Our being was actually our 'non-being.'"[40] This sense of not-being one or the other can be quite unsettling.

However, our existence at the borderland of cultures allows us to serve as cultural critics and bridges. Because we are part of the culture, but remain to a certain degree outsiders, it is easier for us to critique the cultures that we inhabit. In our role, we can, if we choose to, see both the positive and the negative that each culture brings to our context. Even more, we become hermeneutical tools, interpreters of both cultures, better able to distinguish differences and similarities, strengths and weaknesses that allow us to see the unique contributions each culture can offer to the other. In return, we also serve as cultural bridges, helping each culture understand the other better. Our location at the border of cultures and languages provides us with this unique standpoint, a vantage point that allows us to see each culture more clearly.

Yet, our cultural perspectives can become skewed, and given the human predicament, our strength at being in the borderland of cultures can easily become a liability. This occurs when our sense of cultural identity becomes eroded as the dominant culture dismisses our culture and the contributions of our culture as being inconsequential, backwards, or nonexistent. It also becomes a problem when we are forced to take on the values and identities of the dominant culture, but recognize that we will never be fully accepted as a part of that culture we are asked to emulate. Liberation theologies help us understand the need for theology to contend with socioeconomic and political oppression. Black theologies and Feminist theologies have made us aware of how racism and sexism oppress and dehumanize us. But there is another level of oppression that operates at the cultural level, destroying our identity and our self-understanding by degrading and effacing the culture that creates us. Latino/a theologians help us see cultural oppression and its dehumanizing power. If our cultural contexts make us who we are, the denigration of our culture is also the denigration of who we are.

Being in Community with God and Each Other

Human beings were created to be in community. The book of Genesis tells that God saw that it was not good for Adam to be alone, thus creating a helpmate for him (Gen. 2:18). Whether it is in terms of our family or of our extended community, we are social and communal beings by nature. For Latinos/as, our sense of community is strongly bound with our sense of identity. We value our family, our barrio, and our church as the contextual locations for our identity.[41] To be human for us cannot be separated from our participation in our respective communities—that is, both our ethnic and faith communities. We define ourselves and find meaning for our lives from the particularities of our contexts. We are the products of our barrio, our church, and our family. These are more important to us than universal and abstract categories.

One of the most significant aspects of our community is the church. It is also one of the most significant symbols of God's presence in our midst. In many communities, the church serves as the central point of the community, where people go to celebrate and grieve, finding both solace and support.

Often, the local church is the center of educational initiatives, the source of information, and the vehicle for political action. Churches in some barrios serve as a refuge from gangs and violence. In others, they are the place where the people connect to their culture through participation in traditional celebrations and through the preservation of language and stories. Regardless of their affiliation, churches bring the community together.

Traditionally, ecclesiology understands the church in terms of its catholicity (universality), apostolicity, oneness (unity), and holiness. Whether we see ourselves as either Catholic or Protestant, these defining marks are central to understanding the church as a whole. At times it may seem that the unity and universality of the church are absent from the Latino/a context. Protestants often define themselves in opposition to Catholics, deriving much of their identity from that which they perceive as distinguishing them from the Catholics—whom they believe to be idolatrous and unsaved, in need of conversion. On the other hand, some Catholics perceive Protestants as radicals who have not only broken with the true faith, but who also have abandoned their cultural and family traditions.

The apostolicity of the church comes under question too, as each group vies for what they feel is the true claim to apostolicity. Catholics see themselves as apostolic in their traditional succession and safeguarding of the tradition. Protestants, on the other hand, argue that they are in line with the true apostolic faith of the early church, recovered through their adherence to the Scriptures. We might even add Pentecostals, who might argue that the true mark of the church is attested to by the gifts of the Spirit. Even the holiness of the church might come into question given our age of sexual scandals and cover-ups that have plagued not only the Catholic church, but many Protestant congregations as well.

However, in trying to understand how these defining marks function, we need to make some key distinctions. The first is between the ideal of the church as it should be (the invisible church) and its particular instantiations in congregations and individuals (the visible church). We may never fully live the ideal, but we participate and strive toward it. The church is fragmented in its particular instantiations, but bound by its faith in God. The oneness of the church is not found in its individual members, but in Christ (John 17:20-23; 1 Cor. 12:14-20). While there is diversity in the church, our unity comes in relationship to Christ and by the Spirit who binds us into oneness, even if we don't always see eye to eye. Using the value we place on families in Latino/a culture as a model, González illustrates this by pointing to how family members might squabble with each other, but retain a sense of unity that cannot be easily broken.[42] Similarly, the holiness of the church does not depend on any individual member of the church. It depends on

God. While we strive to be holy, we are sanctified through God's grace and presence in our lives.[43] In the same manner, it is God who sanctifies the church.

Likewise, the catholicity of the church does not mean everyone adheres to the same beliefs, perspectives, and practices. Instead, as González argues, the word "catholic" etymologically does not mean "universal." It means "according to the whole," a concept that embraces and celebrates diversity. According to González, this definition does not lead us to strict orthodoxy, but calls us to dialogue, which opposes the raising of one particular point of view to an absolute, while recognizing that all our knowledge of God is partial, contextual, and from a given perspective. We even find in the Bible four different Gospels, each with a unique perspective that does not necessarily harmonize with the others in every detail. Yet, they provide a far richer basis for understanding our faith and a stronger historical witness than if all said exactly the same thing.[44] As we may know from courtroom dramas, when witnesses have identical stories, their stories become suspect. But when they have different stories with some common motifs, they build a much stronger case. The plurality of perspectives and views enriches the church and guards against an idolatrous lifting of a single perspective over the whole. In contrast to the traditional definition of apostolicity, González also traces the etymology of apostolicity, which actually refers to being sent out. Using this definition of apostolicity, this characteristic of the church coincides not with succession or adherence to the original faith of the apostles, but rather with the mission of the church.[45] For Latinos/as, the church is active. Faith is not something you have; it is something you do.

Just as the image of God is not in an essence that we have, but is in what we do, the ontopraxis of the church allows us to encounter the invisible church in the actions of the visible church. Of course, not all of the church's actions reflect the presence of God or reveal the true church to us. In the name of the church, we have engaged in wars and unimaginable acts of violence. We have condoned crusades and the violent conquest of lands, including the American continent. We have persecuted people, tortured heretics, and allied ourselves with political and commercial interests. We have raped women and children. We have committed all these atrocities under the banner of the church. But that is not the locus of the church, even if done in the name of the church. The church is where we find God, and we do not find God in such acts.

To understand the church, we must look at the mission of the church in the apostolic sense of being sent out to bear the gospel. The church has been a saving grace to many in the barrios and ghettos of our country, providing a place of refuge and serving as an advocate for the causes of those suffering under the weight of injustice. Churches have provided education and health services to countless people throughout the world. At times, churches have stood against the violence and corruption of governments and corporations, even while others in the church have allied themselves with these forces. The church's identity is in its action. The church can reveal Christ through its actions, but it can also become demonic through its actions. However it is through its actions that we can truly encounter the one holy, catholic, apostolic church. Through its love and through its acts it serves as a sign of the coming reign of God on earth. A particular church can incarnate the universal, just as we too can embody the image of God through our actions. In our ecclesiology we must not ask what the church is, but what the church is doing. For only in knowing what it is doing can we truly know what the church is.

As a symbol and forebearer of God's reign on earth, the church also has a teleological component. It foreshadows and prophesies of what is to come. While fragmented in its present form, like a true symbol, it points beyond itself to a future hope. It is in this hope that we also find a sense of unity. While Latino/a congregations might look at different denominations with distrust and suspicion, we do see a hope in the future that can draw us together. Theologically, there is a sense of a new ecumenism alluded to by Elizondo and González where we find common ground not by doctrinal agreement and shared practices, but by a common struggle and hope for liberation and justice that beckon us to a common goal. While this reality might not be present in the people of our communities and churches, it is becoming more manifest in the theological dialogue of Latino/a theologians, and it is hoped this is a sign of things to come.

A People of Faith

Some denominations see Latinos/as as an object of evangelism, a people who lack church and spirituality. The contrary is true. Latinos/as are a people of deep-seated spirituality. It may not be evident in our affiliation with the institutional church at times. For most of us, it is not the institutions that are the source of our spirituality. We may participate in the church because we are spiritual, but we do not derive our spirituality simply by our participation in the church. In part this is because we do not have a rigid dichotomy between the world and the spirit as we might find in other Christian groups. We might use the language of world and spirit in reference to the sacred and the profane. But it is not a dichotomy between the physical world and the spiritual. For most Latinos/as all of creation is invested with spirituality and

God's presence. The miraculous is real and not necessarily supernatural in nature, since we tend to think that miracles are a very natural part of God's world.

Because we have this deep sense of God's presence in our midst and in the midst of the world, we do not always find our spirituality tied to the traditional conventions of the institutional church. Thus, our spirituality can take many forms. For some, these forms might even be beyond the bounds of traditional Christian practices. They might encompass native religions, the use of *curanderos/as* (healers), or traditional African religions such as Yoruba in the practices of *Santeria*. In these religious expressions, we may find empowerment and connection to primal forces of the holy, expressed through these categories. It is also as likely that we might not see any contradiction in adhering to these different faith practices and Christianity, defining ourselves as part of both. Although not unheard of, this type of syncretism might be less common among Protestant denominations. However, this does not mean that other spiritual expressions cannot be found in Protestant denominations, which often appropriate certain spiritual practices from Pentecostalism. By the same token, the deep sense of spiritual presence found in Pentecostal traditions often resonates with the cultural, spiritual, and liberation concerns of Latinos/as, which explains to some extent Pentecostalism's rapid growth in the Hispanic community.[46]

At times, the willingness of Latinos/as to cross religious borders is comparable to our ability to cross cultural and political borders, our ability to exist in more than one tradition. Often, the cultural composition of the church or particular connections with a group bear more weight in the decision to become involved with a particular group than any rigid sense of denominational identity. Even for those Latinos/as who might not identify with a given church or religious tradition, a sense of spirituality seems to pervade our lives, in part infused by the spiritual nature of Hispanic cultures. This does not mean that Latinos/as are necessarily and inherently more spiritual than other people. Nor that we should naively assume that all Latinos/as are religious, spiritual, and noble. Rather, it means that our culture tends to foster a sense of spirituality that has at times been lost in the urbanized Western cultures. It also means that there is a mystical attitude toward the world and creation that facilitates the development of spiritual concerns. These spiritual sensibilities manifest themselves in the life-giving activities of women and men, in *lo cotidiano*, in our practices of hospitality, and in our religious rituals and observances. Thus, Christianity as a whole can benefit in seeing Latinos/as not simply as an object of evangelization, but as a subject and source of evangelism and spirituality that can rescue the church from a sterile instrumentalism and intellectualism.

Until That Day

Who we are as human beings is not set in stone. As part of our human predicament, we know that we are not what we should be. But we also know that we are moving toward something, toward an ideal and a hope. The apostle Paul writes in his letter to the Philippians, "I am confident of this very thing, that He who began a good work in you will perfect it until the day of Christ Jesus" (1:6). In this sense, who we are as human beings and the future of the church are all bound up with our hopes for what is to come and our sense that what should be, one day will be. This will take us to our final chapter as we look at the hope for our future, a future that rests with God.

Notes

1. Luis G. Pedraja, *Jesus Is My Uncle: Christology from a Hispanic Perspective* (Nashville: Abingdon Press, 1999), p. 51.

2. See John Ayto, *Dictionary of Word Origins* (New York: Arcade, 1990), p. 145. I first allude to this connection in *Jesus Is My Uncle*, p. 129, footnote 54. The English word *cretin* comes from the Swiss-French version, *crestin*, although this word came to acquire a different and more disparaging meaning.

3. Some of the material in this chapter can be found with more detailed arguments in two of my articles: "In the Face of Evil: Understanding Evil in the Aftermath of Terror," in *Strike Terror No More: Theology, Ethics, and the New War*, Jon Berquist, ed. (St. Louis: Chalice Press, 2002), pp. 187-99 and "Suffering God: Theodicy for the 21st Century," in *Quarterly Review* (Summer 2002).

4. John Calvin, *Institutes of the Christian Religion*, trans. by Henry Beveridge (Grand Rapids: Eerdmans, 1989), Book I, pp. 198-205.

5. Paul Tillich, "Heal the Sick; Cast out Demons," in *The Eternal Now* (New York: Scribner, 1963), pp. 60-61.

6. Ada María Isasi-Díaz warns against assuming that God's identification with the suffering means that God condones suffering, found in *Mujerista Theology: A Theology for the Twenty-First Century* (Maryknoll: Orbis Press, 1996), p. 129. Nancy Pineda-Madrid, in her essay "In Search of a Theology of Suffering, *Latinamente*," *The Ties That Bind: African American and Hispanic American/Latino/a Theologies in Dialogue*, Anthony Pinn and Benjamin Valentin, eds. (New York: Continuum, 2001), echoes this warning, writing that "often 'Christian' reflections on suffering have advanced the idealization of the passive, uncritical resignation to suffering," p. 197.

7. Friedrich Nietzsche, *On the Genealogy of Morals: A Polemic*, trans. by Walter Kaufman (New York: Vintage Books, 1967), p. 39.

8. Irenaeus, *Against Heresies*, in *The Ante-Nicene Fathers*, Vol. 1, A. Roberts and J. Donaldson, eds. (Albany, Ore.: Ages Software, 1996, 1997), 1.25.5, p. 693; 2.20.2, pp. 894-95. Augustine, *City of God*, trans. by Henry Battenson (New York: Penguin, 1972), XI.22: pp. 453-54. More recently, John Hicks has argued in favor of this theodicy.

9. See my article "In Harms Way: Theological Reflections on Disasters," in *Quarterly Review* (Spring, 1997), pp. 5-23, particularly pp. 9-11.

10. Kathryn Tanner argues that if we ignore the interconnected nature of creation and

transcend our limits, we become susceptible to the same havoc we wreck upon the environment. "Creation, Environmental Crisis, and Ecological Justice," in *Reconstructing Christian Theology*, Rebecca S. Chopp and Mark Lewis Taylor, eds. (Minneapolis: Fortress Press, 1994), p. 100.

11. Pedraja, "In Harms Way: Theological Reflections on Disasters," in *Quarterly Review*, (Spring 1997), pp. 11-14.

12. This is well argued by process theologians who believe that God is limited by metaphysical necessity. See David Griffin, *God, Power, and Evil: A Process Theodicy* (Philadelphia: Westminster Press, 1976), pp. 251-74.

13. I first made this argument in "In the Face of Evil: Understanding Evil in the Aftermath of Terror," in *Strike Terror No More: Theology, Ethics, and the New War*, pp. 190-91.

14. Karl Barth addresses the nature of human freedom in "The Gift of Freedom," trans. by Thomas Weiser in *The Humanity of God* (Atlanta: John Knox Press, 1960), pp. 59-96.

15. In Christian existentialism, Søren Kierkegaard calls this despair, a form of defiance in which the self asserts itself, as being fully in control without any form of dependence upon another. See for instance, *The Sickness unto Death*, trans. by Alastair Hannay (New York: Penguin Books, 1989), pp. 98-105.

16. For Barth human freedom cannot be realized in the solitary detachment of an individual in isolation, nor should it be understood as asserting itself. We incorrectly assume that freedom means self-assertion and isolation. *The Humanity of God*, pp. 77-78.

17. Gustavo Gutiérrez, *The God of Life* (Maryknoll: Orbis Press, 1989, 1991), p. 12.

18. Both Schleiermacher and Barth understood freedom as an ability to choose between differing alternatives. For instance, Barth writes "to call a man free is to recognize that God has *given* him freedom." Later on, he writes "man becomes free and is free by choosing, deciding, and determining himself in accordance with the freedom of God." Hence, human freedom is dependent upon God, and the choosing we do is between that given to us and before us. *The Humanity of God*, pp. 74, 76-77.

19. Barth writes on freedom: "Again, man's freedom is a far cry from the self-assertion of one or many solitary individuals. It has nothing to do with division and disorder. God's own freedom is Trinitarian, embracing grace, thankfulness, and peace. It is the freedom of the living God. Only in this relational freedom is God sovereign, almighty, the Lord of all." Freedom exists in relationship, in being free to be for the other. It is not "freedom *from*, but a freedom *to* and *for*." Ibid., pp. 71-72. Also see pp. 79-80.

20. Augustine in *The Many Faces of Evil: Historical Perspectives*, ed. by Amélie Oksenberg Rorty (New York: Routledge, 2001), p. 49.

21. Marjorie Hewitt Suchocki argues this same point in *The Fall to Violence: Original Sin in Relational Theology* (New York: Continuum, 1995), pp. 101-3.

22. Elsa Tamez argues in *The Amnesty of Grace: Justification by Faith from a Latin American Perspective* (Nashville: Abingdon Press, 1993) that the sins of the poor cannot be compared to the sins of the powerful, since the poor feel the brunt of sin against them more than others, pp. 14-21.

23. Ada María Isasi-Díaz, *En la lucha / In the Struggle: A Hispanic Women's Liberation Theology* (Minneapolis: Fortress Press, 1993), p. 39.

24. Orlando Costas, *Christ Outside the Gates: Mission Beyond Christendom* (Maryknoll: Orbis Press, p. 26).

25. Enrique Dussel makes the argument of how power and domination play a role in sin in *Ethics and Community* (Maryknoll: Orbis Press, 1988), pp. 18-26.

26. Gustavo Gutiérrez, A *Theology of Liberation: History, Politics, and Salvation,* (Maryknoll: Orbis Press, 1973, 1988), pp. 16, 103.

27. See Ada María Isasi-Díaz's discussion of this topic in *Mujerista Theology*, pp. 113-15.

28. David Traverzo Galarza, "Sin: A Hispanic Perspective," in *Teología en Conjunto: A Collaborative Hispanic Protestant Theology*, José David Rodríguez and Loida I. Martell-Otero, eds. (Louisville: Westminster John Knox Press, 1997), p. 122.

29. Ibid., p. 121.

30. Virgilio Elizondo, *Galilean Journey: The Mexican-American Promise* (Maryknoll: Orbis Press, 1983), pp. 103-5.

31. Ibid., p. 105.

32. See Anthony Pagden, *The Fall of Natural Man: The American Indian and the Origins of Comparative Ethnology* (Cambridge: Cambridge University Press), 1982.

33. Alfred North Whitehead writes in his ninth category of explanation that "*how* an actual entity *becomes* constitutes *what* that actual entity *is*; so that the two descriptions of an actual entity are not independent. Its 'being' is constituted by its 'becoming.'" *Process and Reality*, corrected edition, David R. Griffin and Donald W. Sherburne, eds. (New York: Free Press, 1978), p. 23. Deciding what possibility to actualize involves a process of activity of relation, elimination, and selection that defines what something is, making it actual, and, in that sense, constituting its being. Emmanuel Levinas also argues that the ethical demand precedes being, especially if we define ethical reasoning in terms of praxis, particularly as activity and not merely as subjective passivity. *Otherwise than Being or Beyond Essence*, trans. by Alphonso Lingis (Boston: Martinus Nijhoff Publishers, 1981).

34. Here I am indebted to Whitehead and Jüngel's distinction between possibility and actuality. I do not speak of potentiality as an essential quality, but as a teleological element inherent in humanity, closer to Aristotle's final cause, but not as an actuality.

35. For more see my book *Jesus Is My Uncle*, chapter 2 in particular.

36. See David Maldonado "Doing Theology and the Anthropological Questions" in *Teología en Conjunto: A Collaborative Hispanic Protestant Theology,*" José David Rodríguez and Loida I. Martell-Otero, eds. (Louisville: Westminster/John Knox, 1997), p. 107.

37. Miroslav Volf, *Exclusion & Embrace: A Theological Exploration of Identity, Otherness, and Reconciliation* (Nashville: Abingdon Press, 1996), p. 66.

38. Ada María Isasi-Díaz provides a good argument in terms of relationships as the key for understanding identity in regards to understanding difference in terms of relationships rather than as exclusion. "A New *Mestizaje/Mulatez*: Reconceptualizing Difference," in *A Dream Unfinished*, Fernando Segovia and Eleazar S. Fernandez, eds. (Maryknoll: Orbis Press, 2001), pp. 203-14. That our actions and relationships continually define our being is also central to my understanding of ontopraxis. Our praxis, and the praxis of others, defines who we are within a context of relationship.

39. Maldonado, "Doing Theology and the Anthropological Question," pp. 109-10.

40. Virgilio Elizondo, *The Future Is Mestizo* (New York: Crossroad, 1992), p. 18.

41. David Maldonado, "Doing Theology and the Anthropological Questions," p. 110.

42. Justo L. González, "In Quest of a Protestant Hispanic Ecclesiology," in *Teología en Conjunto*, p. 93.

43. Ibid., pp. 90-91.

44. Justo L. González, *Out of Every Tribe and Nation: Christian Theology at the Ethnic Roundtable* (Nashville: Abingdon Press, 1992), pp. 18-27.

45. Justo L. González, "In Quest of a Protestant Hispanic Ecclesiology," in *Teología en Conjunto*, pp. 85-87.

46. See Eldin Vallafañes's article, "Spirit without Borders: Pentecostalism in the Americas (A Profile and Paradigm of "Criollo" Pentecostalism)" in *Apuntes* 22/4 (Winter 2002), pp. 124-25.

CHAPTER TEN

THE DAY AFTER MAÑANA

As children, we are afraid of the dark. Actually, it is not the dark itself that we fear. What we fear is what it might hold in its shroud. In that darkness, our fears and nightmares take form and come to haunt us. I think that we never fully outgrow this fear of the dark. It just takes a different shape. The nightmares that once haunted the darkened confines of our childhood rooms, now more mature themselves, take residence in the unknown recesses of our future. Ghosts and goblins are now replaced with doubts, uncertainties, and more realistic torments. Thus, the future frightens us. But it also holds the promise and fulfillment of our many hopes, dreams, and aspirations.

Most of us live with an eye toward the future, sometimes in hopeful longing and sometimes with fear and dread. For the future brings us the grace and promise of the possible—a new start, a new day, where things might be different and where our hopes might become a reality. But the future also means the possibility of loss—the loss of friends, family, status, youth, and so much more. So we look to the future with hope, but also with anxiety, not knowing if it will bring us the fulfillment of dreams or the horror of nightmares. It is a mystery that both fascinates and frightens us. For some, the future is already determined, waiting for us. As a result, we try to get a glimpse into it. We try to divine it, to predict it as best we can. We seek out seers and prophets; we scrutinize the Scriptures for answers, for patterns, for a plan.

Others see the future as open-ended and filled with possibilities, which we can bring into being. But ultimately, all we can really do is have faith.

We tend to think of eschatology as the doctrine of the last things. So it evokes in us thoughts of endings—the end of the world, the end of life. But is it truly a doctrine about endings? I venture to say that is actually a doctrine of transitions, of beginnings, of creation, of new things. It should not be a doctrine shrouded with fear and trepidation about the end of the world. Nor should it be about death and the afterlife. We need to approach it as a doctrine of hope and life, and as a demand upon our present work, for the future is not just about what it brings to us, but also about what we bring to it.

The *Mañana* Principle

In his book, Mañana, Justo L. González, writes about the different ways that we might interpret the Spanish expression *mañana*. For the privileged it is sign of laziness, postponing for tomorrow what can be done today. In contrast to this, González argues that rather than laziness, it is "the discouraged response of those who have learned, through long and bitter experience that the results of their efforts seldom bring about much benefit to them or their loved ones."[1] However, González also posits another possible interpretation for *mañana*, one that looks at the future not in terms of continuity with a past filled with oppression, but rather as filled with a radical hope that the future will be transformed to bring justice, liberation, and life. Seeing that the present is not what it could be, our vision of *mañana*—of what could be, yet is not—serves as a constant judgment on our present. It is the radical questioning of the present by the future as envisioned by God.

González provides through this argument a different way of understanding eschatology. Some see eschatology as devoid of social and political transformation. To them, it is a mere spiritual concern with the afterlife.[2] The primary question that concerns them is where they will be spending eternity and what will be their reward. For others, eschatology simply involves a passive waiting for God to act. To them the world as it currently exists is beyond hope, so they await a time when God will do away with this reality and replace it with another. Some, who might indeed see eschatology as a call to action, are often more driven by fanatical ideas of a violent end of time. Others, like early twentieth-century liberals, see it with a naïve view of human progress and achievement to bring about a utopian reality. In contrast to these, González provides a principle based on *mañana* that judges the present and calls for its transformation.[3]

Taking this principle and applying it to eschatology implies several things.

First, it points us to the teleological dimension of eschatology. This means that eschatology is not merely an accounting of the future. It is also something that has a role in the present. Beyond providing us with hope, eschatology also has a vector quality and a summons. It provides us with the goal for which we must strive. It beckons us into something and provides us with a measure of what is possible. We are called into the future, but not just any future. We are called toward God's future, and in this we find our hope.

Generally, we tend to look to God in the past, reminiscing about what God has done in the past. We seek God through traditions, stories, and past events that define our faith. But most of the biblical accounts tend to point us to a God of the future, using the past primarily to remind us of God's faithfulness and ability to continue in the future that which has already begun. For example, in the Exodus, God leads the Israelites, always going ahead of them, drawing them to the fulfillment of their future in the promised land (Exod. 13:21-22). In the book of Isaiah we are told not to look back and ponder former things, for God is doing something new (Isa. 43:18-19). In the New Testament, Jesus goes ahead before the disciples to Galilee, as well as to prepare a place for them (Matt. 28:7; John 14). This does not merely mean that God lives in the future, having no bearing upon us, or that God exists in a future time. What this means is that God embodies our future.[4] God's grace creates new possibilities for us, regardless of our past. But God also beckons us to bring forth what God envisions for the world.[5]

Because there is a teleological component to all eschatology, calling and beckoning us toward God's vision of the future, there is also an inherent demand for action in all eschatology. Eschatology demands that we work toward actualizing the possibility of God's reign on earth. Most liberation theologies, including Latino/a theology, are teleological in nature, bounded by a future hope where justice and liberation become a reality. Thus, we see in Latin American liberation theology an emphasis on God's reign, toward the hope of a future, which places a demand upon us to change the structures of the present and to work toward bringing forth God's reign. However, this demand is not the same as the naïve view of the early twentieth century that thought that through our work and progress we could bring forth God's reign on earth. The demand of eschatology upon us does not rest solely with us, for inherent in the demand is also the knowledge that God too is working to bring forth this reality. Without God's intervention, without new possibilities for being, we could not do it.

Finally, because eschatology provides us with a radical vision of what might be, it also brings a judgment on the present order. Whether we are able to bring a change in the present status quo or not, the present is still judged by the future because we know the possibility of what might be and recognize that it is not. This future that impinges upon the present, that breaks into our lives and demands change, might not be the same future as imagined in other eschatological works. But it is a future with which we must contend.

Creation and Eschatology

It may seem odd to put a section on creation together with eschatology. Yet, I believe it is the best place for it, because eschatology is not about the end of creation. It is actually about the fulfillment of creation and about creating something new. Unfortunately, some have used eschatology to justify the squandering of resources and the exploitation of creation, such as was the case for former Secretary of the Interior, James Watts, during the Reagan Administration, who argued that conservation efforts were pointless because the end of the world was imminent. Underlying such arguments is a belief that creation has been corrupted by human sin and that the world will be destroyed by God. This belies an inherent and pervasive dualism that sees the material world as inferior and corrupt, in contrast to the pristine spiritual world. Therefore, eschatology becomes the justification for the depletion of resources.

Naturally, such eschatological views of our relationship to creation are problematic. First, Christian eschatological hope is not bound to the destruction of creation. Rather, it points to its fulfillment. As the apostle Paul writes:

> The creation waits in eager expectation for the sons of God to be revealed. For the creation was subjected to frustration, not by its own choice, but by the will of the one who subjected it, in hope that the creation itself will be liberated from its bondage to decay and brought into the glorious freedom of the children of God. We know that the whole creation has been groaning as in the pains of childbirth right up to the present time. Not only so, but we ourselves, who have the firstfruits of the Spirit, groan inwardly as we wait eagerly for our adoption as sons, the redemption of our bodies. (Rom. 8:19-23)

Instead of pointing to the destruction of creation, Paul binds our salvation together with that of creation. Just as we await our fulfillment, so creation awaits its liberation and the birth of a new reality. Through this verse, not only is eschatology connected to the fulfillment of creation, we, too, are connected to it. Instead of a duality, where the material world will be destroyed along with our fleshly bodies, this passage indicates an integral connection between our material existence, creation, and our redemption. Salvation is not merely for humanity. It is for the whole creation, which awaits its liberation that is bound to the redemption of humanity.

There also seems to be an indication in this passage in Romans that the problem is not creation, but human sin. Creation waits for its liberation, but this liberation comes as the result of the redemption and fulfillment of humanity. This means that the subjugation of creation is not the result of decay in creation, but of our actions that are contrary to God's will. Although Genesis portrays God as giving humanity dominion over creation, this rule cannot be separated from the image of God present in humanity. This rule, if truly in accordance to the image of God, would be one of love and care giving, where we tend to creation. In failing to fulfill our proper relationship to creation, we have actually enslaved creation, and its liberation can only come in our restoration to a proper relationship to God and to others.

In losing our right relationship to creation, we lost our sense of a place within creation and become detached and disconnected from it, forgetting that we too are a part of creation and interconnected with it. Instead, because of our pride, we fall prey to anthropocentrism, placing ourselves at the center of creation, everything else revolving around us and created for us. Rather than living in harmony with creation, we live in a state of constant struggle with it. As Leonardo Boff writes, "human beings feel that they are *above* things, rather than *alongside* and *with* things."[6] In turn, we are displaced from creation, becoming alienated from other creatures, while exploiting and destroying the environment. The brokenness of our relationship with nature has dire consequences for us, since we cannot escape our dependence on the rest of creation.[7] The result is a state of war against the rest of creation. Our sin leads us to lose sight of the interconnectedness of all creation and of our connectedness with the Creator.[8]

Another mistaken notion is that creation is somehow static, completed at the beginning of time. Modern science has shown us otherwise, revealing to us a universe that is in flux, constantly changing and evolving. Paul's words in Romans 8 point in the direction of an ongoing creation that contains within its folds teleological and eschatological components. Creation is not complete. It is moving toward something, awaiting its fulfillment, a part of a process begun by God that still awaits its fulfillment, a process in which we too are called to be cocreators with God.[9] Just as a woman in labor awaits birth, creation is still creating, seeking the final moment where it too achieves its destiny and gives birth to what God intends. Thus, creation is bound up with eschatology, but not, as previously imagined, through its fiery end. Instead, like the hope of humanity, creation too awaits its transformation into something new and different.

In the final chapters of Revelation, creation does not cease. Instead, it continues in a new heaven and a new earth. While, we might interpret these passages as the destruction of the old and the appearance of a new creation, it can easily be interpreted in relation to redemption, where the old becomes transformed into something new. Rather than the destruction of creation, it is possible to interpret these passages as the fulfillment of creation, where in our human restoration creation too becomes restored. Thus, in the same way that our old nature passes away and we are made new in our relationship with God, so is the case with creation.

A proper understanding of creation is important to Latino/a theology for several reasons. First, we understand the earth and all that is in it in a sacred manner. Creation is not something alien and separate from God or from the realm of spirituality. Rather, creation is infused with God's presence and with a deep sense of spirituality.[10] For some of us, our indigenous ancestors were keenly aware of seasonal cycles and held a deep reverence for the earth. Others, whose lifeblood was drawn from cultivating the earth, also held a deep sense of respect for nature. In the mysteries of the created order, in the celebration of life, in lo cotidiano, we find a sense of the holy and of the sacred that connects us to the rest of creation and to God.[11]

It should not be a surprise that the apostle Paul writes in Romans that creation reveals God's power and majesty (Rom. 1:20). Some interpret this passage in terms of a proof of God's existence through creation's purpose and analogy of being, as does Aquinas, or in terms of its design, as does Paley. But for Latinos/as, the revelation inherent in creation is not in those arguments that are based on nature's design and majesty. Rather, the revelation inherent in creation has more to do with its sacredness, organic interconnectedness, and the spiritual presence inherent in it. For the most part, we do not question the sacredness of the Scriptures and traditions that contain an accounting of God's revelation in history. Likewise, we should value the inherent sacredness of creation where we also can encounter God's revelation, which calls us to a deeper respect of creation than what we display in our utilitarian and exploitative treatment of it. The intuition of Latinos/as, who see the creation as sacred and spirit-filled, is not the mark of a superstitious and backward people, but a model to be emulated.

Second, the destruction of creation and of the environment tends to affect Latinos/as and other minorities in a greater and more disproportionate way than it affects dominant groups in our society. Those with the least resources in society are usually the most vulnerable to the destruction of our natural resources and of our environment. It is the workers in factories and in fields that are most commonly exposed to toxic chemicals and wastes. Similarly, these plants are seldom located in the middle of affluent suburbia. On the contrary, they are typically located in poor neighborhoods that border industrial areas. It should not come as a surprise that in most Two-Thirds World countries, potable water is a rare resource, often the victim of pollutants. The affluent can find some level of protection from the toxic elements that are dumped into the environment, while the poor are more susceptible to their ravages.[12] Toxic waste is not dumped into suburbia, but it easily finds its way to the barrios and neighborhoods where the poor and the marginalized live. Thus, we must take seriously the sacred nature of the environment and begin to work toward the healing of creation instead of its destruction. Rather than seeing eschatology as a justification for the rape and exploitation of nature, we need to move toward a theology of liberation that includes all creation and a view of eschatology that includes the fulfillment of all of creation—an eschatology of life, not destruction.

The Reign of God

Because we are often hesitant to address eschatological themes with our congregations and fail to engage the church-at-large in our writing, ministers and theologians are often left behind. Instead, eschatological themes are dictated more by popular culture and fiction than by sound theological scholarship and doctrine. Thus, eschatological themes are reduced in the public eye to a limited array of sensationalist, radical, and often unsound theology. In reality, there are many perspectives on eschatology among Christians, with a wide range of beliefs about the meaning of God's reign and the afterlife. The same is true about Latinos/as and their eschatology. There is a wide range of perspectives, varying from denomination to denomination, from church to church, and from individual to individual. To assume that there is one eschatological view or that somehow we have a special insight into God's reign and eschatology would be wrong.

Some Latinos/as believe in the rapture, the taking of Christians out of the world before the end times, a belief grounded more in popular visions and dispensational views of the eighteenth and nineteenth centuries than on biblical doctrine. Others do not believe in it. Some believe in one form of millennialism or another, while others reject it. Some are dispensationalist, believing in different dispensations of grace throughout history, supposedly traced throughout the Bible. Latinos/as often share the same popular views about the end of times that circulate throughout society and the church at large. Thus, to speak of eschatology in terms of a uniquely Latino/a way does not mean that this is necessarily the eschatology embraced by the people. Rather, it is an attempt to understand eschatology in light of our experience and culture to see what our perspective can offer to the church as a whole.

If one of the key components of eschatology is its teleological component (pointing us toward a goal and calling us to action), then it is important that we attempt to understand what our goal is. We can see this in Jesus' preaching, particularly in regard to the coming of God's reign. Jesus' prophetic message was directed toward the establishment of God's reign, a reign with specific characteristics that are often overlooked in our eschatologies. But it is these characteristics that provide content to eschatology. Generally, we tend to dislodge God's reign from history by either spiritualizing it or by locating it at the end of history, thus minimizing its demand upon us. In contrast Jesus' message seemed to indicate a historical locus for God's reign—a reign that had both present and future dimensions. It was a reign that was already made present, having entered history in Jesus and his followers, but which still awaited its full actualization.

In the words of the Lord's Prayer we catch a glimpse of the expectation of God's reign upon earth: "Thy Kingdom come, Thy will be done on earth as it is in heaven." If we look carefully at these words, we see what the reign of God entails. First, some would claim that God's reign is what awaits us in heaven, a place to which we should strive to go. However, it is clear from the words of the prayer that the location of God's reign is upon earth and that it is an expectation that awaits its fulfillment in history. After all, when we pray we do not say, "Take us to Thy kingdom." Rather, we pray, "Thy Kingdom come." This locates the Kingdom of God where we are, not in a distant place far removed from our reality. Second, in asking for the coming of the Kingdom, we pray that God's will be done on earth as in heaven. Could it be that the coming of God's reign is tied to doing God's will on earth as in heaven, where God already reigns? It is exactly that. God's reign comes about through doing God's will.

The next question, of course, is what God's will entails? Often, those in positions of power claim the validation of God's will, but that is not necessarily the case. God's reign and the early church's insistence upon the lordship of Christ not only served to affirm Jesus' status, but also served to condemn the economic, religious, and political structures of power that were in place. Jesus was tortured and murdered by the political and religious power structures of the time as a subversive and a heretic. For the early church to claim his lordship was to make a claim against the very power structures that rejected and condemned him. The early church rejected any claim of divine validation for these structures of power—whether they were social, political, economic, or religious in nature. Instead, these affirmations of Jesus' lordship identified and allied God with the silenced victims of society. Through these early affirmations the church validated Jesus' message and God's presence with him. These affirmations exemplified the *mañana* principle, as God's reign leveled a judgment upon the structures of society, calling for a radical change.

What God's reign entails might be open to debate, but some common characteristics can be drawn together from the prophets, the Sermon on the Mount, the Last Supper, and other New Testament passages.[13] These prophetic words are not simply oracles of a predetermined future reality. They are a plan for action, a goal that beckons us toward making God's reign a reality through us and actualizing it in our lives.[14] Throughout Jesus' preaching we see a concern for the poor, the outcasts, and the marginalized. Those who have no place in society, who are excluded and minimalized by power structures of domination will find a place in God's reign. Similarly, there is a deep concern for actively seeking peace. God's reign does not come about by domination, force, and coercion. It comes through the patience and gentle persuasion of God's love. Finally, God's reign affirms life and the dignity of all creation.

These characteristics provide us with some guidance on how we should understand God's reign. Latino/a eschatology affirms creation, life, and love over destruction, domination, and death. For instance, Ada María Isasi-Díaz rejects the term Kingdom, which evokes images of domination, hierarchy, and male dominance in favor of the term kin-dom, which evokes the interconnectedness and inclusion of everyone into God's reign. While I believe the subversion of our power structures of domination in society, evoked by the use of terms such as God's reign and references to Jesus as King, are important, I also believe that Isasi-Díaz's terminology points toward the same ideal—one that subverts the hierarchical structures of power, domination, and death that control our society. Inherent in both we find a shared vision of God's reign as fashioned through love, inclusion, and empowerment. Rather than seeking conformity and sameness, the diversity of gifts shared enriches the whole. Instead of lifting one person, group, or culture, all are brought together in God's love.[15]

In terms of the *mañana* principle, the reign of God is not merely a portent of things to come; it is a call to action in the here and now.[16] The reign of God comes about in our doing, its being dependent upon our praxis. In loving one another as God loves us, we begin to bring forth God's reign upon earth by living in accordance to God's will for us. If we love one another, we will seek everyone's welfare. Instead of creating structures that see human beings as objects to be used for gain, we will work to promote the dignity of all creatures and seek equity and justice for all. We replace structures of death and violence, with structures that affirm life. As the martyred Latin American liberation theologian, Ignacio Ellacuría, writes:

> Not that it is evident what the fullness of life consists of, still less how full-
> ness of life is to be achieved. But it not so hard to see what it does *not* con-
> sist of and how it will *not* be achieved.... To seek life by taking it away from
> others or without concern for how others are losing it, is certainly the nega-
> tion of the Spirit as giver of life. From this perspective, the basic Christian
> message of loving others as oneself,...of preferring to give rather than
> receive, and of resolving to give all one's property to those who are poorer,
> are utopian ideals.... With it, not only is there a drive to seek something
> radically new, but some lines are drawn for the attempts to begin anew.[17]

These ideals inherent in Christianity and this demand to love one another
beckon us to work to change the structures of society and to create new structures that promote life. But the reign of God is not limited just to humanity.
God's salvation encompasses all of creation, as we enter into new relationships with creation and with God. Thus, we also seek an end for the exploitation of nature and work for its preservation. By working toward transforming
our relationships and our present structures into new ones that reflect God's
will, affirm life, and are driven by love, we bring forth God's reign on earth.

Such a task as bringing into fruition the reign of God seems monumental
and unattainable if dependent upon our efforts alone. But it is not. God
stands with us in this task, providing us with new possibilities when all seem
exhausted and guiding us in spite of setbacks. God works at our side and
through us—often in spite of us.[18] If we understand God's defining characteristic to be love, then we must recognize that God does not bring about this
aim through coercion or sheer power. Instead, God works through us and
with us in history to bring forth change, empowering us to make the vision
of God's reign on earth a reality. The status quo of our present structures of
domination, coercion, and inequity can never exhaust or close the possibility of change and transformation. God's grace continually opens the future
for us as a new possibility for bringing forth a new creation and for being
made anew.

God's reign also judges the present. God's judgment upon us is not one of
condemnation, but one rooted in God's love. In love, God rejects the structures of hatred, death, and violence that we have created. In its place, God
provides us with the possibility of life. In the end, it is death, condemnation,
and hell that are thrown into the lake of fire (Rev. 20:14). If death and Hades
are destroyed, what is left if not life and love? God's will is that no one will
perish and that all find life (John 3:16-17). God's love calls us all toward its
embrace. But we are free to choose. Thus, it is not God who condemns us. It
is we who condemn ourselves. God desires and gives life. But in rejecting
God we reject life and embrace death. By promoting economic structures
that rob people of their lives and wreck havoc upon creation, we embrace

death. In choosing to live by hatred and violence, we embrace death. God's reign and love stands as a judgment against these structures of death and destruction that are our legacy.

Life After Life

At times, it seems that theologians today often are afraid to speak of the resurrection or of life beyond death. In a world driven by scientific methodologies, academic detachment, and philosophical inquiry, such topics seem to be taboo, tinged with superstition, relics of a premodern time. Instead, we prefer to demythologize the Bible of these vestiges of a "simpler age." Yet, most of our fears seem to reside with the battles of past centuries. In current scientific circles, quantum mechanics and relativity theories point to a reality that is far more complex than the rigid laws of Newton's mechanistic universe. We live in a world that is intricately interconnected, where the line between matter and energy is fuzzy and fluid, and where observation, cause, and effect are no longer simple equations. Our current worldviews are more open and complex than the simple dualities of ages ago. Postmodern theories no longer accept simplistic academic detachment and philosophical foundations. To speak of resurrection and life in spite of death can no longer be construed as a precritical and premodern worldview. While we might refrain from speculating on the nature of a resurrected body or what life in spite of death might mean, we must continue to affirm the belief that in God life will triumph over death.

Throughout the ages Christians have shared a belief that affirms life over death. This belief extends to what occurs to us after the end of our daily earthly existence. However, there is no agreement on how our lives are affirmed in spite of death. Most Christians do hold to some belief of life beyond death, but the shape this life might take varies from person to person, and at times individuals hold on to views that are contradictory in nature. Of course, part of this problem is that the Scriptures themselves seem to provide different views regarding what awaits us beyond death.

In the Hebrew Bible, notions of life beyond death are not prevalent. Emphasis is placed on this life and immortality often relies on the preservation of one's memory and legacy through one's descendants. Other views suggest a sense of collective immortality, where one lives through one's people (Gen. 25:8).[19] Other passages seem to suggest different views regarding one's state beyond death. References to our return to the dust of the earth seem to indicate that there is no individual sense of immortality and that life ceases with one's death (Gen. 3:19; Job 10:9). A similar sentiment seems to echo in

Psalm 6:5 where the psalmist cries: "No one remembers you when he is dead. Who praises you from the grave?"(NIV). Similar words are uttered later by King Hezekiah: "For the grave cannot praise you, death cannot sing your praise; those who go down to the pit cannot hope for your faithfulness. The living, the living—they praise you, as I am doing today; fathers tell their children about your faithfulness" (Isa. 38:18-19 NIV). Other passages refer to Sheol, a term that at times seems to refer to death and at other times to a shadowy existence beyond death, possibly even associated with hell. Yet, other references seem to indicate a sense of deliverance from death (Ps. 16:10) and some form of existence beyond death (1 Sam. 28:8-15).

In the New Testament, the prevalent notion of life beyond death is the resurrection. This does not mean that other views are not present in the New Testament (1 Cor. 15). Some passages tend to suggest the immortality of the soul or an existence in paradise or hell, while others tend to suggest that one's soul will sleep until the resurrection (Phil. 1:21-24; Luke 23:43; 1 Cor. 15:51-52; 1 Thess. 4:13-14). While most Christians, including Latinos/as, will affirm that we believe in the resurrection, most of us probably also believe that our souls are immortal and that upon death we will be with God. The resurrection then becomes something deferred to the end of times.

Rather than belaboring the merits and problems inherent in some of these beliefs, I think it is more important that we understand their implications, particularly in light of the experience of Latinos/as and other marginalized communities. First, while a belief in the immortality of the soul might provide a certain sense of consolation to those who face death and suffering in their lives, it also presents a number of problems. Biblically, the human soul is not a disembodied spirit, but a living soul with a bodily reality (Gen. 2:7). Generally, our views of immortality tend to come from Socratic and Platonic views of the body as the prison of the soul rather than from biblical accounts.[20] Inherent in such views of an immortal and disembodied existence are dualistic and hierarchical tendencies that elevate the spiritual over the physical. As a result, the concerns of our embodied reality and our care for the environment become subjugated to inordinate spiritual ideals. In turn, we diminish the value of the physical world and of our bodies, which we begin to view as inferior and corrupt—a belief that inevitably extends to those who labor with their hands and bodies, as many marginalized groups do. Eventually, such views open the door to the exploitation of nature, the rape of the environment, and apathy toward the physical needs of individuals and communities.

Since all human experience comes through our embodied reality, one might also ask what a disembodied immortal existence would be like. For instance, Lucretius states in his argument against the immortality of the soul:

"If the spirit is by nature immortal and can remain sentient when divorced from our body, we must credit it, I presume, with the possession of five senses."[21] But these senses of sight, smell, touch, taste, and hearing are all connected to physical processes, which are connected to our body and would cease upon death. Even if we were to have a sense of vision, to hear the thoughts of others, and to feel emotions as a disembodied soul—simply to exist for eternity in a state where we are unable to touch, to smell, to taste— would be hellish enough, and even worse if our other senses were absent.[22] By the same token, to understand immortality as a continuation of our life on earth—with all its memories, emotions, regrets, and emotional scars— would be more of a hell than a heaven, especially for those living at the margins of society. For the most part, it is those who live a life of privilege and lack of want who might actually want an enhanced continuation of the present order and of their current life. Everyone else would hope for a radical change.

This brings us to the biblical concept of resurrection. In the Gospels, it is not the empty tomb that points to the resurrection, but Jesus' appearances. But in most of the resurrection narratives, from the grave to the Emmaus road, people don't recognize Jesus right away. While the words and actions of the risen Christ allow people to recognize him as the same person they knew, there is some difference in his physical appearance that prevents people from immediately recognizing him. In the garden, Mary does not recognize the risen Christ until he speaks to her (John 20:14-16). On the road to Emmaus, they do not recognize the mysterious traveler as the risen Lord until he breaks and blesses the bread (Luke 24:16-31). The continuity between the person they knew and the risen Christ only becomes evident to the disciples through Jesus' words and actions.

What is consistent in these accounts is that there is a bodily reality to the resurrected Christ. The Gospel of Luke, for instance, makes a point of telling us that the disciples were afraid of Jesus "and thought that they were seeing a spirit" (Luke 24:37). However, the narrative also makes it clear through Jesus' words and actions that they are not seeing a Spirit, but rather a person of flesh and bone who takes food and eats it in their sight (Luke 24:38-43). How we understand the bodily presence of the resurrected Christ might be open to theological debate, but its importance would be difficult to dismiss without significantly altering the nature of our faith.

However, in speaking of resurrection, we must be careful to note that it is not the same as the resuscitation of the body. It does not imply the return of the soul to a lifeless body nor the reconstitution of our present body (1 Cor. 15:35-50). Just as Paul, in 1 Corinthians 2:14, contrasts our natural human nature to our spiritual state in relation to God's Spirit, the contrast between our present body and our resurrected body is in terms of relation to God.[23] For instance, in 1 Corinthians 15:44, the apostle Paul contrasts our present bodies—what he terms the animal or natural body ($\psi u \chi \iota \kappa \acute{o} \nu \ \sigma \omega \mu a$), driven by instincts and natural desires—with the resurrected body, which is a spiritual body ($\pi \nu \epsilon u \mu a \tau \iota \chi \acute{o} \nu \ \sigma \omega \mu a$). However, the contrast is not between a physical body that enslaves us and a disembodied soul, detached from any bodily existence. Rather, it is between our present body and the resurrected body. In both instances, Paul uses the Greek word $\sigma \omega \mu a$ (body). The contrast is between two states of bodily existence—one in accordance to the present state of humanity, human nature, and one in accordance to the resurrected body, a new state of being, which exists in accordance to God's Spirit, truly reflecting the image of God as was intended. The difference is in context—one defined by our present context of sin and violence, the other defined by the context of God's reign, love, and life.

Belief in the resurrection affirms the ultimate triumph of life over death. Inherent in it is a recognition that being a Christian does not mean we will circumvent death and suffering. On the contrary, resurrection comes only to that which is dead, left behind, and forgotten. It is God's affirmation of life in spite of the machinations of death. Our life, hope, and dreams might be swallowed by death. But resurrection affirms that death will not be the final word. The resurrection validates and gives meaning to what has been discarded by the prevalent power structures that dictate our values. Jesus—condemned, tortured, and murdered—is resurrected. The resurrection is God's judgment against our present world order and its structures of violence, domination, and power. The resurrection is God's rejection of death as the finality of life, of silence as the end of dissent. Hence, it empowers us to take action knowing that life will triumph over the power of death that seeks to silence us and rob us of hope. The resurrection does not circumvent death; it transcends it. Through it we encounter God's grace and gift of the possibility for life in spite of death. Through it we encounter an affirmation of the goodness of our creation and the possibility for our transformation and re-creation.

In Latin American theology, the resurrection serves as a hope and as a promise of a future in which the structures of death will be replaced by those that affirm life. It is a hope that empowers us to confront the powers of injustice and oppression, even when we know that our struggle for life will inevitably take us face-to-face with death. Thus, it allows us to hope against hope.[24] Similarly, Latino theologian Virgilio Elizondo speaks of the resurrection as a principle of joy and hope that empowers us to confront the power structures that oppress and dehumanize us. Thus, the resurrection is essential to the faith of Latinos/as. By our hope in it, we are able to overcome our fears and find our voice to make a claim against those who will enslave and silence us.[25] The resurrection is God's affirmation of life that empowers us to face the pharaohs of today—the pharaohs and Caesars of oppression, economic injustice, racism, sexism, and marginalization that enslave us—and demand our liberation. The resurrection empowers us to face all forms of violence, suffering, and death to bring forth God's reign on earth. The resurrection is a judgment on the present and a call for action. It is a vector that points us to embrace and affirm life in spite of death. In it lies the promise not only of our transformation, but of the transformation of all creation.

The resurrection also affirms the significance of our work and hopes. The ideals for which we live do not die with us. The grave does not silence our work for God's reign. We can say to some extent that Christ continues to live and work in history through us. We can say that Christ continues to be embodied in our lives and at work in creation through the Spirit. Similarly, our lives' impact on the world does not end with our death. Our lives continue to have repercussions upon history and upon all of creation. Objectively we are immortal, our lives a datum of history, a fact that continues to ripple throughout time. But we are also subjects of history, affecting history beyond the scope of our present earthly existence. In God, our lives, our dreams, our hopes, and our affirmations continue to be preserved and continue to influence history. We are not forgotten. All that we are, all that we have invested with meaning, all that we have sought to bring about in accordance to God is not lost. We might die, but everything we are continues to live in God and in the lives of those who continue our work.

Finally, the resurrection is also not just something that awaits us in our future. It is something that we live today. Our baptism symbolizes our participation in the death and resurrection of Christ. In it, we have left the past and embraced our future. We have died to our former self and have begun to live the new life in accordance to the resurrection. In us, the resurrection is a reality as we find a new beginning, a new lease on life, a transformation that breaks with the old and provides us with a glimpse of the new, of what could be.

Que Sera, Sera

The Spanish adage, *que sera, sera*—whatever will be, will be—is fairly well known, immortalized through song. Some might interpret this adage as fatalistic, or as a call to live for the moment without regard for the future. But I do not believe that either is the case. Rather, I think it is a statement of faith. In Matthew 6:34 we are told not to "worry about tomorrow, for tomorrow will worry about itself. Each day has enough trouble of its own." In a sense, this passage is both an affirmation of faith and a guide to how we should approach eschatology. What will be, will be. Rather than worrying about what the future might bring, we should focus on the present. We can become obsessed with speculation about life after death, about the end of the world, and about what our future holds. But if we trust the one who holds our future, our faith alone should sustain us. Of course, this does not mean that we should ignore the demand that the future exerts on us. The passage in Matthew is preceded by a call to seek the kingdom of God. Thus, we are called to action. But we are called to action today. We are called to bring the reign of God into our lives and into our world today.

It has been my hope through the pages of this book to introduce you to theology from a Latino/a perspective, with the recognition that all theology comes from a given perspective. Each of these perspectives helps enrich us, broadening our understanding of God and of each other. My intent is not to claim that Latino/a theology is superior or more spiritual than any other theology. On the contrary, my claim is that no theology is superior or more spiritual than any other. Latino/a theology has unique insights to offer the whole of the church, which in turn can provide us with a deeper sense of our faith. In the same manner, I invite others to do the same—to explore theology beyond the limits of one's own culture and to enter into dialogue with others so that we might grow.

Latino/a theology is young as far as theologies go. It is growing and changing, moving in new directions. New voices are entering the dialogue each day. We are slowly moving from a time of self-discovery and self-affirmation to a second and even third generation of scholars who are leading us to explore new directions. While we might have been more self-aware of our own standpoints and biases in the development of our theology, we also have blind spots. With new generations of scholars come new elements that allow us to become more self-critical and to interrogate ourselves even further. This in turn will only serve to strengthen us, for theology must always be aware of its biases, its cultural perspectives, and its limits, continually engaging in self-reflection and growth.

Que sera, sera might serve us well as an eschatological maxim, calling us to trust God with the future and work to make the reign of God a reality in the present. But it could just as well serve as a theological maxim, calling us to recognize that no theology is ever a finished product, but rather is constantly changing and moving, a theology of the way, which at times surprises us. But this road that we are on is taking us somewhere and it does have a destination—the fulfillment of the reign of God. It is toward that aim that we work, holding to the faith that in God we will find our ultimate fulfillment in the fullness of time; and through God, whatever will be, will be.

Notes

1. Justo L. González, *Mañana: Christian Theology from a Hispanic Perspective* (Nashville: Abingdon Press, 1990), p. 164.

2. Ibid., p. 165.

3. Ibid., p. 166.

4. Eberhard Jüngel speaks of God as being act and possibility and, in this sense, God as being the source of our possibility, and thus, also of our future. Thus, for him, God's being is in the future and God embodies the future for us as what is possible. *God as the Mystery of the World: On the Foundations of the Theology of the Crucified One in the Dispute between Theism and Atheism* (Edinburgh: T & T Clark, 1978), p. 50.

5. Here, I am alluding to Alfred North Whitehead, who speaks of God's lure, calling us toward actualizing certain possibilities for us. *Adventures of Ideas* (New York: Free Press, 1933, 1961), pp. 166-67. Whitehead sees a progression from a view of God as a coercive agency, to a Platonic ideal where God works through divine persuasion, through ideals that bring forth change in the world. It is this that he sees revealed in act in the foundation of Christianity.

6. Leonardo Boff, *Cry of the Earth, Cry of the Poor*, trans. by Phillip Berryman (Maryknoll: Orbis Press, 1997), p. 70.

7. See Katherine Tanner in "Creation, Environmental Crisis, and Ecological Justice," in *Reconstructing Christian Theology*, Rebecca S. Chopp and Mark Lewis Taylor, eds. (Minneapolis: Fortress Press, 1994), p. 100.

8. Leonardo Boff, *Cry of the Earth*, pp. 81-82. This notion of the interconnectedness of all creation also echoes with Alfred North Whitehead's philosophy, where all beings in the universe are interconnected through an extensive continuum where everything is interrelated and interconnected, *Process and Reality*, corrected edition (New York: Free Press, 1978), pp. 65-66.

9. Boff, *Cry of the Earth*, p. 83.

10. Ibid., pp. 152-54. Boff argues in favor of a panentheism, that is, that although all things are not God as in pantheism, God is present in all things, hence rupturing the dichotomy between immanence and transcendence where God and the world are mutually transparent to each other. In many respects this also resonates with the work of Alfred North Whitehead, particularly in the last chapter of *Process and Reality*.

11. Ibid., p. 116.

12. See Boff's argument that the poor are the most vulnerable to the injustices of the exploitation of natural resources and the destruction of our environment. In return, he calls for a connection between liberation theology and ecology that is not driven by consumerism and is mindful of our ecosystem. Ibid., pp. 110-14.

13. Ignacio Ellacuría, who was martyred by the political establishment in El Salvador, writes about these characteristics and their call upon us in "Utopia and Prophecy in Latin America," *Mysterium Liberationis: Fundamental Concepts of Liberation Theology*, ed. by Ignacio Ellacuría and Jon Sobrino (Maryknoll: Orbis Press, 1993), pp. 290-91.

14. Ellacuría writes that "to actualize means to give present reality to what is formally a historical possibility and, as such, what can be taken or left, what can be read in one way or another." However, the actualization of the reign of God does not merely depend upon us. It also relies upon the ongoing work of the Spirit in us and in history. Ibid., p. 293.

15. For more on this concept of God's reign, see chapter 5 of my book, *Jesus Is My Uncle: Christology from a Hispanic Perspective* (Nashville: Abingdon Press, 1999), pp. 110-22, where I elaborate on the themes of God's reign, utopia, and diversity.

16. Mortimer Arias argues that the reign of God is experienced as action in *Announcing the Reign of God: Evangelization and the Subversive Memory of Jesus* (Philadelphia: Fortress Press, 1984), p. 19.

17. Ellacuría, *Mysterium Liberationis*, p. 306.

18. Ibid., pp. 292-93.

19. This reference might allude to a life beyond death, but it might just as easily refer to a collective sense of immortality where one lives on in one's people.

20. Plato, the *Phaedo,* as cited in *Immortality,* ed. by Paul Edwards (New York: Macmillan, 1992), pp. 73-82.

21. Lucretius, *De Rerum Natura,* book 3, as reprinted in *Immortality.* Ibid., p. 85.

22. John Hospers has an insightful account of what it might be to awaken without a body and the unintelligibility of such an experience within our realm of thought in *An Introduction to Philosophical Analysis* (3rd edition, 1988) as reprinted in *Immortality.* Ibid., pp. 279-81.

23. In *Mañana,* González points to a similar contrast between the spiritual and the natural or unspiritual in regards to 1 Corinthians 2:14, where the word ψυχικὸς, translated as natural or animal state in both this passage and in 1 Corinthians 15:44 does not refer to an inferior material reality. Instead, González argues that the word used could be better translated as "soulish" if such a word were to exist in English, which would mean in accordance to one's human nature. By the same token, the spiritual to which Paul contrasts this word refers to living in accordance not to the human spirit, but to God's Spirit. González, *Mañana,* pp. 158-59.

24. See Julio Lois's account of the resurrection in his article "Christology in the Theology of Liberation," *Mysterium Liberationis,* pp. 184-86.

25. Virgilio Elizondo, *Galilean Journey: The Mexican American Promise* (Maryknoll: Orbis Press, 1983), pp. 115-17.

SCRIPTURE INDEX

SUBJECT INDEX

Abelard, Peter, 107, 149-50, 156
Acosta, José de, 29
ACTHUS, 37
Adoptionism, 136
AETH, 37
African Americans, 74, 77
African Religions, 81
African slaves, 30, 116
Africans, 175
Alexandrine, 137
analogy, 69-70
Anselm, 53, 149, 150
Antiochene, 137
Apollinarius, 137
Aquinas, Thomas, 69, 192
Aquino, María Pilar, 36
Arianism, 117
Arias, Mortimer, 204n. 16
Aristotle, 58
Athanasius, 134
atonement, 107, 149-51, 167
Aztec, 30, 60, 79

baptism, 160-61, 201

Barth, Karl,
  definition of God, 119
  on dogmatics, 52-53
  and freedom 184n. 16, 184n. 19
  on gender, 113
  and God's Word, 26n. 30
  on language about God, 94, 97-98
Barton, Paul, 45n. 19, 45n. 23
Bell, Daniel M., 46n. 38
Bernard of Clairvaux, 107
Bhabha, Homi, 25n. 17
bicultural, 74
bilingual, 74
Black theology, 34, 77, 178
Boff, Leonardo, 115, 191
Brueggemann, Walter, 46n. 46, 47n. 47
Bultmann, Rudolf, 53
Butler, Lee H., 48n. 63

Calvin, John, 147, 166
Catholic, 81-82, 115, 162, 179
Chalcedon, Council of, 137-39
Charismatic, *See* Pentecostal